Acclaim for DAVID FROMKIN'*s*

THE WAY OF THE WORLD

"[*The Way of the World*] certainly has the virtues of conciseness, and the giant steps he has chosen—from 'becoming human' to 'achieving rationality' to 'ruling ourselves'—are wisely chosen. . . . An achievement."
—*The New York Times*

"*The Way of the World* [is a] superbly crafted historical analysis of the story of humanity and civilization."
—*Bookpage*

"Fromkin is a skilled raconteur with a keen eye for telling anecdote and a conquistador's power to cover vast swaths of territory in a short amount of time."
—*Publishers Weekly*

"*The Way of the World* is an appropriate reminder that good scholarship and good reading are not mutually exclusive. In telling the human story so well, it makes a significant contribution to our understanding of ourselves." —*The Boston Book Review*

"Mr. Fromkin is good at getting the reader to turn the pages." —*The Economist Review*

DAVID FROMKIN

THE WAY OF THE WORLD

David Fromkin is Professor of International Relations, History, and Law at Boston University. He is the author of *In the Time of the Americans*, a History Book Club selection, and *A Peace to End All Peace*, a national best-seller, which was a finalist for both the National Book Critics Circle Award and the Pulitzer Prize and was singled out by *The New York Times Book Review* as an "Editors' Choice," one of the thirteen "Best Books of the Year." He lives in New York City.

Also by DAVID FROMKIN

THE WAY OF THE WORLD

THE WAY OF THE WORLD

From the Dawn of Civilizations to the
Eve of the Twenty-first Century

DAVID FROMKIN

Vintage Books
A Division of Random House, Inc.
New York

FIRST VINTAGE BOOKS EDITION, JANUARY 2000

Copyright © 1998 by David Fromkin

All rights reserved under International and Pan-American Copyright Conventions.
Published in the United States by Vintage Books, a division of Random House,
Inc., New York, and simultaneously in Canada by Random House of Canada
Limited, Toronto. Originally published in hardcover in the United States
by Alfred A. Knopf, a division of Random House, Inc., New York, in 1998.

Vintage and colophon are registered trademarks of Random House, Inc.

The Library of Congress has cataloged the Knopf edition as follows:
Fromkin, David.
The way of the world: from the dawn of civilizations to the eve of
the twenty-first century / David Fromkin.
p.   cm.
Includes bibliographical references and index.
ISBN 0-679-44609-5 (alk. paper)
1. World history. I. Title.
D23.F76 1998 98-14574 CIP
909—dc21

Vintage ISBN: 0-679-76669-3

Author photograph by Jerry Bauer

www.vintagebooks.com

Printed in the United States of America
10   9   8   7   6   5

To Wallace Sellers

*—who told us how to fail and now
has shown us how to succeed—*

Contents

PART ONE: PAST

1 : BECOMING HUMAN

Tens of thousands of years ago, in a cave in southwestern Europe, a shaman clad in bearskin told tales of past and future to his rapt followers. A flickering flame cast moving shadows on the wall. Blood had been spilled; spirits had been invoked. Speaking in a low, hypnotic tone, the shaman made life and death, the seasons of the Earth and the movements of the sky, intelligible to his people. He retold familiar stories of the tribe to which they belonged: its wanderings; the long-ago ancestor from whom they had descended; and the destiny that had been foretold for them.

"Can you do that for us today?" asked the Wall Street hedge-fund manager over a luncheon in midtown Manhattan. He had been told that I was teaching at a university and was challenging me. "Can you tell the story of humanity in the universe and make it whole?"

"Well, actually, yes, I can," I said, "though of course I have to do it in my own way." My way of telling it—though it begins with the creation and multiplication of civilizations, and their lives and deaths—concentrates mostly on the lines that led to the only civilization still surviving, the scientific one of the modern world, and on the prospects before it.

. . .

How do you tell the story of Mankind? Oddly, I used to know some-one whose job it once had been to answer that question. It was my friend Walter Fairservis, and the reason he had to answer the question was that he was helping to design a new Hall of Asian Man for New York's American Museum of Natural History that would pro-vide a panorama of Asian history.

Walter, who died a few years back, was an anthropologist and archaeologist, but above all an adventurer: a forerunner in real life of the fictitious Indiana Jones. He was a big man, an outdoors type with a weatherbeaten look, rumpled and shaggy. His special field of scholarship was the origin of civilizations. He excavated mainly in Egypt and in Pakistan, but he also roamed the rest of the world, whether on camelback or jet airplane, comparing the beginnings of ancient times in one place with those in another.

Asia is the continent on which human civilization first appeared; its flourishing is a long story, too big to be told comprehensively. Fairservis recognized that the most he could do was to select displays that would get a few of the most important points across to viewers.

Visitors had a choice of two entrances to the exhibition. One took you through chronologically, beginning with the origins of human life and culture. If you followed this path, you came away with a sense of how much material progress the human race has made in its relatively short life span.

The other entrance, as I remember it, displayed a marketplace in central Asia as it might have appeared in the time of Marco Polo (a bit before 1300 A.D.), with goods from an enormous wealth of cul-tures. From there, you could choose your path to whichever culture most interested you. Viewers came away not only with a sense of the broad range of civilizations contained in Asia alone, but also, it may be assumed, with an idea of the extraordinary variety of human soci-ety in the world as a whole.

Material progress, and the variety of cultures: here were two ob-servations about the history of the past that were important and true. Visitors could observe for themselves, and draw their own conclusions. It seemed to me that this was about as much as you could communicate successfully in the course of one visit.

I try to do something similar. I focus on an aspect of human experience: on *change*, in particular with regard to the way we organize and govern ourselves, and how we deal with the issues of war and peace and survival. I concentrate on some of the turning points in history and look at where they have led, and where they will lead in the future if we continue on the same path. Narrated in such a way, the turns in the life of the human race form a story that can be outlined in no more time than it takes to tell a tale, as a shaman would, around an evening campfire.

Like those who first put their hands and minds to the writing of history, Herodotus and Thucydides, Greeks of the fifth century B.C., I will deal essentially with the high drama of battle and politics. If instead I were surveying the history of art or science, of literature or music, I would work from a different outline and would have a different tale to narrate.

Telling one story necessarily means not telling another. Little will be said in the pages that follow about artistic creation or spiritual wisdom; there are no discussions of Shakespeare or Dante, of Mozart or Beethoven, of Leonardo or Michelangelo. The tale of how human beings have organized themselves in separate independent societies that sometimes cooperate but more often clash with one another, needs to be told on its own if it is to be told at a manageable length.

A glance at the table of contents shows that I conceive of a dozen radical turns as having brought us from the African forests of millions of years ago to the world of the 1990s and beyond. There is nothing special about the number twelve; another historian, organizing matters otherwise, would do it in some other number of headings and permutations. What follows is only a view from one person's perspective.

Perhaps there were, are, or will be other universes, but we can know nothing of them. It is *our* universe that we speak of as *the* universe; we look to its birth for the framework of our beliefs and institutions.

The stories of creation told by the shamans of nomad tribes and the priests of earlier civilizations were factually untrue, but they held meaning. In the full sense of the word, they were myths.

Uniquely, the civilization to which we belong at the end of the twentieth century tells a tale of creation that is true—which is to say, unlike all others, it is based upon evidence. But the story changes all the time, as new evidence comes to light. Moreover, it is incomplete, and in its incompleteness it cannot tell us what—if anything—creation signifies. Our scientists tell us *what* happened, but they haven't a clue as to *how* or *why*. Is the universe a cosmic accident or the result of a cosmic design? Science doesn't know; so we may believe whatever we choose.

A peculiarity of the modern world, as regards our account of genesis, is that only the relative few who are scientifically literate know and understand what "we" believe. Few are conversant with today's cosmogony—our story of creation—or cosmology, our knowledge of how the universe functions. More than half the adults in the United States do not know that every year the Earth orbits around the sun. Yet a scientific elite is expanding the frontiers of their own knowledge to an extent that seems almost miraculous. Recently, *The New York Times* reported that scientists have looked back 11 billion years into space and have photographed the universe as it was then—"some 85 percent of the way back to the beginning of time." Since then astronomers have peered even further.

The age-old vision of life and creation that would have emerged from a shaman's songs and tales in times past would have been familiar to the tribesmen to whom he chanted. The modern vision, when occasionally we catch sight of it, comes to most of us as surprising news. Of course scientists themselves disagree, even about fundamental issues. Some of them take the view that the universe holds to an essentially cyclical course and therefore had no beginning and will have no end. Others believe it was brought into existence by a Creator, who had no beginning. The most striking current theory, however, is that there *was* a beginning, and that it came with a Big Bang.

Billions of years ago—astronomers continue to disagree about the date but most place it somewhere between 11 billion and 15 billion B.C.—our universe exploded into existence. From the detonation came space, time, matter, and energy.

In its first second, the universe began to expand and it continues to do so. For all we know, it may go on expanding forever. Its size today can be described but not imagined. Our estimates of it have to be enlarged repeatedly. At last count there were perhaps a hundred billion stars in our galaxy, the Milky Way. Early in 1996 we learned that there are fifty billion such galaxies in the sky; previously we had thought there were "only" ten billion. And more space is being created all the time.

Our tiny corner of the universe—the corner dominated by our local star, the Sun—took shape long after Creation. The solar system, the Sun and all that revolves around it, emerged less than five billion years ago.

The Earth is an assemblage of waste materials left over from the creation of the solar system: bits of debris that whirled about aimlessly in space, and then collided, smashing into one another and merging, like so many lumps of scrap metal crushed together by a compactor. The Earth came into being 4.6 billion years ago, just after the birth of the Sun.

Life on our planet seems to have sprung up from the then-molten Earth somewhere between 3 and 4.2 billion years ago. We think that it took the form of single-celled microbes, organisms without a nucleus, that lived in a kind of "primeval soup." One of these was able to replicate, becoming the germ of all future life; from it all else followed.

But, again, we don't quite know how. For although we believe that this simple germ of life spawned many species, we haven't yet solved the riddle of how cells with a true nucleus came into being. We do have some clues, however.

New evidence suggests that the minute organisms from which the animal kingdom emerged may have "crawled or slithered between grains of mud or sand in primordial waters." Eventually they may have reached out to make use of the light of the sun and would have split water—and released oxygen. It was not until nearly 600 million B.C. that they developed the beginnings of skeletons and enough substance to leave fossil remains for us to find, vestigial remnants of what came before us.

Upheavals continued to alter the Earth's geography radically. Continents were on the move. Life's existence was jeopardized on at least five occasions by mysterious catastrophes, "extinction events" as they are called, such as the one that is widely believed to have brought an end to the dinosaurs. These events occasioned a proliferation of species that could adapt to the changes. It was not until long afterwards—after the last catastrophe, and billions of years after life began—that primates appeared, and then, much later still, took the first steps in the direction that eventually led to humanity.

So it isn't the case, as traditional cosmogonies would have it, that human beings were created "in the beginning." On the contrary, the first humans, and even their immediate forebears, entered a universe well into its prime, and a solar system in its middle years. Almost all of time past was over before the human story started. In terms of the billions of years since the universe began, the human race has only just barely made its appearance.

For a scientist, that can be disappointing. "We are living . . . long after most of the exciting things have happened," an astronomer wrote recently, in terms that could be construed as expressing a complaint, or at least a regret. But for those who are drawn to the drama of changing times and places in which people were both remarkably the same as, and fascinatingly different from, ourselves, all of history's excitements, its trumpets, banners, and pageantry, were yet to come.

We have managed to learn some important things about the functioning of both the universe and ourselves. In the universe, everything always moves; there is no such thing as standing still. The planet on which we dwell continuously rotates and revolves, and the star system to which it belongs rushes through space at an unimaginably high speed, taking us with it.

It should be dizzying and yet we are unaware of the motion. So a second thing we have learned is that we are incapable of perceiving accurately what is happening around us. Our senses deceive us. They bombard us with false reports. Like an intelligence network infiltrated and controlled by the opposition, they continuously supply us with disinformation.

Life is a story that each of us tells to his or her self; and it therefore is a tale told by an unreliable narrator.

One of the other major truths we have learned about the universe is that at all times everything is in process of transformation. Gases become solids; mass becomes energy; one species evolves into another.

Metamorphosis is the perpetual activity of the universe. When tales were told in ancient Greece of maidens whom the gods transformed into streams, or of youths who became constellations in the sky, skeptical philosophers regarded them as fantasies or superstitions. For Ovid, a contemporary of Caesar Augustus, they were the stuff of poetry. Apuleius, the Roman novelist who related a tale of having been turned into an ass by witchcraft, did so in the spirit of a street-corner entertainer; he was making fun of such superstitions.

A belief in metamorphosis once was scoffed at; now it is a central premise of modern science. Evidence recently reported from Lake Victoria in Africa shows that three hundred unique species of cichlid fish came into being in the last twelve thousand years, and that a new species can develop in a mere twenty generations. In the Galápagos Islands off the South American coast, where nearly twenty species of finch evolved over the course of more than four million years, the size of the beak of a finch has been observed to evolve over the course of as little as three years. An experiment with lizards in the Bahamas has shown evolution following predictable paths in developing bodily changes over the course of not much more than a decade. But whether the changes occur so quickly that we notice them, or so slowly that we do not, everything is always turning into something else.

. . .

One of the oldest stories that have come down to us is a tale of change from the Bronze Age. It is about a victorious king who returns home after twenty years of war and wandering. A goddess turns his men into swine; it is only one of the metamorphoses he witnesses. All about him, things and people are not what they were and not what they seem. To learn how to make his own way home, a fellow warrior, becalmed near Pharos island off the coast of Egypt, seeks out the Old Man of the Sea. To force the Old Man to help, he must seize him when he beds down to sleep, and hold on to him while he changes shape. "He'll try all kinds of escape," advises a friendly goddess, "twist and turn into every beast that moves across the earth . . . but you hold on for dear life, hug him all the harder!" And so it happens.

> First he shifted into a great bearded lion
> and then a serpent—
> a panther—
> a ramping wild boar—
> A torrent of water—
> a tree with soaring branchtops—

Only when the weary Old Man resumes his own shape does the warrior release him and obtain his counsel.

And that, it seems to me, illustrates the rooted fallacy that keeps us from understanding continuing change. We believe that underneath shifting appearances there is something true and unchanging. To us, the Old Man was himself all the time; he only seemed to look like a serpent, a panther, and a wild boar. They were disguises. So, too, the men the goddess turned into swine really, in our eyes, remained men; it was just that they were trapped in the bodies of pigs.

In the familiar fairy tales, the frog is a prince who has fallen victim to a wicked spell. A persistent theme, certainly in Western culture, is the search for what is permanent and unchanging beneath shifting appearances; but it now looks as though there is no such thing. Our cosmology tells us that what changes all the time is not appearance but reality. We find this hard to believe.

Our remote primate ancestors were some sort of apes. They dwelt long ago—more than twenty million years ago—in the forests that covered Africa. In the manner of most primates, they would have clustered in groups—a disposition that was to serve them well. Four-legged eaters of fruit, weighing perhaps between 90 and 110 pounds, they clambered up and down trunks and swung from branches. They lived in the lofty boughs of the trees whose fruits they ate.

How we got from there to here, from then to now, and from them to us is the first, longest, and most obscure episode in the human story. The exact nature of the process is debated still. What is incontrovertible is that the genealogical line that eventually led to us passed, en route, through many curious creatures, and a great many that we still are unable to identify.

The road that winds away from the primates of the African forests was taken in perhaps 7 million B.C. Seven million years ago—some say six, or even five—the break took place between the apes in Africa whose descendants were to become human and those whose progeny were to become chimpanzees. What our ancestors did at the crossroads was to take the first step of the many that eventually would transform the offspring of apes into people. That step was a step indeed: it was to walk on two feet.

Prehistorians have found a trail of that long-distant past—literally so—in the northwest of what is now Tanzania in East Africa. The trail is ninety feet long. The footprints—made some 3.5 million years ago—of three people, a child and two adults, were found in it. Preserved in volcanic ash, they are the prints of bipedal "hominids"—creatures on the human family tree. Other such steps date from about 1.5 million years ago.

In the summer of 1997, scientists announced that in South Africa they had discovered the fossilized footprints of an anatomically modern human dating from 117,000 years ago. Between the earlier, prehuman footsteps and these more recent, human ones, what transpired, unseen by us in the darkness, was the birth of the human race.

Bipedalism—walking on two feet—was a transforming, but not defining, event. What we have learned in past decades is that our humanity—the traits of mind, heart, and body upon which we pride ourselves, and which we regard as the most significant things about us—emerged not at the beginning of the evolutionary process, but quite recently.

Why was it useful for our nonhuman ancestors to be able to come down from their treetop homes to walk on the ground? It is by no means evident what advantage being able to stand up and walk on hind limbs would have conferred on an ape in 7 million B.C. Yet it must have held some benefits, for once a species of two-legged ape came into being, other species of two-legged apes did too. An upright posture, the free use of arms and hands, and a prehensile thumb were to prove their value, but not until much later—not, in fact, until after the passage of millions of years.

It may be that the forests of Africa began to die out, perhaps giving way to savannahs. If so, bipedalism would have provided the option of exploiting either one. With abundance no longer as available in the boughs of trees, with forest life no longer quite so easy, it would have offered an alternative; it would have opened up a way out of the forest. Anthropologists used to emphasize the possibly shrinking prospects of life in the forest, but now stress the attractive new vistas offered by the savannah. If that scenario is true, then our primate ancestors would have come down from the trees of Africa to face an uncertain future of altogether new challenges and opportunities on the ground. On their own two feet, abandoning the gardens in which they had lived, they would have walked away from the orchards of Eden.

Millions of years elapsed between the time when our ape ancestors became two-legged and the time when they started to develop a large brain. It took that much time, which seems long to us but is short in evolutionary time, to fully accomplish the radical anatomical changes that were needed to accommodate an upright posture. These are not years about which we know a great deal. We have little physical evidence to go on, the remains of a few humanoid skeletons from between 3.5 and perhaps 4.4 million B.C., and none at all (as yet) that are older.

Modern views of the origin of our species take as their starting point the revolutionary theories of Charles Darwin (1809–1882). Darwin, a young Englishman at loose ends who had taken up an interest in natural history, obtained an appointment from the Admiralty in 1831 to ship aboard the HMS *Beagle*. The *Beagle* was charged with, among other missions, surveying coastlines in southern Latin America and visiting various islands in the Pacific. Its voyage lasted five years. Darwin's careful records of his observations during the trip supplied him with the basis upon which he theorized for the rest of his life.

Darwin was a pioneer in exploring the question of why, over time, species change. The explanation at which he arrived, the theory of natural selection, is his claim to immortality. He believed that evolutionary changes occurred only over almost unimaginably long periods of time, but we now know that they can take place more quickly. Indeed, "evolution" is a somewhat misleading term for a process that works in large part by leaps and discontinuities, however tiny. Darwin was frustrated in his effort to understand how genetic changes occur: "What the devil determines each particular variation?" he demanded. He imagined that in the body there must be some sort of alphabet that he could not read. He was right. As the author of a recent work on evolution has written, "Today, biologists call Darwin's invisible characters 'genes.'"

A human being has tens of thousands of genes, spelled out in about three billion "letters." It is a triumph of modern biology to have learned how to go about deciphering the language, which has made possible some of the most exciting science of our time.

Here is what scientists tell us about heredity.

We inherit from our parents not so much specific traits as a range of possible characteristics contained in our genetic code. It is as though you and your parents sit down together to a game of fortune, with you playing at a combination of their two roulette tables. The numbers that come up for you will be different from theirs. Only the tables will be the same. Sex complicates and marvelously expands the possibilities. The intermingling of the genetic codes of the male and female in a couple offer an almost endless number of combinations. The traits that the children inherit can vary widely from those of each parent.

Then there are the wild cards. The frequency with which these are dealt turns out to be an important clue to understanding the process. The wild cards are called "mutations," a term coined by the Dutch botanist Hugo de Vries (1848–1935). They are errors in copying that occur when the genetic materials within us are damaged, as they often are by environmental stresses and shocks, and by atmospheric forces such as the radiation of the sun, and then imperfectly repaired by our enzymes. What results is that we transmit to our children hereditary traits that, paradoxically, we do not have ourselves and did not inherit from our ancestors.

New traits are being born all the time, whether by accident or by divine design, and Creation, instead of having come to an end on the seventh day, is continuous and, indeed, continues today.

The result is a dazzling variation in traits springing up in all living things all the time. Variety is essential to the process of natural selection through which nature keeps life going. The way of the world—our world—is to promiscuously propagate differences. Like a jazz musician improvising variations on a theme without exactly repeating it, life throws up a welter of smaller or larger genetic variants that are much the same, but not entirely the same, as what already exists. In fits and starts, nature repeatedly proposes new options; those that are an improvement sometimes supplant the others. Occasionally, violent changes in the environment call for entirely new qualities; given sufficient variety, some species will have the luck to possess hitherto useless abilities that allow it to adapt to new circumstances, while yesterday's winners go under.

If a population becomes physically divided, each half eventually may become a species of its own as, pointed in different paths by the luck of the genetic draw, generation after generation, each travels further along its own road. The process, though initiated by chance, seems to be driven by a certain logic. Of the unimaginably large number of options that life on Earth has proposed, only a minuscule proportion have been taken up and adapted, have had the chance to become a species. And of this tiny band—the more than three billion species that have existed—only a mere 1 percent, thirty million, survive today. The survivors are not necessarily bigger or stronger; they are either luckier or more adaptable. They happened to possess the traits that were called for when accidental changes in the environment took place, or else had the ability to develop such traits. That seems to be what humans did by acquiring big brains.

Between 2.5 and 1.5 million years ago, the brains of our ancestors suddenly jumped enormously in size. This had an immense effect. The human brain may be the most complex object in the universe; ours today contains a trillion cells. The most astonishing manifestation of this enlarged neurological capacity is consciousness. Yet what is it? When and how did we get it? Is it a mechanical connection or a divine spark? We don't know, but it is the defining characteristic of humanity. When did we become the only creatures to live with the knowledge that someday we are going to die?

Our newly large-brained forebears discovered how to manufacture tools and weapons that allowed them to butcher animals and become meat-eaters on a regular basis. Like their useful thumbs, their distinctive brains opened up new opportunities.

For perhaps a million years, beginning in about 2 million B.C., the older type of ape continued to exist alongside the newly emerging, big-brained ape-man that scientists call the *Homo* family. But by 1 million B.C. or thereabouts, all the various other two-legged species had become extinct. All that eventually remained of the upright primates—of the experiments in bipedalism that nature had been conducting since 7 million B.C.—was this *Homo* family from which we spring. Whether or not there were many branches on the family tree remains subject to investigation and interpretation.

Found alongside the remains of *Homo erectus* were the first hand axes. These ax-wielding creatures were more man than ape. We think that members of *Homo erectus* were the first to manage and use fire, to make tools to a preconceived design, and to hunt, as it were, professionally. Their bodies were not dissimilar to ours, and they ran as we do. Yet they too eventually fell by the wayside, victims of evolution, though controversial new evidence suggests that they may have existed as recently as thirty thousand years ago.

Fossils provide evidence of a wealth of humanlike beings who lived during the past half-million years. Some of them overlapped with our ancestors. The human race, *Homo sapiens*, which put in its appearance more than a hundred thousand years ago, was one of several species that were quite similar. An astonishing recent archaeological find in northwestern Australia suggests to some that creatures earlier than modern man created art. The gifted and cultured Neanderthals, now believed to have emerged in about 230,000 B.C., seem to have been, as we believe ourselves to be, descendants of *Homo erectus*. We are inclined to believe that they were the first creatures to bury their dead, though with what purpose in mind we do not know. What may have been a flute was found recently in one of their caves and is estimated to be somewhere between forty-three thousand and eighty-two thousand years old; it haunts us with the possibility that Neanderthals may have invented music.

Neanderthals may have been cut off by advancing glaciers in Europe, for they evolved separately from other descendants of *Homo erectus*. By the time they encountered anatomically modern humans, the Neanderthals had become a distinct, separate species— a not uncommon result of geographical separation over long periods of time. For the final ten thousand years of their existence, they coexisted with modern humans in Europe and the Middle East, and perhaps alongside *Homo erectus* as well. For whatever reason, Neanderthals, among the last and closest of the other humanlike creatures, vanished from the Earth by about 30,000 B.C.

What happened to them? Recent studies by genetic biologists seem to show that they did not interbreed with humans: this was not the cause of their disappearance. A persuasive case has been made for the proposition that they were eliminated, as were so many species before them, by the inexorable Darwinian logic of natural selection. Computer studies have shown that if population A has a mere 2 percent competitive edge over population B, population B

will disappear completely within as little as a thousand years. It is very likely that this was the fate of our Neanderthal brothers. Yet the shadow of Cain unavoidably falls over our speculations. We cannot rule out entirely the possibility that the Neanderthals, and perhaps others, disappeared from history because humans exterminated them. As so often is the case in studying the distant past, we are reminded of how little we know.

We know only in the most general way when *Homo sapiens* first appeared. Of the situation of the first humans, and of the battles and wars, wanderings and returns, that must have been their experience during the tens of thousands of years that followed, we know nothing. Since they could not write, we can never know the thoughts and beliefs that animated them, or the hopes, hates, loves, and dreams of either public or personal life: 95 percent or more of the history of our species remains a blank to us.

Physically, humans could not have been any match for many of the beasts that stalked them through the long night of the Paleolithic world. They must have been haunted by terrors of every kind. Vulnerable as they were in many ways, they would have been more hunted than hunter. Our surmise is that by functioning in groups, our first real ancestors eventually won the war for survival. Their tale brings an end to the story of our genesis.

What would a shaman of today tell the human species about its origins? And what follows from the modern scientific account of genesis? Genetic biologists tell us that all life on our planet has a common ancestor. A blade of grass, a field mouse that runs across our path, a flower and the insects that it tempts, fruits and vegetables, the fish that swim and the birds that fly: all are our distant cousins. But, this side of sentimentality, I know of no way to respond to that information. It is, I think, a truth without consequences. Illuminating our origins does nothing to light up today or tomorrow.

We are wrong to believe that the ground upon which we stand is stationary; similarly, we are wrong to think that beneath fleeting appearances there is something unchanging, and in my view it is also untrue that we can learn about ourselves by questioning the primeval sludge from which, billions of years ago, the germ of life emerged. These are typical errors that result from flaws in our instincts, in our sensing apparatus, and in what we believe to be our common sense.

At some stage or another, adopted children often develop an obsession with tracking down their biological parents. They are convinced that only by learning the identity of their parents can they learn their own. They are mistaken, but it is a very human mistake to make. We are not our ancestors; we are ourselves.

Who are we? A look at the beginning of life on Earth shows that no creature existed then that bore even the slightest resemblance to us. Only in part did the founding germ even engender us; in very large measure we come from mutations—from individual acts of new creation—that span the three or four billion years from the emergence of the first living cells until today. Everything is always in the process of becoming something else; as we change, the old self is discarded.

So who are we? We are not, I believe, those who initiated the chain of being that eventually engendered us: that long line of creatures stretching from the primeval slime billions of years ago to ourselves. Their reproductive efforts helped to move the process along, but they stayed behind; they did not themselves ever go on to become human. One after another, they ran their race and then, before expiring, passed along the torch of life that eventually was handed to us. We carry it still. The torch is the same, but the runner is different.

The human race, anatomically modern *Homo sapiens*—born, we now think, between 100,000 and 200,000 B.C. in Africa[1]—hit the ground running. It displayed unique endowments early in life. A human

1. It looks as though the race was born in northeast Africa and then spread to the other continents. In this, the human race seems to have been following a pattern. A number of other manlike species also may have been born in northeast Africa and then spread to other continents; but not everybody agrees, and the debate continues. An alternative theory is that *Homo erectus* was a direct ancestor of *Homo sapiens*; that *Homo erectus* wandered from Africa to Europe and Asia; and that *Homo sapiens* then sprang from *Homo erectus*. In other words, modern humans evolved independently on the three continents, according to this alternative theory.

being had not only a large brain but a larynx: a voice box. Humans could speak to one another. Along with consciousness, the magical gift of language is chief among man's attributes, its nature and the date of its appearance still debated. A persuasive view is that language caused a quantum leap in the ability of the group to work together and to develop culture, making all else possible.

Art is another magical gift: the discovery of Ice Age cave paintings in a grotto called Chauvet, in the Ardèche region of France in December 1994, reveals masterful art dating from more than thirty thousand years ago, long before we had thought early man capable of such sophisticated expression.[2] Somehow the childish or amateurish first stabs at art that we expect to find continue to elude us. Instead, in more than 200 caves of southwestern Europe, of which Chauvet is the latest to be discovered, we come face to face with mature manifestations, tens of thousands of years ago, of two characteristics of humanity that were new under the sun: individual genius, and a cultural tradition within which it must have flourished.

We have a tendency to regard the arts as products of civilization rather than an innate impulse. The evidence instead seems to show that they are basic to our nature, for they flourished *prior* to civilization. They are among the first unique manifestations of humanity.

The naturalistic art of Chauvet is based on an observation of animal movements so extraordinarily accurate as to argue the existence of a body of knowledge handed down through generations. Pointing to the same conclusion is this art's aura of spiritualism and magic: of spells and incantations; of ceremonies of renewal; of rituals marking or welcoming the seasons; of prayers for divine favor. Like the caves of Lascaux and Altamira, discovered earlier, it looks to be more shrine than museum, embodying some system of beliefs that in all likelihood was transmitted through time.

Other relics of the Ice Ages also support the view that knowledge was inherited through a more or less organized society. Ice Age markings engraved on pebbles and other surfaces were recognized

---

2. *The New York Times* reports the discovery in northwest Australia of tools and rock art provisionally dated between 100,000 and 200,000 B.C., long before modern man is supposed to have occupied Australia. If these dates are confirmed, new puzzles in the study of prehistory will have to be solved.

as notation systems a few decades ago by Alexander Marshack, now of the Peabody Museum at Harvard University. Decoding them, Marshack discovered that the notations kept track of sequences of events that recur: the regular patterns of animal, bird, and fish behavior tied to the seasons, for example, and the many cycles of birth and death, rising and falling, that are to be seen on the earth and in the heavens. This is information gleaned from observation over long periods of time, and therefore is the sort of knowledge that typically is acquired by transmission through generations.

So for the explorers of prehistory, quite a lot of things that must already have happened come together by 30,000 B.C. at the grottos of Chauvet. Perfectly preserved by a prehistoric landslide that sealed them off, these caves contain at least 263 breathtakingly vivid portraits of animals: lions, bears, mammoths, woolly rhinos, bulls, horses, elks, and a panther. Most of these were frightening predators. A world that must at one time have been terrifying, unpredictable, and incomprehensible seems to have been mastered and made understandable. There appear to have been both language and art; individual genius and group traditions; systems of magic and of belief; intellects that functioned by organizing events in time sequence (otherwise put, people who knew how to tell a story). This would suggest a more or less organized society that thrived by communicating information, member to member and generation to generation, and that tightened bonds and loyalties by social food-sharing around the campfire.

Students of prehistoric man have suggested that for humans such food-sharing was not accidental, but took place on a regular and systematic basis, and that it was a central experience shaping development. It could have been the basic cooperative enterprise: a behavior pattern of not merely living together but also working together, conducive to the development of culture. It would have led to the first routine division of labor: between the women, who gathered plants, and the men, who hunted animals. The food would have been brought back to a home base and consumed there. Social life would have developed around the rituals of dining together.

Anthropologists disagree as to when this hunter-gatherer mode of life took hold. Some still believe that it can be traced back to

Homo erectus, one or two million years ago. Some think that our forebears essentially were scavengers and that real hunting began more recently, with the human race and its contemporaries, perhaps about thirty-five or forty thousand years ago. But the latest excavations show that humanlike creatures of some sort were engaged in systematic big-game hunting at least 400,000 years ago.

Almost all primates live in groups. Their doing so is facilitated by inherent dispositions to dominance and deference that support a hierarchy in which each knows his or her place, and in which one individual tends to lead and the rest to follow.

A leader may be indispensable, but his necessary functions in prehuman days were few. Among chimpanzees, the leader tends to go first. Among primitive peoples who survive today, leadership can play a similarly minimal role. Lucy Mair, a pioneer in anthropology who taught at the London School of Economics, long ago described such casual governments as those of the Nuer of the southern Sudan—"Among them certain persons are leaders in the sense that they are respected, and people will wait to see what they do and then follow suit"—and those of the Turkana of northern Kenya: "The . . . belief that the very oldest men can curse offenders . . . appears to be the only approach to government that they have."

Yet so far as I know, no society, human or chimpanzee, has ever been able to live without some sort of leadership to give it direction. The English word "government" derives from the Latin *gubernare* and the Greek *kybernaien*, both of which meant "to steer (a ship)." That is what leaders and governments do: they set, or maintain, a given course for the ship of state.

There *are* creatures that operate as a group without leadership, but they still need to have something else to guide them. Ant societies, for example, have an organization that rivals ours, and even display such sophisticated behavior patterns as the division of labor; but ants are, in effect, robots, guided by the hidden hand of instinct. They are programmed by an inner "computer" to react in a specific fashion to what they encounter. "Practically every behavior pattern that ants exhibit," reports a student of the subject, "is based on their responses to a limited number of tactile or chemical stimuli."

Humans are not genetically programmed to perform appointed tasks; we are told to do so by other humans. To work together effectively, we follow the leader.

Whenever it took place, the development of a society based on hunting had to impose new demands on its members and on its leadership that would have affected both in important ways.

Engaging in a common enterprise for the first time meant taking the giant step from merely living together to working together. Operating as a team would have strengthened cohesion and communication. It would have opened up the way to irrigation canals, pyramids, cathedrals, skyscrapers, and rockets to the Moon. It is not that groups can do these things better than individuals can; it is that individuals cannot do them at all. Groups can transcend time, creating a culture that endures through the ages and the generations. Culture, a product of spiraling interactivity, dwarfs the sum of what all members of the society can contribute individually. From earliest times, humans demonstrated an amazing organizational ability that drove them forward.

The development of the group enterprise—many individuals working together as one—would have created a revolutionary new force in the world that might well provide, at least in part, an explanation of how the human species came on so fast and so strong.

An explanation is required. Along with human beings, a restless energy somehow had been born into the world, something unique and without precedent. The speed of human achievement in those formative years of the race is hard to credit, and yet new evidence of it is found all the time. Was there some divine intervention, differentiating men from beasts? If not, then the only plausible explanation is that it was the awesome effect of a collective, cohesive effort.

The quantum leap from the condition of merely living in a group to actually functioning as a group may have caused the acceleration of history in the last 100,000 years of the human race, but what caused that leap to be made? Was it the extent to which language facilitated leadership? For language must have made an enormous difference.

Hunting as a team would have presented new challenges to leaders, and also new vulnerabilities. Chiefs would have been called upon to show skills in tracking, ambushing, trapping, and killing prey; lacking such skills, they might have been called upon to step down in favor of someone more able, or be eliminated.

Adroit leadership would have become more central to the cohesion and success of the group. All other members would be affected by the quality of their leadership, which would determine how well they ate or whether they ate at all. In that sense, everybody would have been drawn into politics, into an interest in the question of who should lead. Successful leadership would have united tribes more than ever before; unsuccessful leadership would have divided them. Politics would have taken on a new intensity and a new edge.

The changing role of leadership in such a society is suggested by observation of the Nambikuara, a primitive tribe in the northwest of twentieth-century Brazil. Claude Lévi-Strauss, the French anthropologist, reported that *"Uilikande,* the native word for chief, seems to mean 'the one who unites' or 'the one who joins together.'" Lévi-Strauss argued that members would secede from a failing group, and would coalesce in forming a new group around a successful leader. If prehistoric foragers followed a similar behavior pattern, then in hunter-gatherer days the role of leadership in the making of society must have been growing.

In a sense, the evolution out of ape and into man finally achieved fruition in the late Ice Ages, some twenty-five or thirty thousand years ago. Humans had grown into their modern anatomy: they had become us, *Homo sapiens sapiens.* Better than any other species, they had adapted to the exigencies of the Ice Ages. They had learned to cope with winter. They had managed to either find or erect shelter. They had learned to wear clothes. They did not merely use fires but made them as well. They had art—and also industry, for it is now believed that the creation of textiles occurred as early as 27,000 B.C. They had language, religion, and notation systems that functioned as calendars. Most important, their foraging way of life was suited to their environment—even if they did quite possibly hunt to extinction such animals as the mammoth and the mastodon.[3] By and large, they lived in harmony with nature. They flourished and multiplied: there may have been a world population of ten million humans in hunter-gatherer days.

Human evolution could well have come to a temporary halt in the Ice Ages. It could have rested until the natural environment changed again, causing the species to move on to some further stage. Then, and not in the 1990s, it would have been a plausible time to predict that history, at least for the moment, had come to an end.

We know that humans of the Ice Ages had been shaped and driven by circumstances. Chance and necessity, or perhaps the will of God, had made them what and who they were. But they were about to assert themselves. They would formulate and pursue purposes of their own, perhaps the first inhabitants of the earth to do so. In a universe in which everything always is changing, they were going to start initiating some of the changes themselves.

The downfall of Adam, the punishment of Prometheus, the disobedience of Pandora: such later tales and myths were to reveal a consciousness that in refusing to accept life as it is, humans might be incurring the wrath of heaven. But it proved to be of the essence of human nature to be willful and curious, to be reckless, to be insubordinate, and to seek novelty.

An account of the human race from the end of the Ice Ages to our own time is the history in particular of one such unnatural endeavor, pursued for thousands of years against enemies from without, and now, for centuries, against dangers from within. It is the throw of

---

3. It is by no means certain that they did so. An alternative theory is that these animals fell victim to disease.

the dice on which we gambled everything: the experiment of civilization.

Whereas genesis—the true narrative of creation, to the extent that our scientists know it—tells us how nature made the earth and the human race, what will commence in the chapter to come is the epic of humanity remaking itself and its world.

2: INVENTING CIVILIZATION

It may have been a change in the weather that gave the human race its chance.

Some ten or fifteen thousand years ago, the last of the Ice Ages came to an end. The ice cap once had held perhaps a quarter to a third of the land surface of the globe in its frozen grip. The global winter, alternately advancing and retreating, had lasted for so long that its season of history has to be counted in millions of years, affecting the climate even of the southerly regions that lay far from its grasp. Now the glaciers melted into lakes and streams, and poured into overflowing seas. The earth, after its long sleep, began to wake. Springtime came to the planet and to the human race. The great thaw could be smelled on the wind; change was in the air.

Whether or not climate was responsible—and opinions differ, as they do about so much of prehistory—life now offered new possibilities to humanity. Sometime between about 12,000 and 7000 B.C., these potentialities began to materialize. They sprouted up conspicuously in the Middle East. The seminomadic hunter-gatherers who hitherto had roamed these lands discovered new ways of doing things. The new way to live was to build a house and settle down.

The new way to get food was to farm. To do both was to work a revolution in human affairs.

Like so much that from time to time would change the world, agriculture may well have been born in the Fertile Crescent, perhaps in the Karacadag mountains in southeastern Turkey.[1] It may have been there that humans first grasped the connection between seeds and plants. Taking wild grains of wheat or barley in hand, humans figured out how to extract the seeds and plant them in the surrounding soil.

Much followed of consequence. Along with the domestication of plants came that of animals: the harnessing of other species to human purposes. This was unique and revolutionary. No other species had, or has, used and trained another species deliberately. Dogs already had been domesticated in hunter-gatherer days. After the agricultural revolution began, at irregular intervals over the course of thousands of years, they were followed into human service by the food animals—goats, sheep, pigs, and cattle—and, considerably later, by the transport animals—donkeys, horses, and camels.

In becoming both farmers and householders, human beings did something unprecedented. In the past, like members of other species, they had adapted to changed conditions in order to survive—they had been pushed and shoved along an evolutionary path by the force of circumstances. Now, for what must have been the first time, a species was altering its behavior independent of external coercions. It was giving up an existing practice of life that still was successful, and in fact was far more in harmony with its environment than the new way. And apparently it was doing so in order to satisfy, not needs, but desires. It seemed to be seizing an opportunity, not responding to a necessity.

Since the change was not necessary, many chose not to make it. Indeed, for thousands of years after settling down began, nomadism persisted on a large scale alongside it. For a time, relations between the two groups were friendly and often symbiotic. Only later did nomadism become a rival and antagonistic way of life.

Growth of agriculture and the spread of sedentary villages are

---

1. Although there is evidence of cultivation at an earlier date in Southeast Asia.

linked with the growth both of food supply and of population, though the causal connections are not clear. However, at some point population grew so large that it could not be sustained without agriculture.

Eventually, the polarity of the settled and the wild came to seem natural. By early modern times the conflict between them, in which first one and then another held the upper hand, looked to be a theme of history. The Arab philosopher Ibn Khaldun, writing in the fourteenth century A.D., saw it as the cycle in which history moves—endlessly. An oasis would become a town; a town, a city. It would flourish and grow wealthy. Then city-dwellers would grow soft with easy living; luxury and selfishness would erode their civic virtue and social cohesion; and greed would cause rulers to raise taxes, driving a wedge between palace and people that would render the city vulnerable to attack from without or sedition from within. Hard, lean warrior tribes would ride in from the desert to plunder and destroy. Afterwards, new cities or dynasties would arise from the ashes.

A parallel theme was the emerging and continuing civil war within agriculture that pitted cultivators against herders: farmers, who settled the land and erected fences, against seminomad shepherds and cowhands, who fought for unconfined grazing land for their animals. This was a perennial theme, enduring from pre-Biblical times up through this century.

It is surprising that the birthplace of civilization can actually be pinpointed. Were modern-day politics to permit, it could even be visited. The streets of its cities are in ruins, and the remnants of its buildings are not impressive: mud-bricks, with layers of reeds and matting indistinguishable to the untrained eye from the detritus of other Middle Eastern habitations of long ago. Rediscovered only in the modern era, its very name was forgotten for thousands of years. But this is where humanity first achieved civilization. The place is ancient Sumer, located in the alluvial plain in the south of what now is Iraq. It used to be called Mesopotamia—"the land between the rivers," Tigris and Euphrates—a place glimpsed by millions of viewers on the television screen just a few years ago when Saddam Hussein's armies fled back across it from Kuwait in the final days of the Gulf War.

The people who came to it, who settled it, and who created civilization, called the land Sumer, so we know them as Sumerians. Their ethnic affiliation is unknown to us. They spoke a language not closely related to any that we are aware of. We are not certain where they lived before they settled Sumer, but evidence suggests that they came from a hill country, perhaps a long way off.

Sumer was a delta, its soil amazingly rich with silt, a gift of the Tigris and Euphrates rivers. But before the Sumerians, its promise went unfulfilled; the rivers flooded at the wrong times. The triumph of the Sumerians was in meeting and overcoming that challenge. They developed irrigation, diverting the overflow when it would be harmful, damming it, taming it, and storing the water underground for use in the proper season.

The success of irrigation over the course of time became connected with the development of a sophisticated organization of society that allowed some fraction of the population—less than the whole of the work force—to produce a surplus of food. That freed others to engage in arts, crafts, and businesses; meanwhile the agricultural surplus, when exported, brought in the wealth to support such activities.

So various and profound were the changes, trends, and factors in the Sumerian accomplishment—the creation of an agriculture-based complex society—that some scholars continue to refer to them collectively as revolutions, the agricultural revolution and the urban revolution, even though they took place over a long period of time. Taken together, as the agricultural-urban revolution, it was one of the two great revolutions humans have made in their condition. The other is the continuing industrial-scientific-technological revolution of modern times.

A millennium after the central technology of irrigation was invented, the agricultural-urban revolution achieved fruition, mainly between 4000 and 3000 B.C.: the millennium referred to by scholars as the "Uruk period." Uruk was the first of the Sumerian urban centers to become a large city. It was the Great Power of its day.

The fourth millennium was a period of urbanization at all levels. For the first time, real cities—qualitatively different from what had been merely large settlements—came into being; but they coexisted, as they do today, with smaller and simpler urban settlements: towns, villages, and the like. Much of the population of Sumer lived in town rather than in the country. In time Sumerian society, like our own, developed its division of labor and what we would call social stratification. There were elites, administrators, professionals, merchants, craftsmen, and practitioners of all sorts of specialized vocations.

The Sumerians either introduced or improved a wide range of basic technologies. Nobody knows for sure where or when the wheel, the cart, and the plow were invented, but the Sumerians used them millennia ago; and even if they did not invent the wheel, they at least improved upon it, adapting it for a variety of uses: pulleys, for example, to draw water.

They developed the essential technologies of architecture and of city planning. They may have invented the corbel vault and the dome. They created mathematical systems, traces of which are with us today[2] in the sixty minutes into which we divide the hour and the degrees in a circle, and the twelve-hour periods into which we divide the day. They used science, especially astronomy and mathematics, as bases of their technology, and in doing so pioneered what we do today. Knowledge, like the floodwater of the Euphrates, was channeled into practical uses.

Above all, they learned how to write, an innovation that soon spread to neighboring civilizations such as Egypt and Palestine. Their method was not easy to employ; they seem to have used as many as two thousand symbols, so that literacy was a skill that only professional scribes could master. But this Sumerian invention was among the greatest of all human achievements.[3] It broke the long

---

2. They devised a decimal system, based upon ten, but developed more fully the sexagesimal system, based on sixty.

3. We believe the invention to be Sumerian in the first instance, though it is possible that it was invented earlier, independently, in China or elsewhere.

silence of the universe, and enabled human beings to communicate with one another across space and time.

The wedge-shaped symbols were impressed in soft clay. The writing eventually was used for a variety of purposes: the Sumerians made long lists of names, for example, in the belief that to name something is to acquire power over it.

The first work of literature—or at any rate, the earliest that survives—comes from Sumer. Its hero was, so far as we know, a real person. His name was Gilgamesh, and he was the ruler of Uruk. He lived in about 2700 B.C. He was credited—though wrongly—with building Uruk's famous city walls. In the centuries after his death, legends grew around him. The legends were woven into oral traditions, and at some point in that millennium assumed written form. Popular imagination eventually turned him into a god, and two thousand years after his death he was still worshipped.

Archaeologists have recovered fragments of Sumerian writings that tell tales of Gilgamesh and his adventures. These took shape as an epic, handed down to us in Babylonian, and most recently rendered into English in 1992 by the poet and professor David Ferry. The early fragments in Sumerian, because they touch on the theme of Gilgamesh's search for immortality, answer the question of whether the inner, spiritual life of early humans was anything like ours. Thanks to the Sumerians, who invented both the science of writing and the art of literature, we know that our principal concern—mortality—was theirs too.

The world's first epic dealt with humanity's first question. Alone among creatures, we know that we are going to die; therefore, alone among creatures, we protest against it. Can we live forever? asks Gilgamesh. And since, as he learns, we cannot, what is the next best thing? The Sumerian answer was: to accomplish deeds that will be remembered. Right or wrong, it was not a primitive or archaic response: there are many who would say the same thing today.

Indeed, among the most remarkable things about the Sumerians is the fact that these were people very much like ourselves. If you and I, suitably clothed and fluent in the language, had strolled through the streets of Uruk four, five, or six thousand years ago, stopping from time to time to chat with its inhabitants, we would have found ourselves discussing familiar subjects. We might have spoken of war or politics, lamented that business had fallen off, or complained that taxes were too high; or we might have speculated on the direction of the prices of goods.

In physical appearance this somewhat short but solidly built people with their black hair and distinctively longish noses would not have differed greatly from those who live close to Uruk today. Statues show Sumerian men stripped to the waist, but in real life they went about fully dressed, as we do. Men would have dressed in shirts or jackets, skirts, and a headcloth. Their flocks were abundant, so their clothes would have been of sheepskin, and also—from a technology hit upon long before—of leather, as well as of cloth in a number of varieties. Often beads, shells, or pieces of metal were attached to their clothes, sometimes to be used as fasteners, sometimes only for decoration. A woman's wardrobe could have contained a variety of garments, among them togas, jackets, veils, ribbons, and types of headdress. At times they would have adorned themselves with ornamental headcombs. They wore bracelets and earrings. Men and women would both have covered themselves with cloaks. Both would have employed cosmetics, and would have applied them in front of mirrors.

Dinner in Uruk thousands of years ago might not have been fundamentally different from what we experience today. It is true that a meal there would have had us doing without a table or chairs, sitting instead on the floor and eating from a common dish. And no utensils would have been provided; each of us would have used the knife we kept in our belt. But the silver serving vessels might well have been magnificent.

The bread would not have been leavened; but neither is the matzo that Jews eat during Passover, and that many choose to eat all year long. In that respect as in others, Sumer's food would not have challenged our notions of what is edible. The dinner menu might have included a range of vegetables, barley, lamb, mutton, pork, fish in abundance, game birds, or the ubiquitous fruit of the palm tree: dates. Some of the food would have been served fresh, some dried or smoked.

We would have drunk our beer through straws from a common container—from the barrel, as it were—or, if we found ourselves guests of the wealthy, we might instead have sipped a wine made from dates. We might have been entertained by dancing and singing, or the music of such instruments as the drum or the harp, the lyre or the cymbal. We might have played board games, or rolled the dice.

Only a short time before, on the scale of evolutionary time, our ancestors had been illiterate savages, wanderers who gathered in the caves of the bleak Ice Ages. How did the Sumerians become so much like us so quickly? How did Tarzan, after so brief a preparation, manage to put on the manners as well as the clothes of Lord Greystoke?

A plausible explanation of such explosive progress is that, as a result of the teamwork that language makes possible and that group organization develops, culture grows exponentially, which is to say, by geometric rather than arithmetical progression.

The elements that go into the making of a civilization had been present for a long time. Art is at least as old as the human race; we see it on the walls of caves and in the masks and designs of primitive human tribes. Music, if the Neanderthal flute[4] is what we think it is, may be even older than we are. But it is in cities that not only do these arts flourish, but also the arts of living, of manners, and of refinement.

In the social sciences, civilization means the complex organization of society. In the humanities, it means a coherent outlook; an ideal held in common by those who belong to the same society; a shared vision, expressed in sculpture, painting, architecture, literature, philosophy, and other manifestations of the human spirit.

It is not easy to define, but we know it when we see it; and, however it may have been achieved, we recognize the first civilization in the city-state of Uruk.

---

4. See page 16 above.

. . .

The ascent of humanity from tribal life to city-dwelling was associated with progress in many, but not all, aspects of life. Two of the darker features of early society survived not merely into the first civilization but practically into our own time.

One of these is slavery. In the cities of the Sumerian plain from which civilization first emerged, slave girls from the Iranian highlands were as normal an import as timber. The institution of slavery was basic to later ancient civilizations, and survived into modern times. It was stamped out only in the nineteenth and twentieth centuries.

The second is that women, though allowed to own land, ordinarily were not included in the political process. Goddesses were powerful figures in the pantheon of ancient religions; yet their roles were not reflected in everyday life. From time to time women became rulers, but this was the exception rather than the rule. The king-makers, oligarchs, elites, and decision-makers almost always were men, as were the electors when republics came into being. It was only in the present century that many democracies gave women the vote. In a number of countries they still do not have that right.

In scale as well as structure, the cities of Sumer were different from the communities of earlier humans. In its days of glory, Uruk covered 1,100 acres and contained an estimated twenty-four thousand inhabitants: maybe more. It had outgrown the social units of hunter-gatherer days, which may have been a loose alliance of twenty or twenty-five groups of twenty-five members each. In Sumer the family-based clan or tribe had been replaced by a territorial unit: the city-state, which included the surrounding territories as well as the city proper.

Sumer's maintenance and administration of a system of ditches and canals eventually both required and produced sophistication in government and in the administration and recording of a complex system of land titles and user rights. Sumer's majestic public structures, too, bore witness to the existence of a centralized authority, endowed with the power to adjudicate, administer, impose or organize cooperation, perhaps conscript, and tax. Scholars estimate that Uruk's rectangular White Temple, which stood on a terrace forty feet high, must have taken fifteen hundred men five years to build. It was a public-works project that called for purpose, planning, and perseverance.

Like the other cities of Sumer, Uruk was surrounded by a wall of sun-dried brick; Uruk's stretched almost six miles, with over nine hundred towers. It was a heroic achievement; little wonder that in later days the citizenry ascribed it to godlike Gilgamesh, though in fact it was constructed some six centuries after his time.

We know little of Sumerian government and politics. Formal leadership, like so much else, seems to have emerged in the Uruk period (4000–3000 B.C.), along with writing and the potter's wheel. In its early days, Sumer was a theocracy. Cities were dedicated to the gods; and priests, in interpreting the divine will, provided effective authority. Gradually, though we do not know how, secular figures emerged whose lead to some extent and in some circumstances was followed; the varying titles they received—great man, lord, governor, king—may have referred to varying degrees of importance. It has been suggested that leaders sometimes had to submit their decisions to a citizen assembly for consent or ratification.

In Sumer, by the millennium after the Uruk period, rulership had become hereditary; and in the millennia that followed, as kings eventually tended to claim that they were divinely anointed, and even that they were gods themselves—as did Naram-Sin of Akkad (c. 2254–c. 2218 B.C.)—the religious and secular powers in the state were united in secular hands. This established the pattern of Middle Eastern politics for thousands of years, in which rulers such as the Great King of Persia were worshipped as gods. Western conquerors of the region, Alexander and the Caesars, later were to adopt this practice themselves.

Of the Uruk period, in which civilization first flowered, a leading authority on Sumer has written, "Sadly, it also seems to see the emergence of armies and of organised warfare."

Warfare always had existed, and primitive fighting may have been at least as brutal and bloodthirsty, if not more so, but the armies and the organization of battle came with civilization. The taming of the rivers gave rise to new quarrels. "Because of the imperatives of irrigation techniques, early settlement tended to concentrate in fairly narrow bands along the river courses." Communities were close together, in continuous contact, and in frequent conflict about the grazing land and planted fields that lay between them, as well as about disputed water rights.

Like other primates, humans, by nature members of groups, are hostile to humans who belong to other groups. In the five or six or seven million years of human existence in the wild, that may not have caused a problem, for groups presumably encountered one another only occasionally. That was no longer true after mankind chose to create civilization by closely settling the river valleys.

In the lands between the two rivers, Sumerians had founded city-states next to one another, in inevitably continuous everyday relationship with one another, yet each politically independent and acknowledging no higher authority. In bands, whether of monkeys or men, there always had been politics within the group. What the Sumerians had invented was intergroup politics: politics among independent states, the forerunner of international relations.

In Sumer, priestly authority at first may have been sufficient to keep quarrels in check, not only within the city, but even when conflict broke out between neighboring communities. As of the third millennium B.C., Sumer seems to have become a land of fortified cities. Begun as centers of religious worship and as marketplaces, for economic and social purposes, they became fortresses as well.

The technological revolution of which Sumerian civilization was an expression extended to weaponry. To the last centuries of the Stone Ages humans owed such inventions as the bow, the sling, the dagger, and the mace. To the fabrication of these and other armaments, such as spears, shields, and helmets, the Sumerians, who lived in the Bronze Age,[5] brought their skills in metal-working. Having helped to perfect wheels, they employed them in battle wagons: four-wheeled carts pulled by animals.

Yet in history nothing is inevitable; chance plays a major role, as does error and much else. A string of what look like accidents

5. Scholars disagree as to which people first learned to make bronze and where.

produced *Homo sapiens*. Once we were here, human willfulness and unpredictability entered into the equation. The imperatives of administering a river system should have forced the Sumerians to create a unified central political regime. They resisted the logic; their city-states remained independent.

The pattern of politics among sovereign entities born in Sumer at the dawn of civilization was that of independent city-states sharing a common culture, faith, and language—lacking a central authority to resolve the conflicts that frequently flared up among them—engaged in an ongoing rivalry for security, wealth, and power. Unity and diversity were to be the north and south poles of international relations; and in Sumer, political diversity was at war with cultural unity. It was a pattern that was to be repeated in classical Greece, and that would parallel the structure of politics among states of a different sort in modern Europe.

Alliances must have been vital to the Sumerian system of independent states clustered together. As one state grew too powerful for its neighbors, those neighbors would have to ally against it in order to preserve their independence. That is a policy summed up by the phrase "balance of power." It is a strategy basic to all political systems in which the individual actors strive to remain independent.

Something new in international politics happened in about 2300 B.C.: a Semitic warrior-king, Sharru-Kin, once a high official of the Sumerian city of Kish, a leader now known from the Bible as Sargon, conquered his neighbors to create the world's first empire. He, his sons, and his grandson united under their rule the cities of Mesopotamia—which is to say, today's Iraq and some of today's Syria—and claimed to be lords of a domain that stretched from the Mediterranean to the far side of the Persian Gulf. Later legend had it that the monarchs of Sargon's line were kings of the whole world, from "the sunrise to the sunset."

Sumer, inventor of international politics, had experienced only the balance-of-power politics characteristic of a system of independent city-states. Sargon showed how one city, without destroying the others, could subordinate them so as to create a single imperial state. Systems of states who maintained their independence by a balance of power, and empire: these were the first two patterns of international relations in the emerging civilized world.

A millennium or more after the Sumerians invented civilization in the land between the Tigris and Euphrates rivers, other human beings created it, too. The other three independently invented civilizations in Eurasia did it, as the Sumerians did, in the course of bringing rivers under control: the Nile in Egypt; the Indus in the Indian subcontinent; and the Yellow and Yangtze rivers in China. These were the four independently created civilizations of Eurasia.[6]

The Egyptians were the second to initiate an urban and agricultural revolution. But Sumer traded with the Nile Valley and brought ideas as well as goods so, although civilization was independently created in Egypt, it may have owed at least something to Sumer. The Sumerian fabrication of writing may have inspired the Egyptians to develop their own very different system, or it may be that the Egyptians did this independently as well.

Even more than the Sumerians, the Egyptians were the products of their river. The Nile, which runs for more than four thousand miles, is the longest in the world. Its source, sought for centuries and discovered only in Victorian times, is hidden in the highlands of Africa, south of the Equator; from there it flows all the way to the Mediterranean. Viewed from an airplane, the river valley that cuts through Egypt looks like a narrow railroad track running south–north through the wide emptiness. In effect, this long skinny line of oasis *is* the country.

The Egyptian Nile is close to being one-dimensional: it has length but no real width. There was no way for ancient Egypt to spread out east or west to create metropolitan centers; civilization could flourish only along the narrow line of the riverbank. Such early city-states as may have germinated soon merged along the

6. There may have been a fifth in the Oxus river basin in central Asia. Excavations continue.

north–south axis into two kingdoms,[7] and the joining of the two by about 3000 B.C. created the Egyptian state.

Here, then, was another option in human politics: a centralized state holding the line of the fertile riverbank and controlling the deserts on either side that it dominated. This was a structure that, so long as it held together, brought domestic peace.

Egypt sometimes sent expeditions southward towards the Sudan, but was itself relatively secure from attack; foreign enemies tended to be far away, or to be deterred by natural barriers. But Egypt was brought into international politics by its northeastern frontier—the Sinai-Palestine land bridge to the Middle East—where other early civilizations and powers began to flourish. Egypt could be invaded across that bridge, or could launch invasions from it. The rivalry between the land of the Nile and the lands of the Tigris-Euphrates therefore was played out, time and again, in ancient Palestine; it is a geopolitical theme, revived in modern times, that dates from the dawn of civilization.

Of the four early manifestations of the agricultural/urban revolution, the civilization of the Indus-Harappan civilization, as it is called, after Harappa, one of its cities—has the least to tell us. In large part, this may be because we cannot yet decipher its language. What archaeology has unveiled, in the absence of a decoded written record, is an original civilization somewhat incomplete in comparison with the other three. It began two thousand years later than Sumer and lasted only a few centuries. Its physical remains suggest an outstanding ability to organize large-scale public works. Its cities were planned. Its streets had drains; its houses had latrines.

Unlike the Sumerians or the Egyptians, whose settlements clustered close together, these people of the Indus built their cities far apart, sometimes separated by thousands of miles. Whether for that reason or some other, they seem (again unlike other civilizations) to have not had armies. The late professor Walter Fairservis, excavator

---

7. Such, at least, is the traditional account, though scholars now question whether pre-dynastic Egypt really had coalesced into southern and northern halves.

of Allahdino, a Harappan site near present-day Karachi in Pakistan, who advanced the cause of deciphering the Harappan script, wrote that in Harappan civilization, "There is no evidence for warfare, for alien states, for great kings, or for monumental building on the scale of Near Eastern or Egyptian or Chinese; there is no evidence for large temples, pantheons of deities, slavery, class division, fortifications, elaborate state rituals, palaces, etc. In effect there is nothing comparable to the civilizations of Early China, Pharaonic Egypt or Sumero-Akkadian Mesopotamia." Such as it was, however, it did not entirely disappear, as did Sumer. "In all," wrote Fairservis in his abbreviated, telegraphic style, "there is little to differentiate much of Harappan culture from that of traditional tribal, or aspects of village India today."

The origins of Chinese civilization, though obscure, are better known than those of the Indus valley. In China, as in India, agriculture came much later than it did in the Middle East, perhaps in 5000 B.C., when farmers along the Yangtze River began to grow rice. As in Sumer, international politics arrived with the creation of independent political units along the banks of the great rivers. The two alternatives, as in the Middle East, were rival independent states or empire. In China, as in Egypt, it eventually was empire that supplied the dominant theme, though it was achieved at a later date. Egypt became a unified kingdom in about 3000 B.C. In the Bronze Age, the shadowy early dynasties achieved mastery of some of China, but the country fell apart in the "Warring States Era" (770–221 B.C.). China's political unity traditionally is dated only to 221 B.C., when, as a leading military historian has written, "the able Prince Cheng of Ch'in destroyed the other six remaining states and created a unified empire with perhaps fifty million inhabitants and a standing army of well over 1 million." China's sense of cultural unity, however, had developed thousands of years earlier.

Ch'in, which we now spell "Qin," gave its name to China. Prince Cheng, later known as Qin Shi Huangdi, the "First Emperor," provided the country with its form. He pulled the core of it together by abolishing feudal privileges, installing a centralized administration, and standardizing weights, measures, and language. With the wilderness of the steppes to the north, jungles in the south, the world's highest mountain range to its west, and the world's largest ocean to the east, China was better protected by nature from invasion than were the other early civilizations—even better than was Egypt. Of the threats that did exist, the substantial one was from the mounted hordes of the northern steppes; they invaded China repeatedly even after the First Emperor built the Great Wall. Fearful also of the threat from ghosts, against whom, he believed, the wall provided some protection, he ordered (with only a few specific exemptions) the burning of all books, to keep out the past.

Superstitious, the emperor traveled widely for years, meeting one sorcerer after another, in search of a magic potion that would make him live forever. Immortality of a sort was conferred upon him instead by his accomplishments: the establishment of frontiers and of a type of government in China that would endure for more than two thousand years.

Though favored by geography, Chinese unity—the legacy of the First Emperor—always was at issue and at risk. The burden, over the centuries, of maintaining intact so large a political unit was daunting and at times unmanageable. United long ago, China has had to devote most of its political energies to the overriding task of subduing local warlords and trying to remain a centrally ruled country.

Isolated by the luck of political geography from rival power centers until modern times, China, until recently, was the world's oldest continuous civilization, and the only one that had the freedom to develop on its own, in its own way, and along its own lines for thousands of years.

Egypt as well as China was shielded to some extent by natural frontiers. Geographical circumstances favored political unification; and they were the two original civilizations that achieved it. Their partial isolation also fostered in them a sense that they were worlds of their own: centers of the universe. One major theme of historical scholarship has been that advances were made possible by the cross-fertilization of cultures, but these are examples that suggest just the opposite: the powerful cultures of Egypt and China show how much can be accomplished by the inward-looking who focus on developing individual national genius while somewhat cut off from the world beyond.

Egypt eventually was brought down by its rivals, as both a world power and a distinctive civilization; Persian, Greek, Roman, and Arab conquests over the course of more than a thousand years, beginning in the middle of the first millennium B.C., punctuated its decline and fall. The civilization, religion, and language of the land of the Pharaohs were lost. China, by contrast, managed to absorb the conquerors who came its way, and so was able to continue its run as a distinctive civilization. The wealth of its culture owed almost nothing to the outside world; the Chinese independently invented for themselves, and often earlier, almost everything that the rest of mankind discovered.

Only the peoples of the New World were more isolated by nature than were the Chinese. The Americas were completely cut off. They also lacked some of the gifts of nature that had facilitated the development of agriculture in the Old World. In 5,000 and 10,000 B.C., they did not have the animals or many of the plants of which the peoples of Eurasia and Northern Africa were able to take advantage.

The urban and agricultural revolution may have begun in the hot and humid lowlands of Middle America in about 1200 or 1100 B.C., but flourished for only about six or seven centuries. Known to us as Olmec, the culture sprang into existence around the Gulf of Mexico coast. We do not know what these mysterious people called themselves. Though their art was powerful, the Olmecs failed to develop other necessary aspects of civilization; they did not, for example, invent the wheel. The relation of Olmec civilization to the other complex societies that later sprang up in Mesoamerica remains unclear.

Sometime before 1600 B.C., a great invention was made somewhere on the Mediterranean coast of Syria-Palestine. The inhabitants of that coast, called Phoenicians by the Greeks, were Semites who called themselves Canaanites. It is not inconceivable that this was the work of a single person, an ingenious scribe who could read and write several languages—as was not uncommon on that trading coast that served also as the land bridge from Egypt to the Middle East.

The invention reduced the number of written symbols from hundreds or thousands, which was unmanageable, to twenty or thirty or thereabouts. It consisted of consonants only, until the Greeks adapted it to their own use and put in vowel sounds. From the first two letters, A and B, *alpha* and *beta* in Greek, came the name of the invention: the alphabet.

What choices were available to early civilizations in shaping their futures? To what extent were they compelled by circumstances or by human nature to be similar; to what extent were they free to be different? Variations in economic behavior, in social organization, in political structure, in class division, and religious belief have been examined by students of comparative civilization. The subject is still in its infancy; and while it is clear that a range of options presented themselves to early civilizations, scholars do not agree on the definition of that range or of its extent.

Civilization was created independently in nearly a half dozen places in the first few thousand years B.C., engendering the myriad civilizations that proliferated. Civilizations continued to rise and flourish in the centuries that followed, in Africa, in the Americas, and throughout Eurasia. Humans crossed over from Eurasia to the Americas perhaps twenty thousand years or more before Columbus. During all those tens of centuries they developed in complete isolation from the peoples of Europe, Africa, and Asia. When various "Indians" in Mexico, Peru, and elsewhere conceived of civilization before 1492 A.D., they therefore established it entirely on their own, with no hints or prompting from anyone else.

As civilizations developed, each in its own way, the variety was provided that had driven evolution in nature. Civilizations died but others were born. Some fostered certain kinds of values and exhibited special capabilities; others, others.

Civilizations did not all reach the same level of achievement; of pre-Columbian American societies, for example, only the Maya developed a sophisticated writing system. The animating spirit behind civilizations seems quite different, one from the other. The ruins, for example, of Machu Picchu in the Peruvian Andes, of Angkor in the lush jungles of Cambodia, and of mysterious Great Zimbabwe in southeast Africa present such divergences in visual aspect as to make the point that civilizations are individual and distinctive in character.

In the evolutionary process described in the first chapter as "becoming human," it was the brute traits that came at the beginning and the spiritual ones that came at the end; the first skill was walking, the last one was speaking. So it was with becoming civilized. The Sumerians of the Uruk period gave civilized man, as it were, a body; what still remained was to breathe into him a soul.

3: DEVELOPING A CONSCIENCE

One of the great revolutions in human affairs took place in about the middle of the first millennium B.C. Initiated independently, like civilization, by a number of different peoples far away from one another and unaware of one another, it was the development of a conscience in religion and philosophy.

It is not that people who lived prior to the first millennium were morally deplorable. But their gods were. The early Sumerians and Egyptians, and later the Greeks, believed their deities to be powerful masters, to be feared, bribed, and propitiated, even though their traits were all too human in the worst sense. The gods often were pictured as vain, jealous, foolish, ill-tempered, and unfaithful.

The shift in view from that vision to one in which the universe and its deities were seen to be informed by morality was a kind of revolution. Why it happened, and why it happened when it did, around 400 or 500 or 600 B.C., are among history's greatest mysteries.

Asia was the birthplace of the first religions to focus on moral purpose. Hinduism in India may well have been the earliest of these, although the evolution of its pantheon and the development of its ethical philosophy over the course of many centuries are difficult to date.

The next forerunners were the tribesmen called Hebrews. Whoever they were and wherever they came from, these Semitic people who later formed the kingdoms of Israel and Judea were children of the Middle East. They were of the same extended family as the Akkadians who absorbed the Sumerians, and as the Canaanites with whom they were to be so closely intertwined. In their age-old account of their tribal origins, they asserted that their ancestor Abraham came from Ur. Perhaps this was the Ur we know, near Babylon, or perhaps another. Evidence suggests to scholars that Abraham, his son Isaac, and his grandson Jacob—in the Bible, the patriarchs of the Hebrew tribes—would have lived roughly between 2000 B.C. and 1500 B.C. In their wanderings through time and place, they and their descendants, carrying with them the cultural heritage of the Sumerian plain, must also have been affected by the various other Mesopotamian peoples and cultures they encountered en route to Palestine and Egypt.

The biblical story of the sojourn in Egypt, and of the Exodus under Moses, however close to, or far from, historical fact, clearly reflects an actual encounter of some sort with yet another major civilization: that of the Nile Valley. Whatever happened in Egypt, and whatever occurred afterwards in the desert, and then in the oasis of Kadesh-Barnea, were experiences that had a lasting impact. It is little wonder that findings in archaeological excavations—not in Israel alone but throughout the Middle East—yield information on the history and intellectual and religious formation of the Jews in the fifteen hundred years or so before they put their writings and traditions together in their Bible. The Bible itself adapts tales told by other peoples and in other times whom the Jews had met along the road from Ur of the year 2000 to Jerusalem in the year 1000 B.C.

We can trace the story of the Flood to Sumer. It may even have been based on an actual event in the history of southern Mesopotamia; a flood may have occurred when the sea level rose after the last Ice Age. The waters of the Gulf probably submerged the coast of Sumer, taking back the cities of the waterfront for the sea. To those who lived there, it surely must have seemed that the whole world was being flooded.[1]

The story of the Flood comes originally from Sumerian literature, and we are told that the biblical account of the generations before it was adapted from the tribal records of the Kenites, a traveling tribe of metalsmiths who were by tradition descendants of Cain and who had relations with the Hebrew tribes from about 1300 B.C.

Evidence uncovered in the current excavations at Ebla is said to show that the destruction of several cities of the plain, among them Sodom and Gomorrah, did indeed take place; here, too, the Bible incorporates history.

The relevant observation, however, is not that the Hebrew tribes borrowed; it is what they eventually did with their borrowings. In the retelling, they infused them with morality. The Flood and the destruction of Sodom and Gomorrah were made into tales of wickedness punished; the rescues of Noah and of Lot were examples of heavenly justice saving the upright. The stories were repeated from generation to generation, not as mere literature but as morality tales. Their underlying message was that there is a divine purpose evidenced in the workings of history.

This original view—that there is a design in the history and destiny of the human race, and that the design was created by a moral God—is especially clear in the shape given to the retelling of the flight from Egypt. God redeems His people from slavery and leads them to freedom in a Promised Land: a story able to serve as a metaphor for what all humans can hope for if they follow the dictates of God.

When David united a dozen tribes into a kingdom of Israel and Judea in Palestine around 1000 B.C., merging disparate historical elements into a single Hebrew past for the first time, his new kingdom was associated with the beginnings of a unique religion. It worshipped only one God, even though the existence of other, rival gods seems to have been acknowledged at times. Unlike the pagan gods, the Lord of the Israelites, though originally conceived in primitive if not savage terms, was increasingly as time went on,

---

1. A more recent theory is that the flood in question was that of the Black Sea.

concerned with morality and law. The primacy of moral concerns had already been spelled out in a distinctive sacred law code, carved on stone tablets—the Ten Commandments which, in the biblical account, the Lord had handed down to Moses on Mount Sinai after the tribes came forth from Egypt. By their ethical emphasis, the concise Commandments stood in marked contrast to other early Middle Eastern legal codes, a memory of which the Hebrews may have brought with them from Mesopotamia. The stone tablets were encased within their own gold-plated wooden chest, the Ark of the Covenant, which the tribes carried with them in their wanderings and in their wars.

David captured the city of Jerusalem and made it his capital. There his son Solomon built the Temple, in which the Ark was housed permanently. The religion of the new kingdom remained diffuse, transmitted in various oral traditions and individual sacred writings, and expounded by a line of active prophets.

The practice of the Phoenicians, fellow Semites—as evidenced in much later times by the cemetery at Carthage, one of their colonies—was to kill their firstborn infants as human sacrifices to the gods. This may have been a widespread Semitic custom. The Biblical story in which, as a test of Abraham's devotion to Him, God orders him to kill his son Isaac, but then accepts the substitution of a ram for the boy, suggests some long-ago process in which the Hebrew tribes, with their evolving ethical traditions, civilized the primitive religious practices that they encountered and perhaps even had participated in themselves at some point. In the rituals of the Jewish Temple, what was unique was not that an animal was sacrificed but that a child was not. The rituals reflected a powerful and original belief, revolutionary in its implications: that human life is sacred.

Israel and Judea, only fitfully unified, eventually came apart. The northern ten tribes, collectively the kingdom of Israel, were subsequently devastated, and their people carried away, by the powerful Assyrians in 721 B.C. The ten tribes disappeared, lost to history; their land was resettled by foreigners.

A century later a movement of religious revival and reformation was set in motion in the southern kingdom, Judea, by the appearance of a sacred text that we call the Book of Deuteronomy. It purported to be a lost ancient manuscript, only just discovered in the Temple, in which Moses repeats in detail and elaborates on the laws his people are to obey, and the blessings that will attend them if they do—and the curses if they don't. It was a call to religious revival, which took place to some extent. But it was not until tragedy struck again that the Jews seriously heeded the call and were driven to take refuge in their faith.

The Babylonians, the new dominant power in the Middle East, invaded Palestine and devastated the southern two tribes of Judah and Benjamin in 586 B.C., depopulating Judea, carrying off survivors to an exile that was intended to be permanent. In Babylon, by the waters of the Euphrates, not far perhaps from where their forefather Abraham had started the long journey more than a thousand years before, the Jewish exiles began the work of consolidating their religion in written form, elaborating upon it and, "strangers in a strange land," learning to live a life centered on a faith rather than on a territorial state.

In 539 B.C. Babylon in turn fell to Cyrus the Great of Persia. Under his benign rule, Jews were allowed, if they wished, to return to Judea and to rebuild the Temple. But, as long-hungered-for goals tend to be, it was a disappointment once it was achieved. The Jewish settlers found the pioneering life in Palestine a hard one. Their aspirations had been high, and they were discouraged by living in what the prophet Zechariah called "the day of small things" (4:10).

Fearing the failure of their Zionist experiment, the Jewish community of the Persian Empire eventually sent out a religious leader, Ezra, and a civil one, Nehemiah, under whose leadership in the fifth century B.C. Judea was restored. It was then that the Jews began the process of compiling their sacred writings into an official text that would eventually become known as the Bible.

The Hebrew Bible was a work of many hands, written from many viewpoints, containing elements collected over nearly two thousand years, but as of Ezra's time it was still living, still being modified and added to. It was a diverse treasure, informed by a common sense of the primacy of moral vision and by a striving toward monotheism. It sought to discern the purpose of life, politics, and history in the dialogue between Man and God.

One of the most puzzling coincidences in history, noted at the start of this chapter, is why, in the middle of the first millennium B.C., quite suddenly and all at the same time, charismatic leaders coming from different and unconnected parts of Eurasia, but offering in each case some sort of moral vision, made their entrance on the world stage. Why had the time of the prophets come? Why then and not before? Why had mankind seemingly not heard until then of the great ethical and religious questions that now welled up at so many points along the way from the Mediterranean to the Pacific?

Hinduism in India had anticipated it. Among the Hebrew tribes as well, it was not new, but it had been a long time in coming. What happened in Jerusalem and Babylon between Deuteronomy, in the fifth century B.C., and Ezra, in the third century, was an attempt, not to create, but to define a tradition that already had existed since time immemorial. But in Iran and Greece and China, prophetic voices were also preaching messages of morality and salvation.

Among the first of these prophets was the Chinese sage named Lao-tzu, or the "Old Master," perhaps a fictitious figure, supposedly a court archivist of the sixth century B.C. He was said to have been conceived immaculately, the son of a shooting star. His philosophy was *Tao*—"the way of all life"—and he counseled quietism: being rather than doing. Skeptical of dogma, he refused to reduce his teachings to written form. At the end of his life, it is said, despairing of humanity, he rode away into the desert. The Keeper of the Pass, to whom he said farewell as he left civilization for the wilderness, persuaded him to set down his morality tales in writing, the *Tao Te Ching*.

The first writing claiming to be a record of his life did not appear until five centuries later, tells little, and ends: "No one knows where he died." Historians now date the *Tao* as a more recent work, not composed by Lao-tzu. Many scholars doubt whether he ever lived. Yet Taoism has exerted a major influence in Asia over the centuries.

Zoroaster, the mysterious Iranian prophet and religious reformer, lived perhaps in the sixth century B.C., some three or four decades after the appearance of Deuteronomy in far-away Judea. So, at least, we now believe; though nothing about him is known for certain. He is said to have pictured life as a struggle between the two principles of Good and Evil, in which mankind is called upon to help fight for the Good.

His religion was focused on an afterlife in which the good are rewarded with heaven and the wicked are punished in hell. He foresaw a final end to the visible world followed by renewal and perpetual paradise. Angels, devils, details of the afterlife, and much else that was Zoroastrian evidently went into the making of later Judaism, Christianity, and other religions; but scholars know too little to describe the process with any certainty or precision. Zoroastrianism's watchwords were: "Good thoughts, good words, good deeds." It urged the strong to defend the weak, the rich to feed the poor, and humans to be kind to animals.

The birth of Zoroastrianism in Iran took place at almost exactly the same time as that of Jainism and Buddhism. It was an age of agitation and creative disorder in India. The two religions arose from the social ferment and intellectual soul-searching in the valley of the Ganges during the fifth and sixth centuries B.C. Beliefs were being questioned, authority doubted. Jainism and Buddhism were religious reformations: revolts of the warrior caste against the priestly caste—the Brahmins—of traditional Hinduism.

Vardhamana, called Mahavira ("the Great Hero"), lived from 599 to 527 B.C. and was the historical father of Jainism. He professed to be the last in the line of prophets—twenty-four, according to tradition—who transmitted a message from antiquity. He built his philosophy on the teachings of his predecessors, though to

what extent is not entirely clear. He believed in the timelessness of
the universe: that the world will not end, that it had no beginning
and, therefore, that it had no Creator. His philosophy was elusive.
Reality is so many-sided, he taught, that it isn't possible to arrive at
absolute judgments; one has to say both yes and no. His creed
was asceticism and pacifism; his rule was to not injure any living
thing. All living things, he taught, have souls. We have a far clearer
idea of these ideas associated with his name than we do of his life—
if indeed he was a historical figure along the lines suggested by
tradition.

Over the course of centuries Jainism was almost completely over-
shadowed by Buddhism, founded by a younger contemporary of
Vardhamana's. Siddhartha Gautama was an Indian prince born in
the middle of the sixth century B.C. Like Vardhamana "the Great
Hero" (Mahavira), and like Jesus ("the Savior" or "the Christ") five
centuries later, Gautama became known by his title, "the Enlightened One" ("the Buddha"). All three were figures of whom history
tells us nothing, and of whom tradition tells us much that is incon-
sistent; we must take the details of their biographies on faith, if we
believe in them, because we lack hard evidence. Like Zoroaster,
Gautama linked the practice of virtue in this life to rewards after
death. Buddha preached the Eightfold Path: the right mode of seeing, right thinking, right speech, right action, right way of living,
right effort in every aspect of being, right mindfulness, and right
meditation.

Gautama taught that all is in flux, and that after death comes
rebirth—but that rebirth was not to be desired, for the ultimate goal
was to escape from being. It was this that in the end might be
achieved by the purifying process of living virtuously, by following
the Eightfold Path.

Gautama seems to have addressed concerns current in the India
of his day. The first Upanishads, holy books of the Hindu tradition
in India, may have been composed in Gautama's lifetime, or even
before. They, too, reflect the belief that after death comes rebirth in
some other body, and they too link a fortunate future to good behavior in this existence.

What Buddhism and Hinduism had in common with the other

great faiths that found expression in the same period was the exhortation to live virtuously. Where they differed markedly from the line of Middle Eastern wisdom literature that began with *Gilgamesh* and ran through Zoroastrianism, the Bible in its later stages, and, much later, the Christian Gospels and the Koran, was in the human fears they addressed. The Middle Eastern faiths offered some kind of consolation or hope to people who desperately desired to live on after death. Uniquely, two of the great religions of India set out to do the opposite: to reassure people that they will not have to live forever.[2]

Born perhaps twelve years later than Gautama Buddha, in the middle of the sixth century, K'ung Futzu, known to us as Confucius, lived at a time of political crisis in his native China. For a brief period he served as prime minister of his home state of Lu. Mostly, however, his life was spent searching in vain for a position as head of government in one or another of the Chinese feudal states.

Confucius preached a code of conduct that sometimes is described as a religion, even though he avoided speculation about death, the afterlife, the supernatural, or the Deity. Confucianism dealt with the here and now, and began in politics. But seeing, after long searching and much disappointment, that he himself could not obtain the power to govern, Confucius shifted his focus to education: to shaping the outlook of others who might be given the chance that had been denied to him. His aim was to teach ethics in the broadest sense to those who were going to have the power to govern. Often, like Socrates, he taught by asking questions, obliging his students to find the answers. The object of government, in his view, was to make people content, thus preserving order. He pictured all mankind as children of one family, and preached the importance of helping one another. Centuries before Hillel and

2. There may have been a similar belief in the Greek-Italian Pythagorean faith, according to which a process of purification might release mortals from the wheel of life. Pythagoras lived from about 580 B.C. to about 500 B.C., and none of his writings has survived.

Jesus, he taught the Golden Rule: to deal with others as you would want them to deal with you.

What was true of the other prophets who were his near contemporaries was true of Confucius as well: a tradition, albeit enriching in itself, stands between him and ourselves. Did Confucius really write *The Analects*? Or did disciples, who may have altered his message? We don't know.

Confucius was the founder of only one of the schools of thought that flourished amidst the uncertainties of sixth-century China. He looked back to what he conceived of as a better world, and encouraged his followers to conduct themselves in accordance with the code of an ideal gentleman. A long time later it was objected that this led to an excessive focus on externals, on formalism, and on etiquette.

Yet the living flavor of his teaching is conveyed by such sayings as: "Don't worry if people don't recognize your merits; worry that you may not recognize theirs," and "Do not worry if you are without a position; worry lest you do not deserve a position. Do not worry if you are not famous; worry lest you do not deserve to be famous."

Although it was only centuries after his death that his teachings were taken up as the state religion, it is often said that Confucius, over the course of time, has exerted more influence than anybody else in history. Confucianism shaped Chinese civilization and government, and that of neighboring countries as well. For more than two thousand years, generation after generation of China's tens of millions, and then hundreds of millions, of people grew up in that faith, until the communist conquest in the middle of our own century.

The even larger truth is that, beginning in the time of Confucius and of Deuteronomy, an immense new power walked the earth. The great visionaries of the middle of the first millennium B.C. who opened up new vistas to the religious imagination differed in many respects—some teaching ethics for this world, others tying such ethics to hopes and fears about what happens after death—but all of them struck a responsive chord by offering, in place of the childish religions of early civilization, a moral vision worthy of adults. It was the welling of a spring in the desert, and people, thirsting for a faith in which they could believe, flocked to it.

It transpired that the influence on history, not just of Confucius, but of the other founders of the major religions as well, endured over the ages and eventually far exceeded that of even the most successful generals and politicians. This becomes even more apparent if we add to the Jewish prophets and the mysterious religious leaders of the mid-first millennium—Zoroaster, Gautama, and Confucius—the names of those who later took the Hebrew Bible as their starting point, Jesus and Muhammad. These are all figures about whom we know so little that scholars doubt that some of them even existed. Yet 4 billion of the 5.5 billion people alive today remain adherents of one or another of the religions they founded.

Half a world away from Confucius and Gautama, in the flourishing Greek cities along the Mediterranean coast of what is now Turkey, philosophers who were contemporaries of Zoroaster, Gautama, and Confucius turned toward a rationalist, scientific approach. One of these, Xenophanes, also born in the middle of the sixth century B.C., exposed the folly of the religious beliefs that pictured gods as having human natures: "If horses or oxen had hands and could draw or make statues, horses would represent the forms of the gods like horses, oxen like oxen." He believed that "There is one God," totally unlike humans. But Xenophanes despaired, not unlike Vardhamana, of being able to know the truth of this or anything else; all of human thought, he feared, was mere opinion.

The elusiveness of truth was hinted at, too, in the writings of Heraclitus, another Greek philosopher. He taught, as Gautama did in India at the same time, that everything is in flux: "Everything flows and nothing abides; everything gives way and nothing stays fixed. You cannot step twice into the same river, for other waters are continually flowing on." Pythagoras, still another semimythical figure of that culturally glorious century, established speculative mystical and mathematical traditions that found their way into both astrology and modern science. The secret brotherhood of his followers taught a philosophy of spiritual purification.

The Greeks of the sixth century and earlier were intellectual pioneers. It was the first time that they or anybody else began, as one historian has put it, "to think of space, time, man, and the state in any clear and coherent manner."

Greek philosophy of the time was mostly materialist. In the fifth century, Socrates (and in the fourth century, his disciple Plato) rejected this approach because it did not ask why rather than how, because it did not deal with purposes, and because it did not address what was for Socrates the central questions for mankind: how should human beings conduct their lives, what goals should they pursue, and how can people be made better?

In the dialogues, Plato imaginatively re-created the teachings of Socrates, putting words into the mouth of the great man who had been his teacher. Nobody knows with any certainty where the real Socrates leaves off and Plato begins. Some of the views attributed to the main character may have been those of the author. But it does seem that, like Zoroaster, Gautama, and Confucius, Socrates placed the question of ethics—of the good life—at the heart of his concerns. Like Confucius, Plato sought countries for his students to govern: the ideal that he inspired in the Western world was that philosophers might become kings, or kings philosophers.

But what a professor of moral philosophy at Oxford University has written of him could be said about almost all of the great religious and ethical philosophers of the first millennium—and after: "It is safe to say that no single statement can be made in interpretation of Plato which some scholars will not dispute."

The dawn of philosophy in Greece in the mid-first millennium B.C., which took place as moral creeds were being born in Asia and in the Middle East, occurred at a time when international relations, too, were giving rise to new kinds of questions. The collision of the Persian Empire, expanding westward, with the Greek-speaking world of the Mediterranean brought, for the first time, a moral dimension—a contest of ideologies—into the world of politics.

The Persians, or Iranians, were fierce horsemen who may have come originally from southern Russia or the wildernesses of central Asia.[3] In the last half of the sixth century the Persians went about rounding out their conquest of the entire Middle East. When they reached the Greek-peopled eastern coast of the Mediterranean, they overran it.

The Greeks had settled the Asiatic coast and its offshore islands generations before. Ionia, as it was called, was the wealthiest part of the Greek-speaking world, and the most advanced. For a century or two it was the center of a high culture. Out of the curiosity, imagination, and genius of its city-dwellers came much of what the human race continues to value. Medicine and science flourished alongside the arts. The land of Homer and of Sappho, Ionia invented philosophy and history. It was in the forefront of the Hellenic civilization that gave us prose literature and the theater.

Freya Stark, a twentieth-century British traveler along the coast, wrote that happiness "still hangs unmistakable, elusive, like a sea-spray in the sun, over the coastline." Great wealth brought leisure, and with it the freedom to pursue the good life in its spiritual as well as material aspects.

The Greeks mastered the challenging art of sculpting in marble; at an early stage in doing so, they employed a technique in which the sculpted faces wore an intriguing expression, a look suggesting secret knowledge and an inner amusement. We call it "the archaic smile." It could stand for the Greek-speaking world as a whole in 500 B.C.: perhaps the first civilization to know the full enjoyment of happiness.

Its confidence in the face of life—and death—is reflected in lines ("the greatest perhaps in Greek," writes the classicist D. S. Carne-Ross) in an ode by Pindar written in the fifth century, that Professor Carne-Ross says "have defeated all attempts at English translation." He gives us what he calls the "bald prose of it":

3. The Persians belonged to the largest of the world's language families, the Indo-European. So did the Greeks, whom they encountered. Little is known and much disputed about the parent language from which the dozen or so Indo-European language stocks came. The parent language is believed to have appeared in Eurasia sometime between 7000 and 2500 B.C.

> *Creatures of a day. What is he, what is he not?*
> *Dream of a shadow, man.*
> *But when the radiance granted by Zeus comes,*
> *a bright light rests on men and life is sweet.*

A translator who tried his hand at it renders it:

> *Thing of a day! Such is man; a shadow in a dream*
> *Yet when god-given splendor visits him*
> *A bright radiance plays over him, and how sweet is life.*

In 499 B.C. the Greek cities of the Asian coast and the offshore islands of Ionia threw off Persian rule and reclaimed their freedom. With the Ionian revolt began a war between Persia and Greece that lasted intermittently for about 170 years.

In the war's first phases, tiny Greece, an alliance of independent city-states, beat all the odds by defeating the mighty Persian Empire on the broad plains of Marathon (490 B.C.) and at the narrow straits of Salamis (480 B.C.).

By a supreme act of political imagination and artistry, the Greeks of the fifth century led contemporaries and posterity alike to see their near-miraculous victory as a triumph of Europe's political beliefs over those of Asia. Athens and many of the other Greek city-states were democracies, and even monarchical Sparta believed itself to be governed by the rule of law. The banner under which they fought off the Persian Empire was that of freedom. Persia, on the other hand, was an autocracy, ruled by one man's whim. At least that is what the Athenians claimed. Unaware of the variety of civilizations and political cultures in Asia, the Greeks fixed forever in the world's mind the stereotype of the Great King's empire as the typical oriental despotism.

Herodotus, an Ionian Greek, in exile from the coastal city of Hallicarnassus,[4] writing a half century after Marathon and Salamis, carried this message from his time to ours. His account of the Persian

---

4. Today's yachting center of Bodrum.

wars is the earliest work of narrative history that has come down to us in its entirety. He pictured the two invasions of Greece as episodes in an ages-old quarrel of Asia with Europe: a feud of East and West woven into the tapestry of existence. Cities in the past may well have seen their rivalry with one another as the theme of history, but always it had been on the level of one state, with its patron gods, against another. So far as we know, the Israelite tribes did much the same; in early times they viewed their wars as vindicating the claims of their jealous deity as against those of equally real but rival and enemy gods. Moving from rival gods to rival political faiths, Herodotus, expressing views common in the Greek-speaking world of his time, elevated the wars to the plane of a clash of civilizations and to a battle of ideas and ideals: of freedom versus slavery.

In the second phase of the long war between Hellas and Persia, the victorious Greek city-states fell apart and fought one another, while the Persians remained largely behind the scenes, adroitly bribing and intriguing, encouraging the Greeks to further fratricide. Then, when the Greeks had finished destroying themselves, the Persians stepped in to pick up the pieces.

Thucydides, though he did not live to complete his account, made some of these internecine conflicts his subject, to which we give the overall name of the Peloponnesian Wars. Where Herodotus had an uplifting tale to tell, of ordinary people rising to the greatness of a historic occasion, Thucydides wrote a tragedy, in which men who began as civilized and admirable, in the course of the wars lost humanity, ideals, generosity, and, in the end, all hope, becoming worse than animals. Historians today can point to major omissions in the chronicle of events provided by Thucydides, but the general picture that he painted compels belief.

Of the two main antagonists, Athens at least began with a stated belief in the same high ideals proclaimed in the crusade against Persia. Thucydides put into the mouth of the Athenian leader Pericles, in his *Funeral Oration*, a formulation of those beliefs. Pericles told his fellow citizens that "it was our way of life that made us great." Their state, he claimed, was a democracy that practiced equality:

"Our constitution is called a democracy because power is in the hands not of a minority but of the whole people. . . . Everybody is equal before the law. . . ." Athenians "obey the laws . . . especially those which are for the protection of the oppressed" and place no barriers in the way of talent: "In positions of public responsibility what counts is not membership of a particular class, but the actual ability which the man possesses." Athens, according to the *Funeral Oration*, was an open society: "our political life is free and open" and the "great difference between us and our opponents is our attitude toward military security. . . . Our city is open to the world."

Athenians were not afraid to ask troubling questions about the intersection of morality and politics. Sophocles, an Athenian general about the same age as his friend Pericles, posed this dilemma in his tragedy *Antigone*: Who should prevail if the private conscience of the individual is in conflict with the moral code of the community? And what happens if the code of the community contravenes that of the gods? These were questions that foreshadowed those asked decades later by Plato in recounting the trial and conviction of Socrates.

Great historian that he was, Thucydides told the unflattering truth about the Greek civil wars, in which the darker side of Athenian policy became evident. Athens had turned her allies into subjects; while glorifying the city-state, she had created an empire; and while proud of her own freedom and independence, she had snuffed out that of others.

Thucydides showed the corrosive, brutalizing effect of civil war and class war on hitherto civilized men. In the second year of the war, a plague broke out in Athens that could have served as a metaphor for the moral sickness that infected Greece. Thucydides wrote that "the catastrophe was so overwhelming that men . . . became indifferent to every rule of religion or of law."

One of the most moving moments in the world's literature is the account by Thucydides of an episode that occurred on the island of Melos in the sixteenth year of the war. Melos is a small island in the Aegean Sea, the most southwesterly of the Cyclades chain. It is famous for something timelessly beautiful—a Hellenistic statue of Aphrodite, the "Venus de Milo"—and for something timelessly ugly, the action taken by the Athenians there in 416 B.C.

Melos, though originally colonized by Sparta, had remained neutral in the war between Sparta and Athens. In 416 Athens mounted an expedition against the island. Refusing Melos the right to remain neutral, Athens demanded that it become part of the Athenian empire. In the cynical words put by Thucydides into the mouths of the Athenian envoys, practical men should not waste time talking about guilt or innocence, wrong or right. It did not matter that Melos had done no harm to Athens: "The strong do what they have the power to do and the weak accept what they have to accept."

The Melians put their faith in the gods, but the Athenians scoffed, saying:

> So far as the favor of the gods is concerned, we think we have as much right to that as you have. Our aims and our actions are perfectly consistent with the beliefs men hold about the gods and with the principles which govern their own conduct. Our opinion of the gods and our knowledge of men lead us to conclude that it is a general and necessary law of nature to rule wherever one can. This is not a law that we made ourselves, nor were we the first to act upon it when it was made. We found it already in existence, and we shall leave it to exist for ever among those who come after us.

The Melians pleaded, "Allow us to be friends of yours and enemies to neither side," but Athens refused, besieged the Melians, and eventually won. The Athenians killed the men, sold the women and children into slavery, and then sent their own colonists to inhabit the island they had depopulated.

The Athenians who opposed the war party and who criticized the direction in which their city-state was moving had the gift of portraying the unfolding tragedy of their disintegrating society in universal terms. They were able to illuminate humanity's experience by illuminating their own.

Thucydides, on the sidelines since his dismissal as a general nearly a decade before the Melian expedition, spent the rest of his life working on his history of the war, the first book to provide moral criticism of history and politics.

Euripides, the most modern in spirit of the three greatest authors of Greek tragedy, wrote *The Trojan Women* as the Melian conflict was taking place. The Greek conquest of Troy was the semimythical triumph in which all Hellas gloried, but Euripides showed the hollowness of it, and of all victory in warfare as such.

The play begins by the ruins of captured Troy, and concerns the widows of the Trojan dead, who now are to be given as slaves to the Greek warriors who slew their husbands. The central issue is the fate of the orphaned baby of Hector, Troy's greatest soldier. The Greeks kill the infant by throwing him over the battlements. His tiny crushed body is returned to Hecuba, his grandmother, for the funeral rites. Hecuba appeals to the gods, who do not care, and to the dead, who cannot hear. She tries to kill herself, but is prevented by the guards, and is sent off to slavery.

Gilbert Murray, who brought Greek tragedy to the modern stage a century ago, wrote that the "play is a picture of the inner side of a great conquest. . . . It is a thing that seemed beforehand to be a great joy, and is in reality a great misery. . . . A solitary old woman with a dead child in her arms; that, on the human side, is the result of these deeds of glory."

Euripides' prescience is displayed in *The Trojan Women*, which appeared only half a year after Melos fell. In his drama Athena, patron goddess of Athens, warns the citizens against going too far in their aggressions: "How are ye blind / Ye treaders down of Cities . . . yourselves so soon to die!"

Thucydides, who wrote the Melian Dialogue after the event, hints at a connection to this passage. The first sentence of his next chapter began: "In the same winter the Athenians resolved to sail again against Sicily." It was the Sicilian expedition, as Thucydides already knew, that was to prove the turning point in the war; it was to be the beginning of the end of Athenian glory and power.

In 404 B.C. Athens went down to defeat. Sparta, in turn, was ruined a decade later when its fleet was utterly destroyed by an Athenian commanding a Persian-subsidized armada. The Spartans responded by betraying the Greek cause to Persia, returning Ionia to the Great King. Persia had won.

Plato, a survivor of defeated Athens, wandering through a shattered world in which his mentor Socrates had been given the cup of hemlock—a Cross half a millennium before its time—was driven to imagining utopias. Any morally conscious Greek thinker of the time would have been bound to question existing patterns of politics: the city-state form that led to endemic international wars, the class system that led to perpetual civil wars, both of them products of civilization and arguably inherent in it.

The second phase of the Greek-Persian war was an experience that suggested, in some cases to its survivors, but certainly to succeeding generations and to ourselves, the most basic questions about the nature of humans in a political context. It called into question political goals that were the avowed program not merely of fifth-century Athens but of the twentieth-century Western world. It also raised the question of whether mankind can survive the effects of the warfare that tends to arise within a system of independent states.

Had the cause of the West—democracy, freedom of inquiry and speech, rewards for merit rather than birth—been a mere sham, propaganda in the service of selfish Athenian imperialism? Or had it, on the contrary, been a genuine ideal, but one too fragile to survive the brutalities of politics? Did unending warfare doom mankind to political hopelessness?

The message of the Melian Dialogue was that justice was to be had neither from gods nor from men. But it never had been. The disillusion and despair that characterize the political vision of Thucydides provide, paradoxically, evidence of the moral advance that had taken place in Eurasia in the first millennium B.C. Until then, people had lived in a world without a public conscience. Wars often had turned men into beasts in the past; what was new in fifth-century Greece was that Thucydides, Euripides, and others were shocked by it.

They had formed higher expectations and had framed more elevated standards for humanity—or at least for those of their own culture.

Here was yet another major development in history. It foreshadowed, among other things, the coming of political messiahs, of charismatic leaders promising unity and peace, of Alexanders and Caesars. Human beings now were reaching out for things that were not and never had been on offer in our universe: like the doomed Melians, they asked for justice, and they longed for peace.

4: SEEKING A LASTING PEACE

Sometime in the last years of his life, perhaps in about 408 B.C., the playwright Euripides fled Athens. We do not know why. Perhaps it had to do with the long war between Athens and Sparta, behind which loomed predatory Persia; his tragic genius had illuminated the terrible things that wars do to winners and losers alike. In the end he found refuge in Macedonia.

Macedonia was a kingdom in the north of Greece. It was ruled by a Greek dynasty, and the core of its population was Greek, originally from a river valley northwest of the slopes of Mount Olympus. In Greek mythology, the heights of Olympus were the dwelling place of the gods. The Macedonian Greeks were an exceptionally tall people who lived a rugged outdoor life. Herders whose mascot was the goat, they moved with their flocks from high pastures to low and back again, following the seasons.

The rustic dialect of the Macedonians set them apart. To the Greek city-dweller, the shepherding, farming, and hunting way of life of the Northerners smacked of the barbarian. Macedonians were pictured as uncouth mountaineers who drank, brawled, and gambled. Although they originally were of Greek stock, their bloodline had been diluted; they had assimilated into their population neighboring peoples whom they had conquered.

The typical political expression of Greek genius was the city-state, the Sumerian invention of thousands of years earlier, which when placed in Greek hands had become a work of art; but unlike the other political entities of the Hellenic world, Macedonia was not a city-state but a kingdom. To the rest of Greece, therefore, Macedonia seemed less than Greek.

Its royal house, however, aspired to culture. Like the robber barons of America's Gilded Age, importing European craftsmen to design the interiors of mansions along New York's Fifth Avenue, the kings of Macedonia surrounded themselves with the best in art and architecture that Athens and the other Greek city-states could supply.

Macedonia was a wild highland kingdom of towering mountains, alpine passes, tall forests, and fertile plains well-watered by rivers. It was rich in timber, minerals, horses, and animal life. Winters were bitterly cold, and the summer sun was merciless, but it was a land of abundance: of feasting, of meat and heavy drinking. Life was lived on a large scale.

Its people were warlike, its society archaic. A boy could not eat with the men until he had killed his first boar, and could not dispense with the leather halter around his waist until he had killed his first man.

Macedonia's monarch at the time that Euripides arrived was King Archelaus, usually described as an "able despot." Like such future able despots as Frederick the Great of Prussia and Catherine the Great of Russia, he was pleased to act as the patron of artists and writers. Socrates had declined the king's invitation, but Euripides, whom Socrates much admired, had finally accepted, and at court would have encountered other distinguished guests from the once-glorious city-states of the Hellenic world—among them, in all probability, the greatest of political historians, Thucydides.

It was a portent that, in the wake of the wars that crushed fifth-century Greece, Greek culture should have found patronage in the mountain strongholds of the savage north. The move to Archelaus's court foreshadowed things to come in the fourth century. The cause of Greece, in its long rivalry with the East, was to flee there too, and was to find its champion in Macedonia, half-barbarian though it was thought to be, and even though in the wars that had led to Greece's ruin Macedonia often had been an ally of victorious Persia.

The unlikely story of Greece's comeback—the third and final round in her seemingly endless war of civilizations against Persia—began with Philip II of Macedonia, born in 382 B.C., a hard-drinking womanizer, a warrior and statesman. He was believed to be part Albanian and thus not entirely Greek. He ascended the throne of Macedon in 359, inheriting the kingship unexpectedly at the age of twenty-three, when an older brother was killed battling foreign invaders. Philip temporarily made peace with the enemy, buying time. Later he returned and destroyed them.

Employing military innovations of his own, Philip united and rounded out his kingdom, annexing upper Macedonia (today's independent, formerly Yugoslav, republic) and making it one with what today is Greek Macedonia. Capturing and exploiting mines of silver and gold, he built up the wealth of his resource-rich country to the point where it could afford the vast public expenditures and programs he undertook, including the financing and organizing of a standing, professional army. A master of war and politics, Philip, who wedded often, also was skilled in contracting strategic marriage alliances.

His amazing achievements imposed discipline and unity on fragmented Macedonia. In the surrounding Balkans, he conquered and established the first European empire. He outfought, outthought, and outmaneuvered the independent city-states of Greece, unifying them behind his leadership as their elected Hegemon. He forged not the largest, but the most effective, army the world had known until then.

The next move on his political program, after more than twenty years of preparation, was to lead his Greek-Balkan alliance in a crusade against neighboring Persia. His young son Alexander, born in 356, aspired to a command in that expedition.

.   .   .

A recent biographer of Alexander writes that "Philip hired as tutor for Alexander the best young Greek philosopher of the day, Aristotle"—of that day, one might say in retrospect, or of any other. For encyclopedic knowledge and an ability to organize and classify it, there has never been his like.

The enduring fascination of that relationship—that Aristotle tutored the young Alexander the Great—lies in the summit meeting of talents: the greatest man of thought encountering the greatest man of action. In myth—and somehow the alliance of the philosopher with the warrior does seem mythical—the closest parallel perhaps is with Merlin teaching the young Arthur how to be king.

Were Alexander's quests inspired by Aristotle? Were they premeditated by Alexander? Or was Alexander's mission, which looms so large in history, a design imposed on events only after the fact?

Aristotle and his pupils, Alexander among them, were secluded from the noise and ephemera of the great world. They were installed in Mieza, a quiet, idyllic land of vineyards and gardens in the foothills of one of the local mountain ranges. Aristotle apparently taught his pupils the sciences in which he excelled, including medicine, zoology, and botany.

"Be wary of assumptions," so Aristotle cautioned. "Treat each situation as unique." That is one modern biographer's educated guess as to the sort of advice that the philosopher may have given. According to another, "Aristotle taught [Alexander] ethics and his own views on politics and on the geography of Asia, and perhaps some metaphysics; later he wrote for him a treatise on the art of ruling, and perhaps another on colonisation."

Aristotle himself, at the time, was in a state of intellectual transition. After two decades as Plato's pupil, he was coming out from under his master's teachings, and beginning to assert and elaborate his own doctrines. But we know enough about the development of his thought to surmise the outlook and attitudes that may have informed his teaching during his Macedonian sojourn.

A leading student of these matters has written that "It was a matter of faith with Aristotle that Greece could rule the world if it were politically united." Greek culture was superior to all others, in Aristotle's view. So was Greek virtue.

It would be a mistake, however, to regard Alexander's mind and character as having been shaped largely by Aristotle. Family, circumstances, and Macedonia itself formed him. The young prince was instructed by Aristotle for less than four years, and never saw him again after that.

Moreover, in the ancient world, in which lives often were short, the young became adults early. Childhood in Macedonia ended at seven. At the age of sixteen, Alexander ruled the kingdom as regent while his father was away campaigning. At eighteen, he proved himself as a warrior and, under his father, as a commander in the battle with which Philip broke the resistance of the Greek city-states.

Alexander's choice of heroes to worship shows no sign of outside influence, other than that of his family, and demonstrates the distinctiveness of his character. One of his two chief heroes was Heracles (better known to us, Roman style, as Hercules): a mortal whose bravery, strength, and virtue were such that he was able to transcend his humanity and become a god. According to the "official" genealogy of the time, Heracles was an ancestor of Alexander's on his father's side. Later, Alexander would claim, and perhaps even believe, that he too could become a god.

Alexander's other great hero, Achilles, was considered an ancestor on his mother's side. Achilles, the central character in the Homeric epic poem called the *Iliad*, chooses honor and glory at the price of his life. Moody, passionate, and headstrong, Achilles indeed had the character of Alexander's mother and, as it transpired, of Alexander himself. For while the alcoholic Philip was a jovial drunk, Alexander, in his cups, was driven to dark rages.

The *Iliad* tells of the all-consuming wrath of Achilles when he learns that his best friend, serving with the Greeks in the war against Troy, has died in the fighting, killed by the Trojan warrior Hector. Though he knows that what he is about to do will bring about his own death as well, Achilles throws himself into the battle to kill Hector.

We are told that when Alexander, like Achilles, set out to fulfill his destiny by crossing from Europe to the shores of Asia, he carried with him at all times a copy of the *Iliad*, edited and annotated by Aristotle, that he kept under his pillow at night. In setting out to compete against Achilles, Alexander was aspiring to become, in the heroic vision of the Hellenic world, the greatest human being who ever lived. As one of his most admiring biographers has written, "It was inevitable therefore that Alexander should in due course become one of the vainest men in human history."

An advance guard of Macedonians had secured the passage from Europe to Asia. King Philip was on the eve of mounting his long-prepared and long-planned attack on the Persian empire when he was assassinated. Many had cause to kill him, among them Alexander's tempestuous mother, who had hated her husband for years and who now had been gravely injured by him. In his middle forties, he had become infatuated with a girl of about sixteen, had wedded her, making her perhaps his seventh wife, and had allowed Alexander's legitimacy (and right to the succession) to be questioned. Philip had banished Alexander's friends from court and was making plans to divorce his mother.

Inevitably, she and Alexander were suspected of complicity in Philip's murder. Historians have exonerated them, and most believe the official account, according to which the deed was the work of a former favorite of Philip's who harbored a grievance that impelled him to vengeance.

Through processes of whose constitutional and political details we are ignorant, Alexander succeeded his father on the throne, and was proclaimed king by the clashing of spears against shields.

Everything was in readiness for the war that was about to begin. All that had changed was that Alexander had inherited the command. From his father he also had inherited the mission of leading Greece against Persia, a mission on which he embarked immediately. The new leader was only twenty years old when he set out to conquer the world.

In the spring of 334 B.C., Alexander's armies crossed from Europe to Asia at the Dardanelles. He himself, embarking separately, steered a course towards Troy. He is supposed to have been the first man to land and, in the Homeric tradition, to have hurled a spear into the ground, crying out "that he received Asia from the gods as a spear-won prize."

His forces seem to have numbered no more than fifty thousand, or perhaps less. Against him, Darius, the Great King, could muster a force of perhaps a million, but the numbers are unreliable and need not be taken literally. Persia was able to summon up untold wealth, while the treasury of Philip and Alexander had run dry. It is said that this proved an incentive to the Macedonians: they needed to plunder the Persian Empire in order to support themselves.

Alexander commanded the Macedonians as a king, and the free cities of Greece as Hegemon of their League. His generalship was dazzling in its brilliance. Dealing with issues one at a time and each in its own way, solving a military problem by somehow going around it, taking nothing for granted, questioning, as Aristotle had taught, all assumptions, Alexander at times seemed to be inventing a new art of war in order to wage each battle. He decisively sliced through all of life's Gordian knots.

For ten years after crossing the Hellespont, Alexander led his troops from triumph to triumph. He took the throne of Persia and its empire of the Middle East for himself. He accepted an oracle's claim that he was the son of Zeus Ammon. His soldiers followed him to what they thought of as the ends of the earth—to India—and mutinously forced him to turn back only because the monsoons demoralized them. On the road home—in the Middle East, in what is now Iraq—a misunderstanding of Alexander's intentions led the troops once again to something close to mutiny.

He and they held a ceremony of reconciliation. It took place at a Babylonian city called Opis on the river Tigris: a town that archaeologists still have not been able to find.

Alexander invited about nine thousand to dinner. The guests included not just Macedonians and Persians, but people of other nations and votaries of other creeds. Each table, of course, had its mixing cup. But the huge silver cup placed at Alexander's table, a treasure captured from King Darius, must have drawn all eyes. He was to refer to it in the prayer with which he brought the proceedings to a close.

According to one of his modern biographers, W. W. Tarn, Alexander "had previously said that all men were sons of one Father, and his prayer was the expression of his recorded belief that he had a mission from God to be the Reconciler of the World."

The trumpet sounded. The feast had come to an end; it was time to address the gods. Wine was drawn from the cups. The libation was led by Greek and Persian priests. Then Alexander spoke his prayer.

Its occasion was the seeming culmination of the war of 170 years between Greece and Persia. Or perhaps it had been a war of a thousand years: some would have dated it to an episode long before the Trojan War. For Herodotus, who saw in it the age-old conflict between Europe and Asia, the war between the two was the plotline of history. Now Alexander apparently was bringing it to a close. It could have been said, as it might have been said before and would be said again, that history was coming to an end.

Alexander prayed for the peace between Greece and Persia to endure. According to Tarn (whom most more recent scholars have strongly doubted), Alexander went further and prayed for peace for all mankind. He inspired the hope that there would be no more wars. He asked that all people live in harmony with one another, and that they blend into one another, like the wines in the cup, to become one. From his enormous silver vessel, he poured out the wine as an offering to heaven.

"It was, and was to remain, a dream, but a dream greater than all his conquests," wrote Tarn. Whether the dream in fact was Alexander's is open to serious doubt. There is little concrete evidence of what was said at Opis. The words that Alexander actually spoke have not come down to us, and even the town at which he spoke them has never been found; it lies buried in an unmarked grave.

But by his career, and by the imagery of the mixing cup, Alexander was the earliest historical figure to raise—at least in the minds of people who lived later—the questions of how and whether mankind could achieve permanent peace, and whether such a millennial transformation of the human condition could be brought about by a single being, unless he were indeed, as Alexander claimed to be, the messenger, or the son, of God.

. . .

Alexander, who pushed the art of the possible to its limits, was the first political leader to open up the option of a world-state. There has never really been a second. It has not been within anybody's grasp since it slipped from his. His way to unify the world was to conquer it. Nobody else has been able to do it in his fashion, and nobody has been able to prove that it can be done in any other way. Alexander was unique, admired always but never successfully imitated.

No human ever had won so much. No other person had made himself the master of civilization. Everything was his—and was his when he was young enough so that he should have been able to enjoy it to the full.

From the Libyan Desert to the Hindu Kush he was worshipped as a god, and continued to be so for centuries. He figured in the folk legends of the major religions. More than two thousand years after his death, he inspired both Napoleon and the nineteenth-century Romantic movement of which Bonaparte was the cult hero; but Alexander never suffered a Waterloo, nor was he transported to a St. Helena. He never grew fat or lost his looks. He was the man of the triumphs that never ended and of the youth that never faded.

Alexander the leader is a major figure in the world's political history, but he also deserves a place in history as an individual; as an extreme, a sort of parameter of human potential and experience, a kind of specific answer to the general question about human beings: how far can we go?

For he did go to the limits, and then tried to go beyond them; but it turned out that the limits were real. At Babylon, not long after Opis, he collapsed. Personal demons haunted him. Fits of blackness, anger, and despair overcame him. Disease hovered about in the hot, unhealthy air.

Alexander had taken to the notion that he was the son of a god, but mortality forced itself upon him and broke his heart. His best friend died—Hephaestion, perhaps the only person he loved—and Alexander was as helpless as all humans are in the face of death. He fell into an out-of-control grief that reminded many of the rage of Achilles.

There were limits even to his capacity to consume alcohol, enormous though his typically Macedonian capacity was, though he refused to acknowledge that such limits existed for him.

In the late spring of 323 B.C., Alexander, a victim of physical and emotional breakdown, probably of disease, and possibly of alcoholism, died of a fever in Babylon at the age of 32.

The inheritance was so large that it destroyed everyone who reached to grasp it. From the moment of Alexander's death, the lives of those he left behind—family, friends, comrades in arms—came apart in a welter of plots, poisonings, assassinations, betrayals, and civil wars. One by one, the members of his immediate family, including his posthumously born child, were killed. The Hellenistic world—the name we give to the Greek-ruled kingdoms of Alexander's successors—entered into an orgy of bloodshed. Alexander's passionate and murderous mother, besieged and starved, went to her own death only after having eaten the bodies, first, of her elephants, and then, of her serving women. The empire was dismembered by rival claimants, but their de facto partition of it seemed illegitimate to a world in which the ideal of unity persisted.

"The forty-three years after Alexander's death were years of almost uninterrupted warfare," wrote Michael Rostovtzeff, a pioneering historian of the world that the Macedonian conqueror left behind. "It was not until the second generation of the great ruling Hellenistic families came into power that the idea of separate and independent Hellenistic kingdoms and of a certain balance of power between them took firm root."

In the East, ruled by Seleucus, one of Alexander's officers, the world-conqueror's dream of blending Persians with Greeks was abandoned. Under Seleucus and his heirs, it was the Hellenization of the East that went forward. Rejecting the message of Alexander's prayer, they imposed Greek culture as a way of solidifying their regime, colonizing the Middle East with Greeks in their mistrust of the indigenous peoples. According to Tarn, "to Seleucus a strong state meant the support of his own people. . . . The Seleucid idea was to give to the framework of their empire substance and strength by filling it out with Greeks."

At about the time that the heirs of Alexander's successors were consolidating their Hellenistic kingdoms in Macedonia, Egypt, and the Middle East, a new power was emerging to their west.

Italy—on the fringes of the Hellenistic world, inhabited by Greek-speaking peoples, Latin-speaking peoples, and the mysterious Etruscans, among others—was the political arena in which the republic of Rome was defeating all comers. The Romans achieved mastery of Italy just as the dynasties of Alexander's successors were settling themselves on their respective thrones. It was Rome, and not those successors, that embarked on the next mission which Alexander had marked out for himself: the conquest of Phoenician Carthage, the only remaining Mediterranean sea power. In this, the Romans were Alexander's true successors, as they were to be later when they held out the promise of peace to a world exhausted by war.

The Romans destroyed Carthage, and went on to conquer, at one time or another, the kingdoms of the Hellenistic world, occupying Greece, the Balkans, Egypt, and parts of what now is the Arab Middle East. Eventually they also occupied Spain, much of western Europe, and parts of the British Isles. They held the entire seacoast of the Mediterranean, so that the center of gravity of their empire stretched considerably further to the west than that of Alexander. Their only longtime rival among civilizations was Parthia, successor to imperial Persia.

In the beginning, Rome triumphed because of the character and civic virtue of her people, which expressed itself in the patriotism and fighting spirit of her citizen army; but later, when her armies became professional, she continued to win nonetheless. She triumphed as a monarchy and as a republic in the centuries B.C., and as an empire in the years A.D.

The explanation seems to be that Rome had a sort of national genius for organization. This genius was manifested in the creation of a well-oiled, thoroughly programmed military machine: a "smart" army, as we would say in the computer age, able to function on its own. It also manifested itself in rational civil administration; in the development of a system of laws that remains one of the intellectual marvels of the human race; and in engineering skills that translated into public works of what today we call infrastructure.

There are parts of the Mediterranean world that have never been so well governed as they were by Rome. The Pont du Gard, the spectacular aqueduct-bridge the Romans constructed nineteen centuries ago to bring clean water to the city of Nîmes, reminds us not only of the marvels of engineering and architecture that Rome was able to achieve, but that what Rome built endured.

"All this to carry the water of a couple of springs to a little provincial city!" wondered the American novelist Henry James, who found in the course of his French travels "a certain stupidity, a vague brutality" in what he termed the typically Roman disproportion between means and end: "The end is so much more than attained." But he missed the point, or at any rate, the Roman point; to a progressive civilized government, the provision of infrastructure is everything, and nothing exceeds in importance the supplying of clean, fresh water to urban populations.[1]

Another visible and tangible result of Rome's good government that survives the millennia is her road network. As I have written elsewhere:

An appropriate monument to the special grandeur of ancient Roman government and to its distinctive genius is the remnant of its comprehensive network of highways, which continues to serve public needs even today. Surviving the ravages of time and history, throughout the lands that once formed its empire—in Britain, in continental Europe, in northern Africa, and in western Asia—traces still remain of roads that were constructed during the Roman administration of public affairs. In many of these lands the system of roads has never again been so good. In others, such as France, the system has been retained and improved, modern highways have been built on top

---

1. Ecologists today worry that unclean water and the diseases it breeds may doom the increasingly city-dwelling populations of the Third World. See Chapter 11, below.

of the ancient ones. Among the many pleasures of driving to the French Mediterranean is the knowledge that below the surface of the pavement lies a heritage of two thousand years, and that across the centuries, shades of the ancient world— poets and philosophers, consuls and senators, circus charioteers, and clanking legions on the march—have traveled along that same Roman road to the sea.

The Roman Empire, achieving its greatest size during the reign of Trajan (98–117 A.D.), overextended itself. Trajan drove the empire beyond its limits; the price of his victories was economically unaffordable, and Hadrian, his successor, voluntarily pulled back to more defensible frontiers.

By the time of Trajan and Hadrian, there no longer were, for practical purposes, any Italians in the Roman army: less than 1 percent. Even the emperors increasingly were drawn from the provinces. The Empire in many respects had ceased to be Roman and had been transformed into a multinational organization, functioning with the support of the provincial notables and the leading families of the Mediterranean cities.

Between the second and third centuries, increasing danger from barbarian hordes, and civil unrest and rebellions, drove the emperors to increase the size of their standing army to several hundred thousand men. The military machine was disproportionate to civilian society.

Like the British Empire of modern times, the Roman Empire had come together without plan or forethought. But once in place it seemed to fulfill a purpose: it brought some measure of peace, for centuries, to the Mediterranean world. It represented a step toward achieving that unity of civilized humanity that was to become a persistent theme of utopian thought in the Western world. No polity had come close to doing such a thing before on an enduring basis. From Spain to Iraq, and from the Sahara to the Rhine, the propertied classes enjoyed and shared a common high culture and style of life. These were not goals that Rome had formulated or pursued, or even fully appreciated once they were achieved. But afterwards, when they were lost, they were regretted bitterly, and seen by many as the proper aim of human society.

Even those who enjoyed the benefits of the peace that Rome, at the height of her power, brought to the Mediterranean and parts of the Middle East displayed what a historian of the later empire, A. H. M. Jones, has called "passive inertia," which "was probably in large part due to the fact that for generations the population had been accustomed to being protected by a professional army. The civil population was in fact, for reasons of internal security, forbidden to bear arms. . . . Citizens were not expected to fight."

According to Jones, "The Roman empire seems never to have evoked any active patriotism from the vast majority of its citizens. . . . Rome was to them a mighty and beneficent power which excited their admiration and gratitude, but the empire was too immense to evoke the kind of loyalty which they felt to their own cities."

In ceasing to be a republic and a city-state, Rome had lost a citizenry that participated actively in public affairs. The entire burden was borne by hired hands, which was an expensive way to do public business.

Over time it transpired that the empire cost too much. Like Alexander's empire, Rome's was created entirely by an army. The commonwealth was not a joining together of people who chose of their own volition to federate and become one. The army garrisons stationed throughout the empire were there to keep invaders out but also to keep Rome's subjects down. The army was needed not only to defend and attack but also to occupy and police. As Rostovtzeff observed, "Without such an army the world-state could not continue to exist, it was bound to fall to pieces. . . . The army had to be permanent and had to be an army of professionals [since the] military technique of that age was too complicated to be learned" by short-term citizen conscripts. "This being so, the army must be adequately paid."

But paying them adequately proved to be beyond Rome's resources; the very army that made the empire possible became too great a burden for the empire to bear. Rome was centered on the Mediterranean, which, as Peter Brown has written, "had always been a world on the verge of starvation." Behind the shoreline of the

Middle Sea run mountain ranges in the north and deserts in the south, cutting off the possibilities for farming. Food was the basic source of wealth in the ancient world, and the Mediterranean, once its population had filled out, was constantly short of it. There was a real question whether it could afford civilization: the Sumerian system in which the countryside was so rich that it could support the life of the cities. Roman farmland was rich enough, but it was depleted by heavy taxation.

In late Roman times, the static agricultural economy of the empire, staggering already under the weight of subsidizing the cities, broke under the burden of also paying for the upkeep of an enlarged army and civil service. In the third and fourth centuries, larger armies were needed as never before, to protect against a new enemy—emerging German confederacies such as the Franks, the Alemanni, and the Goths pouring out of the north of Europe. The best the empire could do was to increase the number of its military units while reducing the number of men in each.

Desperate expedients were tried. Brown quotes the complaint that "there were more tax-collectors than taxpayers." Land that had once been cultivated was abandoned by its owners, who fled to the cities to avoid paying taxes on it. Raising taxes to punitive levels proved ruinous. So did debasing the coinage: the Roman currency lost 99.5 percent of its value during the inflation of the third century. Diocletian (245–316, reigned 284–305), the iron man among third-century emperors, decreed that all prices must remain the same. He might as well have ordered the winds not to blow or the Atlantic tides not to rise.

To tax and to requisition its subjects, the government had to be able to find them. Diocletian's solution was to freeze the entire population in place: nobody was allowed to move. In the words of Rostovtzeff, Diocletian and his colleagues "never asked whether it was worth while to save the Roman Empire in order to make it a vast prison. . . . A wave of resignation spread over the Roman Empire. It was useless to fight, better to submit and bear silently the burden of life with the hope of finding a better life—after death."

Alone at that time Christianity, a proselytizing Jewish sect in the process of seceding from Judaism, seemed to tender hope to a Roman world in despair. It was the only religion that convincingly offered the prospect of living on after death—and in a better world than this one. From its origins in Palestine in the first century A.D., it had spread throughout the Roman Empire. Roman persecution of Christianity rose to a climax during Diocletian's reign, yet it continued to flourish and win new adherents.

Cities decayed; commerce withered away. The empire seemed to have grown too large to govern. In the words of one historian, the emperors "lost all control of the vast machine."

Diocletian's successor, Constantine the Great, planted the seeds of the future by moving the capital to the Greek-speaking East, first selecting Troy, but then settling on the site of Byzantium, which was to be called Constantinople, today's Istanbul. Even more momentous was his decision to change his religion, abandoning Mithraism for Christianity.

Constantine may have had a greater impact on history than any Caesar since Augustus. Ascribing to the favor of the Christian god the battlefield success that enabled him to unify the Roman world under his leadership, Constantine became a convert. Eventually, the empire's subjects followed suit, and in the end Christianity became Rome's state religion. Rarely has a change in one person's convictions had such dramatic consequences for so many people over so wide an area.

As for his project of building a new capital for the empire in the Greek-speaking East, in the short run it added one more parasitic capital city to the crushing costs of the empire, but in the long run it increased Rome's life span by a thousand years.

The sack of Rome by Alaric and the Goths in the summer of 410 A.D. marked the beginning of the end of the Latin-speaking western empire. At some point later in that century, the Latin empire, based in Italy, expired.

The Greek-speaking Eastern part, centered on Constantinople, though savaged by the hordes of Attila the Hun, survived. So did Christianity, with its gradually spreading organization and its mass following within the safe confines of the eastern empire.

The unity of mankind and perpetual peace, ideals perhaps inspired by Alexander, appeared to the peoples of the empire to have died with Rome. Certainly Europeans later looked back upon the

Pax Romana as having been real—and contrasted it with the international anarchy that followed after the fifth century A.D.

A more enduring peace was realized at the time on the other side of Eurasia. China's unity was often shattered over the course of millennia, but unlike Rome, destroyed once and forever, China always was put together again. Invasions succeeded, but the invaders were then invariably absorbed into China's syncretic culture. For China, as for Europe and the Mediterranean, a central government tended to bring law, order, stability, and peace; but for China that meant one government for one people, while for the westerners it meant something much more difficult to achieve, one state in which many peoples would live in equality and harmony. Within her protective natural frontiers, and in her unique local circumstances, China could aspire to unity as an attainable goal, while for the West such a goal was elusive.

But China had nothing to offer others except cause for admiration. Believing her own culture to be central, and that of others peripheral, China took little interest in the rest of the world and had no message to offer it. China's way was for China alone.

For better or worse, therefore, China was spared the soul-searching that Europe went through when the western empire fell. Rome had been thought eternal, and in fact had ruled her world longer than had any other power: in the West, she held sway for about 10 percent of the time since civilization began, and in the East, more than 25 percent. She would remain supreme, one of her historians had prophesied, "as long as there are men."

When she fell, it seemed to the peoples she had ruled as though the civilized world had come to an end. Pagans could explain what happened; in their view Rome had abandoned her gods, so they had abandoned her. Christians had more difficulty in supplying an explanation.

A century before, a Christian rhetorician had argued that if Rome perished, "who can doubt that the end will have come for the affairs of men and for the whole world?" When the news that Alaric had sacked Rome reached Bethlehem, St. Jerome declared that "the brightest light on the whole earth was extinguished," and that "the whole world perished in one city."

Had the experiment of civilization, launched originally by the Sumerians of Uruk and taken up since then by one group after another, now proven to be a failure?

The lights had gone out all over Latin Europe and the western Mediterranean. Classical civilization had failed and seemed to have no future; in the fifth century A.D., and for the five hundred or a thousand years thereafter, the outlook was bleak for the peoples to whom Rome had once brought unity, government, law, and peace. Yet that perspective was misleading.

For the rest of the world, and for humanity as a whole, life on earth had been, and continued to be, a success story. Over the course of tens of thousands of years, humans not only had survived—which in itself was an extraordinary success—but had defeated all other species, and subjugated many of them so that they served human purposes. Inventing agriculture, they had put nature to work as well. Instead of continuing to dwell in caves, the best shelter that nature had hitherto offered but not what mankind had in mind, they created their own environment: they built and inhabited cities.

Working together, they had created complex societies capable of organizing vast projects. The material progress they had made was wonderful, their spiritual development even more so. Morality was either God's gift to humanity, or humanity's to the universe.

The innate tendency that allowed humans to progress was the loyalty of individuals to others in their group, accompanied by the hostility they felt to members of other groups. This allowed groups of individuals to become cultures, to pool resources of mind, muscle, and imagination in order to expand powers and extend dominion.

Variety and competition were the engines of progress, as they always had been in the state of nature. And for the non-European world, the five hundred to a thousand years after the fall of the western empire witnessed an unparalleled flowering of civilization. The rich kingdoms and empires of Africa and the Americas, and those that flourished in such abundance in Asia and the Middle East, provided a wealth of achievements and high cultural manifestations never seen before, and China meanwhile rose to a peak of civilization unmatched by any country. Byzantium, guardian of Rome's flame as well as that of Greece, preserved high culture until Constantinople's demise in the fifteenth century.

Warfare had ruined Greece and, in a different way, Rome, but in the rest of the world it had been brought under control by empire. High civilizations tended to achieve imperial unity within their own spheres. Each brought some sort of stability and peace to its own world.

Such was the past. The wonder of ancient history was not that one civilization, that of Rome and the classical Mediterranean, failed, but that so many others succeeded, many of them brilliantly.

What was about to happen in humanity's next phase—the modern world that began in Europe about a thousand years ago as rational science broke away from magic, and commerce started to break the shackles of feudalism—was somewhat the reverse of what had gone before. All other civilizations would fail; only one—curiously enough, the successor to Rome—would succeed.

PART TWO: PRESENT

5: ACHIEVING RATIONALITY

The modern world had its beginnings sometime in our own millennium; its first stirrings in science, invention, and commerce can be detected from about 1000 A.D. For our purposes, the main thing that happened in modern times was the scientific, technological, and industrial revolution. It was this revolution that made the world modern.

Of course there are parts of the world that, even today, remain relatively untouched by modernity. But they are not competitive; they cannot provide the way of life or the standard of living that populations covet in the consumer age; they cannot achieve the military and industrial power that science makes possible; and therefore they risk falling by the way, as others have before them. Indeed the history of the modern world can be seen as the tale of how, out of the many civilizations that flourished in the year 1000, all but one succumbed in the course of the next thousand years. Even traditional Confucianist China, which had overcome all other challenges, was unable to meet this one. Only the Roman Empire's progeny, by inventing first one new civilization and then another, made the running. What follows, therefore, is their story alone.

. . .

On a blackboard in a high-school classroom, a teacher wielding a squeaky piece of chalk used to outline the periods in European history that followed the sack of Rome in 410 A.D. and the fall of its western empire in 476. There were the Dark Ages and the rest of the Middle Ages. They were followed by the Renaissance. Then, soon after, came Reformation and Counter-Reformation, the wars of religion and the settlements reached at Westphalia in 1648, from which sprang the secular and independent nation-states of today.

Such was European history, as earlier generations learned it in school. It was not a bad outline, as such outlines go. Of course it will not stand up to scholarly scrutiny today. The Dark Ages, we now see, were by no means so dark. The Middle Ages were much more than a span of time falling between two eras. The classics of antiquity were not so completely forgotten as to warrant the description of their revival as a Renaissance. Nor indeed, once we look more closely, can we speak of the rebirth of classical culture and learning in Europe as a singular event: as *the* renaissance. Indeed we find renaissances in other times and places. Reformation and Counter-Reformation also are categories that mislead; for there were differences of the greatest importance within, and not merely between, the Protestant and Catholic camps. And there were people who belonged to neither side.

Outlines of history drawn in order to simplify run the risk of oversimplifying. The old-fashioned scheme that I have called to mind illustrates the danger—and so may the one (I am all too well aware) I am chalking here, chapter heading by chapter heading, on my own blackboard.

The passage from the classical Mediterranean to the world of today can be pictured as having taken place in three giant steps: first Rome, then Christendom, and now the modern world.

At the high noon of their civilizations, Rome, Christendom, and the modern world all can be seen as distinctive and coherent, each quite different from the others, each representing special ways of thinking, behaving, living, and organizing society. But, as history is given to overlap, one civilization rising while another falls, we often are obliged to watch more than one at a time.

Our interest in the rise and fall of Rome and Christendom, and of the rise and possible future fall of the modern world, is more than academic. We want to discover the causes, circumstances, and conditions of the birth, life, and death of the civilizations in a line with ours in order to look ahead at what is in store for us.

In listening to the story of the long waning of Rome, and of what came afterwards, and then of what came next, we ask many of the same questions as did Edward Gibbon, most famous of historians, and find ourselves engaged across the years in a sort of dialogue with him.

Edward Gibbon (1737–1794) was an English gentleman commoner. His father possessed a modest but adequate fortune. When Edward came of age, he was given a settlement by his father that provided him with a small but independent income. Later, upon his father's death, he inherited all that his parent had possessed. He lived on the income from his inheritance thereafter.

Physically, his was a precarious existence. His five younger brothers and his sister all had died within a year of birth; and Edward, a weak, sickly child, was himself thought unlikely to survive. Yet not only did he do so, but at the age of twenty-two, commissioned a captain, he proved able to serve for two and a half years in the local Hampshire militia during one of Britain's frequent wars with France.

He was unattractive. He grew up to be, in a biographer's description, "less than five feet tall, with a big head, bulging forehead, round eyes and a small squat nose between chubby cheeks." The Duchess of Devonshire, encountering him at the end of his life, wrote that "he is very clever but remarkably ugly."

Infirmities, of whose causes he and his doctors were unaware, had something to do with the unattractiveness. During his service in the militia, he suffered a hernia, but neglected it. It dragged down his stomach and twisted his digestive tract. The situation of his internal organs was complicated by cirrhosis of the liver, which he acquired by drinking madeira, not enormous quantities, but more than his system could cope with. With his insides malfunctioning, he became grotesquely fat. In the end, he seems to have been unable to see below the obesity of his torso to the enormous tumor in the region of his genitals that killed him, and that he believed to be a swollen testicle.

He claimed to friends that he had at one time contracted a venereal disease, apparently both to give himself an excuse for having no observable sex life and to boast that he had engaged in sexual intercourse at least once in his life—which perhaps he had not.

Physically, then, his was a terrible life. From earliest childhood he took refuge from it in books. As a young man, he sought a subject on which to write. During a Grand Tour of the Continent in 1764, while visiting Italy, he found it. He began research at once, and started writing his book in 1773. Immersing himself in his art, he became the person he chose to be: the historian of Rome.

He lacked, of course, the depth of resources available to scholars today, as well as the breadth of reference: in his time nobody had heard of Sumer, or a range of cultures and civilizations that had lived and died outside Europe before the Roman ascendancy. But in a sense the limits of his information were an advantage; because his material was manageable, he could see it whole. In fact, his was perhaps the last era in which one person could master the entire literature on a vast topic; and Gibbon did so. His scholarship was not original, but it was comprehensive and judicious. His literary architecture and style were informed by genius. From the moment his first volume appeared, giving the English language the phrase "decline and fall," it was acclaimed a classic. Macaulay's *History of England* may be the only opus that can contest with Gibbon's *The Decline and Fall of the Roman Empire* the title of grandest and greatest historical work in the English language.

As Gibbon saw it, the era in which he lived had achieved a different, and higher, kind of concord than had Rome. Of the poles of international politics—unity and diversity—Rome had stood for unity: for empire. The Europe that had emerged from the Peaces of Westphalia as a continent of independent dynastic and territorial states, like the city-states of ancient Greece, stood for political diversity, though within a cultural unity.

But modern Europe had achieved even more. Having at Westphalia turned their backs on extremist politics and religious wars, the countries of Europe had successfully pursued moderation. Even wars, as they conducted them, fought by mercenaries and to a considerable extent according to the rules, were limited; a shared goal was to not interfere with commerce and not injure civilians. In Gibbon's words, "in war, the European forces are exercised by temperate and indecisive contests." In peace, he wrote, the lack of unity was good for competition; it meant that "the progress of knowledge and industry is accelerated by the emulation of so many active rivals." The historian was conscious of his good fortune in having been born "in a free and civilised country, in an age of science and philosophy."

It was a world, in his view, that had the best of both unity and diversity. He saw "Europe as one great republic, whose various inhabitants have attained almost the same level of politeness and cultivation." A balance of power maintained the political stability of Gibbon's world; and he argued that whatever its fluctuations, no matter whether one's own country was on the way up or on the way down, "these partial events cannot essentially injure our general state of happiness, the system of arts, and laws and manners, which so advantageously distinguish, above the rest of mankind, the Europeans and their colonies."

Modern Europe provided a model of excellence. For a European of the eighteenth century, the only other such model, besides classical Greece, was ancient Rome—the subject of Gibbon's study.

The Roman Empire at its zenith embodied, to the European imagination both in Gibbon's age and before, a kind of ideal of what a polity ought to be. The empire brought unity and peace to the Mediterranean world and to its European and Middle Eastern appendages. To the residents of that enormous area it provided the protection and convenience of a comprehensive and uniform system of laws so reasonable that, as later codified, it was identified by scholarly commentators as the epitome of rationality.

Rome developed a homogeneous Mediterranean way of life that took root from the Sahara to the Rhine and from the Atlantic to the Persian Gulf; though there was a shift in weight, over time, from the traditional Latin to the rising Greek aspect of its culture, providing some sort of recognition of the disproportionately large portion of the empire's wealth supplied by the Greek-speaking East.

In the East, Rome's rivalry with Parthia, and then with Parthia's successor, Sassanid Persia, in which the stakes were control of the known world west of China and India, gave to international politics a bipolar structure, not unlike that in our own century between the United States and the Soviet Union. Like the Cold War, it promoted stability. The empire's domestic political structure produced similarly felicitous results. Rome had found some kind of balance between central authority and provincial leadership that allowed local notables to enjoy a sense of participation in government—until soldier-emperors had to push civilians aside and institute Prussianizing reforms in response to the calamities of the third century. But by then Rome's days of happiness were long since gone.

Gibbon believed that Rome achieved its zenith in the age that stretches from Nerva to the Antonine emperors (98–180). Historians today find little reason to dispute his judgment; they, too, tend to fix 180 A.D. or thereabouts as the end of Rome's great days, close to the edge—perhaps 200 or 220—from which the descent began. In the year 200, the Roman world apparently still felt secure; persons, property, frontiers, and values seemed relatively safe from attack from within or without.

Of course in 200 A.D. a Christian, if apprehended, could have been executed. Nor was life much better for a Jew or a slave. For that matter, the Antonine world was not entirely peaceful; why else was the philosopher-emperor Marcus Aurelius always campaigning on the frontier? Nor were the laws, for all their excellence, completely satisfactory; their fundamental flaw was that the emperor was above them.[1] Even the vaunted road system was not fully

---

1. This was true in practice. The same result was achieved in theory by a ceremony at the beginning of each new reign, the coming-out of officials called lictors, who (in lieu of the popular assemblies under the republic) would pass a law transferring the people's power to the new emperor.

effective, at least insofar as the economics of transport were concerned; animal-drawn carts remained so slow and inefficient compared to ships that, as the historian Peter Brown tells us, in the Roman world "It cost less to bring a cargo of grain from one end of the Mediterranean to the other than to carry it another seventy-five miles inland."

But for all of the qualifications that one would want to make to the assertion that the era of the Antonines marked the end of a golden age, it probably remains mostly true. Gibbon was justified in holding up Rome at its zenith as a political ideal; it came close to achieving what other political entities showed no sign even of desiring. As Brown recently reminded us, "The Roman empire was one of the very few great states in the ancient world—along with China—that had so much as attempted to create an oasis of peaceful civilian government among societies that had always lived by war."

What—between 200 and 500 A.D.—went wrong? To Gibbon, as to students of Western civilization ever since, this was the most important question in history. It was only in modern times that the world of Europe and the Mediterranean had seemed to find its way again, and to regain its equilibrium. Is it possible, Gibbon asked, as we do, that whatever happened to bring down Rome will bring us down too?

The immediate cause of Rome's downfall, as Gibbon recognized, was invasion by barbarians.

"The savage nations of the globe are the common enemy of civilized society," he wrote, "and we may inquire with anxious curiosity, whether Europe is still threatened with a repetition of those calamities which formerly oppressed the arms and institutions of Rome." From 410, when the Visigoths raided Rome, until 1683, when the Turks attacked Vienna, wave after wave of invaders had overrun the continent. Might civilized humanity arise some morning to find barbarians once again at the gate?

Gibbon thought it unlikely, for "The reign of independent barbarians is now contracted to a narrow span; and . . . cannot seriously excite the apprehensions of the great republic of Europe."

Cautiously, however, he added: "Yet this apparent security should not tempt us to forget that new enemies and unknown dangers may *possibly* arise from some obscure people, scarcely visible in the map of the world."

Historians disagree as to why the western Roman Empire collapsed. Gibbon himself cited a number of reasons. One of his most persuasive explanations was that too many things had to go right for Rome to continue to endure: her survival for so long, not her demise, is the unlikely event requiring explanation. In recent times a number of historians have stressed one of Gibbon's other persuasive explanations: that Rome's armed forces were not a military match for the German tribes that took the field against the empire in the fourth and fifth centuries.

What happened in Europe in the millennium and a half after 200 A.D. that led up to modern times was that tribes from out of the wilderness swept away the defenses of civilization—and not once, but again and again, so that in retrospect, we can see that one of the things that were happening following 200 A.D. was a centuries-long duel between city-dwellers and warrior nomads,[2] in which, as Rome disintegrated and Christendom started to emerge, the survival of cities and civilization in the West was called into question. In the twilight of western Rome's empire, especially at its fringes, it looked as though the warrior nomads would prevail. Certainly it appeared that way viewed from such marginal holdings as Roman Britain.

In the time of the Republic, Julius Caesar, venturing westward, had brought sections of the far-off British Isles into the orbit of civilization. Later, under Claudius, they became part of the Roman Empire. As distant outposts, however, and expendable, they were abandoned by Rome in her last days. In the first decade of the fifth century, the legions, having proclaimed their general to be the new emperor, pulled out and crossed to the continent to help him face a barbarian threat in Gaul. An appeal from Britain to send back the troops proved futile: Rome had none to send. From Italy the emperor authorized the Britons to defend themselves.

---

2. An experience similar to the pattern of history discerned by Ibn Khaldun. See page 28, above.

Roman Britain was a province of twenty-eight walled cities, but authority and security departed with the legions. Those who had treasures buried them, and a century of civil war began.

Towards the end of the century, foreigners threatened the British Isles. The Celtic inhabitants of Britain retreated before German coastal settlers called Saxons, some of whom may originally have arrived as mercenaries in the service of Rome or of Rome's British allies. According to folk traditions, a local leader then arose who turned the tide. The folktales suggest that, though a Celt, he fought what had once been Rome's battle. Supposedly he defended many of the values of the culture that Rome had adopted. Apparently he was a champion of Christianity. The Germans, on the other hand, were steeped in north European mythology.

The Celtic war leader and his men seem to have fought on horseback and wearing armor, which enabled his few followers, moving from one trouble spot to another, up and down Britain, to defeat the more numerous Saxon infantry time and again. His seemingly decisive victory over the Germans in about 500 A.D. at a place called Mons Badonicus won for Roman Britain a final half-century of Roman peace. We do not know where Mons Badonicus was; nor do we know anything about the chieftain who won the great battle there.

Legend calls him King Arthur. Scholars continue to debate how much truth there is at the core of his legend. Mons Badonicus, and the peace that it brought to Britain, seem to have been real enough. But whether or not such a fifty-year reprieve was won, Celtic Britain at a later date, in the sixth century, went down to defeat, surviving only in Wales, but everywhere else submerged by a tribal wave of Saxon, Angle, and Jute invaders.

In German-ruled Britain, Christianity vanished. Towns and their culture disappeared. It was the same story elsewhere: lights were going out all over the world of classical antiquity. One frontier post after another fell silent; one bastion after another was stormed; one province after another was overrun. Arthur, if that was his name, and the other defenders of the Latin order who, in their respective lands, held off the waves of invaders from the north, fought in what was, in their time and for a long time thereafter, a losing cause.

· · ·

From Uruk in 4000 B.C. to Rome in 200 A.D., the story of ancient history had been the continuing and practically uninterrupted enlargement of the area within which urban cultures flourished. It was reasonable to believe that the expansion would continue until one day there would be no more wilderness, and that the whole of humanity would dwell within the ambit of civilization. That was the vision that Rome, especially in her Christian phase, offered to her world, and that to some extent China offered to hers.

With the decline and then the fall of the Western empire, European-Mediterranean history turned around and went in the other direction. The frontier contracted and then collapsed. Imperial armed forces pulled back to positions more easily defended—and then were ousted from those.

It would not have been unreasonable for the peoples of Europe and the Mediterranean to believe that the frontiers of civilization would be rolled back all the way to their beginnings, that the irrigation works of the Nile would be wrecked by savage tribes, that the world of cities would disappear, and that a return to a hunter-gatherer existence was at hand. At best they were aware only dimly that civilization on other continents continued not only to exist but to flourish.

An age of nomad-warrior victories, almost though not entirely unique to unhappy Europe, had begun. It was to last for more than a thousand years. Coming from the East, it began on the Chinese frontier north of the Great Wall, in the fourth and fifth centuries A.D. It was initiated by the Huns, a people who for obscure reasons decided to ride west. In their path were the mostly German tribes and confederations of southern Russia and of Europe north of the Roman border.

So frightful was the onslaught of the Huns that the Germans in their way fled like animals from a forest fire. Among those who decamped were the western Goths—the Visigoths—who were driven to seek new lands for themselves inside the Roman frontier.

This brought them into a series of conflicts with the Western empire that eventually brought about the sack of Rome by the Visigothic leader Alaric in 410 and the deposition and death of the last Latin Caesar in 476.

The Goths initially came in search of pastureland on which to settle, within the Roman frontier, safe from the Hun predators at their backs. So far as historians can judge, it was not their original intention to put the empire or its cities to the torch. When they clashed with the authorities, they tried to take over the state, not dismantle it. It was only when the peoples of the empire would not accept them as Roman rulers that they acted as alien rulers. They had fallen under the empire's influence long before and to a considerable extent were already Romanized. That is one view of these events.

Whether or not this somewhat benign picture of the Germans at the time is accurate, it is undeniable that eventually some of the tribal rulers adopted a variant of the Roman religion, Christianity.

The mass migrations sparked by the Huns brought turmoil to Europe and the Mediterranean as the Western empire tottered and then collapsed. Vandals, fleeing the Huns, raided what now is France, looted Rome, took Spain, and established a kingdom in agriculturally rich North Africa.

In the end the Huns found fertile lands on which to settle in the Danube Valley of Central Europe. But the nomad wars that they began went on. German tribes hitherto barely known to history—Burgundians, Lombards, Sueves, Franks, Alemanni, as well as Visigoths, Ostrogoths, Vandals, and the like—together with such occasional non-German allies as the Alans, driven from the south Russian steppe by the Huns—marched from one conquest to another, capturing cities and kingdoms, looting them, and moving on.

The Avars, another central Asian tribe, played the role of Huns in the sixth century, prompting Lombards to move into Italy, and driving before them the Slavic peoples, who were forced to fight their way into the Balkans. Much is still to be learned about these Slavic migrations. In the following centuries fierce Bulgar warriors followed their precursors into eastern Europe. After 1100 a movement of Frankish peoples into Slavic lands brought about an enduring conflict between Germans and their eastern neighbors that lasted well into the twentieth century and played a role in igniting the First and Second World Wars.

The Arabians in the centuries beginning with the 600s burst forth from the isolation of their desert peninsula animated by a spirit quite different from that of German tribesmen. They accepted the beliefs and traditions of Jews and Christians as a beginning, but were inspired by the recitations of Muhammad, a merchant of Mecca in his middle forties, to believe that he was the latest and final prophet in a line that ran from Abraham through Moses to Jesus, and that what he brought to mankind in completing the religion of monotheism was the message of God: *Allah*. The forces that Muhammad assembled, and that rallied to his successors when he died in 632, did not set out, as Mongols later were to do, to destroy cities, trade, or agriculture. Muhammad's native city of Mecca itself was a trading community, and indeed served as the commercial center of the Arabian trade route; while Yathrib (later named Medina), to which he migrated in 622 and where he first found support, was an agricultural center.

On camelback and horseback, inspired by the teachings of Muhammad, the Arabs rode on under the Prophet's successors to conquer almost all of the Middle East, North Africa, Sicily, most of the Iberian peninsula, and parts of central Asia and northwest India. In Europe, Arabian armies crossed the Pyrenees into southwestern France; and an Arab raiding party penetrated as far north as the Loire valley before being turned back at the battle of, some say Poitiers, some say Tours, in 732.

In the ninth and tenth centuries, Europe reeled before the horsemanship of raiding invaders called Magyars, who eventually dominated the Hungarian plain, and before the longboats of the Vikings from far-north Scandinavia, whose seamanship was such that they could mount surprise attacks almost anywhere from unexpected directions.

Traders who terrified Europe as raiders, the Vikings brought about the collapse of one attempt at establishing political order after another. History records them as looters of monasteries, striking at the coasts of Ireland, Britain, and France with such frequency in the ninth century that, in the words of one historian, "monasticism became virtually extinct and . . . libraries almost totally destroyed." They demolished all but one of the independent British kingdoms and brought down the empire that had been Charlemagne's. Penetrating the rivers of Europe, they devastated cities in Germany, Flanders, and France, though beaten in their attack on Paris in 885–886.

Yet as ocean-ranging explorers and traders, they created their own world in the north. They brought down kingdoms but established others. Rurik the Rus, founder of the principality of Kiev, gave his name to the eventual Russian state of which he was among the creators. William the Conqueror, a Norman (which is to say, a descendant of Norse settlers on the peninsula later called Normandy, in northern France) reshaped what was to become Great Britain. In the unlikely setting of southern Italy, Sicily, and the Mediterranean, Norman civilization fusing with native Islamic elements was to flourish in the eleventh and twelfth centuries, having developed a cultural outlook that took much from the Muslim East.

The tenth century marked, not the end but the beginning, of another cycle of nomad invasions. As Eurasia entered the second millennium A.D., new hordes galloped out of the wilderness of northern Asia towards the lands that had been Roman—or Parthian—in the long-ago world of the Antonines. Turkish war bands were prominent among them. By the twelfth century, some of them had allied with Mongols.

Of the nomad-warrior invaders of Europe, the seemingly invincible Mongols were most clearly the enemies of civilization, bent on leveling cities to the ground and turning their avenues back into grazing land for flocks. Like the Huns before them, they came from the steppes of northeast Asia. In the thirteenth century they swept over Eurasia like a hurricane, bringing wholesale death and destruction in their wake. Never had slaughter and plunder occurred on such a scale. Those Turkish and Turkoman tribes who allied themselves with the Mongols, especially those who later followed Tamurlane, also seem to have intended to raze civilization to the ground. But the last of the Turkish invaders adopted more traditional goals: the Ottoman Turks captured Constantinople in 1453 not to destroy it but to enjoy it and rule from it.

Despite the profound differences between them, the successive waves of "barbarians" who overran the formerly Roman lands for more than a thousand years had certain things in common. They were toughened by having lived an outdoor life in harsh, unforgiving surroundings. They were experienced in making war. They were hungry, whether for grazing lands or for plunder.

But the history of the nomad wars is obscure. The fall of the Western empire was both the effect and the cause of mass migrations of peoples about whom we know relatively little because they were illiterate—their stories, if any, come to us only from their often uninformed or misinformed victims.

In the migrations, everybody seemed to be in motion. Nobody stayed put. Westerners were going east; easterners were going west; northerners were going south; and the road of empire that led from Asia to Europe eventually proved to be a two-way street. The disorder of post-Roman Europe was that of a world that has been shattered.

When the Western empire crumbled, its peoples were driven to create new and better defenses; a recurrent theme of the millennium was the war between those who manned the walls and the barbarians who sought to breach them. The defensive dispositions eventually led to a new way of life in which people gave up freedom for security. It was called feudalism, and in its economic aspects, manorialism.

European society retreated, regrouped, and reorganized into a mosaic of local self-defense units. These were centered on strongly fortified castles, often located on a dominating high point. The lord of the castle and his knights were heavily armored cavalrymen whose skills in the use of lance, shield, mace, and other military equipment took years of apprenticeship to acquire and whose maintenance in arms was costly. The expense of the system was borne by the peasantry in return for land and for protection.

In their slowly evolving new way of life, Europeans functioned within a network of contracted obligations. Farmers were granted land, and were bound to it, and to their state in life, by the oaths they swore to the warrior-lord who served as their protector. They owed to him a large portion of the produce of their labors in the field; they were obliged to perform military service under his command for a set number of days per year (for example forty days per annum in the England of William the Conqueror after 1066); they were obligated to pay certain fees to him; and they submitted to (and he provided them with) his justice. The warrior-lord himself took an oath of fealty to a higher warrior-lord, accepting a grant of land from him and agreeing to serve him and obey on call in return for his protection.

The whole thing was a gigantic pyramid, in which everyone was guaranteed safe tenure of that station in life to which he had been born, and a call on the support of his superiors, in return for obedience and submission to, and economic and military support of, those above. Such, simplified and systematized, is an outline-model of feudalism and manorialism: a spectrum of arrangements that varied with the landscape of local circumstances and conditions.

By about the time of the Arab, Viking, and Magyar invasions, the warrior nobles of the evolving feudal era were able to provide Europe with a considerable measure of protection.

Feudalism, with its knights in armor and its code of chivalry, was the way of life of a new civilization, which had come into being as that of western Rome was coming apart. The new civilization—Christendom—was in large part the handiwork of the bishops of Rome.

Their achievement was the work of centuries. In one respect, Patricius—Saint Patrick, a bishop of the fifth century born in northern Britain—showed the way. Until his time, Christianity, which had become Rome's state religion, had restricted its activities to the empire. No attempt was made to convert other countries; it was supposed that one day Rome would annex them, and then they would be acquired for Christianity too. Saint Patrick changed that. He actively converted the pagan Irish on the other side of the frontier.

During the centuries that the barbarians were triumphing on the battlefields of formerly Roman western Europe, missionaries were winning over the barbarians to Christianity. The astonishing result was that by the year 1000, the Roman church held sway over more of western and northern Europe than had the Roman Empire at its zenith. Rome's fall was paralleled by the rise of Christendom.

At the same time, the bishop of Rome had been rising in the worldly politics of that era, both within and outside the Church.

In Christianity's first centuries, the bishops of Rome did not, as was later to be the case, rank supreme among the princes of the church. When Leo I, whose "pontificate" lasted from 440 to 461, staked out, for the first time, a claim for the occupant of his Roman bishopric to be considered a *papa* within the Church, he was asking only for age and experience to be given their due weight.

The conservative Leo held a weak hand; some might have said an empty one. Rome had lost its position as imperial capital to Constantinople. Wealth, power, and population were centered in the East, as was Christianity. Latin still was the official language of the empire, but one would have ventured the guess that at least in the East it soon would be replaced by Greek. The head of the Christian faith was the emperor, as Constantine, who adopted it, demonstrated in convening the first conference of representatives of the entire Christian world;[3] and the emperor resided in Constantinople, whose catholic patriarch, by reason of physical proximity, was the bishop who had his ear.

---

3. At Nicea, in what now is Turkey, in 325, to define the nature of Jesus Christ in respect to the Godhead.

Leo, however, made a strength of his weakness. He spoke for the Latin-speaking past and for the dying West, which set him apart from the other clergy and endowed him with a unique authority. The powerful bishops of the East, in their rivalry with one another, courted his support.

After centuries of dealing with the barbarian tribes who had become the masters of western Europe, the popes found champions of orthodoxy in the Franks of France and Germany, who crushed their fellow German and fellow Christian—but Arian— Goths. An alliance was established. The Frankish kings drove the Lombards from central Italy, and donated territory there to the popes.

The Frankish state endured over time, and seemed to offer stability. On Christmas Day 800 A.D., at St. Peter's in Rome, the pope crowned the ruler of the Franks, Charles the Great (Charlemagne to the French, Karl der Grosse to the Germans), as emperor of the Romans, which helped raise the standing of the pope against the bishop of Constantinople; as capital of the West, Rome could be said to rank with the capital of the East, as could its bishop.

After Charlemagne's death, however, his empire fell to pieces, prey to attacks by the Vikings. But the collapse of their military sponsors gave the popes renewed strength in their political authority. Like a recovering patient deprived of crutches who discovers he can walk without them, the Church of Rome brought itself to take worldly affairs in hand.

The ambitions of the papacy were well served by the defeats of its temporal partners. The feudal system that developed in Europe following the Viking raids was ideally suited to priests who aspired to be rulers. The disintegration of power and the dispersion of sovereignty characteristic of feudalism enabled the popes to dominate the secular leadership of Europe.

The millennium that began in 1001 A.D., its wonders eagerly awaited by the Christian world, saw the popes at the height of their power. Appropriately in the Alps, at Canossa in 1077, the hitherto rebellious emperor Henry IV knelt in submission and humiliation before Pope Gregory VII. And the Church-inspired First Crusade (1095), officially aimed at invading the Levant to replace Muslim rule of the Holy Land by a Christian one, proved to be a success.[4]

An unintended effect of the Crusades was to bring Europeans, just emerging from their Dark Age, into contact with the Muslim world: a civilization steeped in classical Mediterranean culture as well as in the early classics of the Arab caliphates. This was one of the great episodes of cultural pollination. It brought back their own heritage to Europeans, and deeply influenced their intellectual, artistic, and scientific rebirth. From the Muslim world, and from the Greek world of Orthodox Constantinople in its last centuries, Europe drew its inspiration and its new orientation.

In retrospect, one can see that the European mind was beginning to look ahead.

Christendom was the civilization of western Europe under the spiritual, and to a large extent temporal, leadership of the pope. Among the bases of his supremacy were the diffusion of power among secular rulers, resulting from the structure of the feudal system, and a spiritual frame of mind that led the masses of the population, when appealed to by both sides, to heed the call of the princes of the Church rather than those of the princes of the state.

Why Christendom declined and fell is another of history's great questions. As in the case of Rome, there are more answers than one. Among them are the development of new technologies of both production and destruction that rendered feudalism obsolete; the birth of capitalism beginning with the rise of towns in the eleventh century, which had the same effect; and the new ways of thinking, materialist and rationalist, that undermined the fabric of a theocratic order.

Then, too, it was dragged down by its association with feudalism. Christianity preached a message of peace; but feudalism—paradoxically, like the barbarian raiders that the feudal system was created to

---

4. But from that high point, things degenerated. Six more crusades (1144, 1187, 1201, 1219, 1229, and 1270) and the Children's Crusade (1212) all, more or less, proved to be failures. The taking and looting of Christian Constantinople by the warriors of the Fourth Crusade showed the impurities in the mix of motives behind Europe's surface religiosity.

protect against—existed through warfare and could not survive without it.

Rome was remembered for having brought peace and security, but after its fall and Christendom's rise, things were quite different. The centuries that followed were a time of violence and disorder. The formerly Roman world was in a state of almost continuous warfare. The wars were self-perpetuating: to survive, feudal leaders had to attract to their service the most skillful members of the warrior elite; to attract such warriors, leaders had to offer them wealth and property; and to continue to obtain new supplies of land and booty with which to reward their followers, they had to engage in ever new wars.

The warfare continued even after the anarchy of the long post-Roman twilight gave way to the early modern world. The military historian Geoffrey Parker has written that

> between 700 and 1000 A.D., the surviving western chronicles scarcely mention a year in which hostilities did not break out somewhere, and wartime outweighed peacetime by a factor of about five to one. . . . In the sixteenth century there were less than ten years of complete peace; in the seventeenth there were only four. . . . During the sixteenth century, Spain and France were scarcely at peace; while during the seventeenth the Ottoman Empire, the Austrian Habsburgs, and Sweden were at war for two years in every three, Spain for three years in every four, and Poland and Russia for four years in every five.

The confusion and turmoil resulting from almost continuous warfare was compounded in the immediate post-Roman years by the number of monarchs leading their armies onto Europe's battlefields. A historian of these times tells us that "in this period there were probably over two hundred kings in northern Europe" alone. Nor were these typically monarchs who enjoyed long reigns. Their sway tended to be ephemeral, as did their kingdoms: who today has heard of the warrior states of Axum, Neustria, or Austrasia?

If anything, the confusion grew worse as what once were called the Dark Ages, the first few centuries after the fall of the Western empire, gave way at about the turn of the millennium to the rest of the Middle Ages. Feudalism, because the sovereign power normally possessed by monarchs was distributed throughout the noble class, made medieval Europe into a drama with a large cast of players. Nobles, as well as so-called rulers, played major roles in war and politics.

In our time, instruction in history often is stereotyped by those who are bored by it as a meaningless recital of names, dates, and places. Detailed accounts of what happened in western history between the death of Rome and the birth of modern Europe risk falling victim to this stereotype; all too often kings were here today but gone tomorrow, their acts proved purposeless, their campaigns achieved nothing, their battles were indecisive, and their desires and policies were of no concern or relevance to the modern world.

But the shattering of Rome's centralized authority opened up centuries of turbulence, movement, and political experimentation that, for all their confusion, proved to be creative and regenerating for society. Like the role of a hostile nature in the evolution of species, the turmoil offered a continually various host of options. If there is much in the shifting conflicts of the warlords of the time that need not interest or detain us, there also are to be found some of the germs from which the modern world has grown.

Not least of these was a reaction against the anarchy, volatility, and violence of those years. The modern world was born with a dream of the stability, peace, and unity that, as we know now, China aspired to for herself, and Rome, for all mankind. But the modern world may have forgotten some of the positive aspects of conditions in medieval times. As a scholar has recently written, "the history of the Middle Ages leaves us, above all, with a sense of the extraordinary vigour and creativity which derives from the fragmentation of power and wealth . . . competing and expanding."

Even the dreadful plague known as the Black Death had a somewhat positive effect. It struck Europe in the 1300s—brought, it is believed, from China by fleas that lived on rats. Its terrible effects devastated and depopulated society, but the death of those with

power, title, and wealth opened up vacancies and permitted movement, heretofore blocked. It was a creative destruction: death clear-
ing the way for rebirth.

In the fifteenth century, the papacy saw its great rival within Christianity humbled: Greek Orthodox Byzantium fell to the Ottoman
Turks. But then a new, internal division arose within Christendom,
when Martin Luther, in 1517, followed by other reformers, attacked
the regime of the popes.

In entering a new round of religious wars in the sixteenth century,
the papacy—to the extent that it had any real choice in the matter—
was running great risks. But perhaps it would have run greater risks
by doing nothing. Protestantism looked to be a mortal challenge
and, because the authority of Rome was so tenuous, it had to be
upheld. Schism within the Church little more than a century before
had produced two rival popes at one point and three at another.
Corruption within the Church, for a time, was notorious.

Material conflicts between Catholic and Protestant were inter-
mingled with spiritual ones, and even at this date are difficult to dis-
entangle. Commercial interests that had come into conflict with
Church doctrine on such matters as usury were inclined to the
Protestant cause, as were German princes seeking independence
from the emperor. Europe was split, with the powerful emerging
new nationalisms and capitalisms generally aligned with Protestantism.

From the middle of the sixteenth century to the middle of the
seventeenth, the conflicts raged, climaxing in the orgy of bloodshed
known as the Thirty Years War (1618–1648), partly an international
war and partly a German civil war, that brought with it epidemic
disease.

So destructive and traumatic were these crusades—wars of the
faith upon which any civilized deity would have had to look down in
horror—that in putting an end to them in the Peaces of Westphalia
(1648), Europe forswore religious warfare. Secular Europe, organized into independent dynastic and national states, is conventionally dated from 1648. François de la Noue, a veteran of the first

phases of the religious and civil wars in France, remarked that "it was our wars of religion that made us forget religion."

During the first half of the second millennium, Europe was beginning to throw off the yoke of feudalism. Improvements in agricultural technology—a new plow that cut a deeper furrow, a more efficient horse collar, and the development of windmill power, among others—created agricultural surpluses, which in turn led to a revival of towns, of trade, and of a money economy. It was a new start.

The growing wealth brought with it a materialist outlook. With so many good things available in this world there seemed to be less reason to concern oneself with the next. People began to look around at new possibilities for themselves. They also started to see the immense potential in others, in the human race as such. It was no great distance from that point to the exaltation of the human being that in the centuries to come was to be called humanism.

Tax collections increased along with the wealth, and enabled rulers to build treasuries with which they could assert independence and create centers of power. Circumstances varied throughout Europe and so did political developments, but these were centuries of movement in which monarchical, baronial, and merchant interests redefined their rights and duties. Centralized kingdoms grew in western Europe, led by England, France, and later Spain, while city-states flourished in Italy, and an elective German Holy Roman Empire held sway over a varying domain in central Europe. Universities were founded at Bologna in Italy and elsewhere, with the encouragement of princes who welcomed the teaching of Roman law, which could be used to counter Church law and to uphold the claims of secular, versus clerical, authority.

Europe's economy changed too, beginning in about 950 A.D. A sharp revival in both population and agricultural production took place at about that time. New lands were opened up for cultivation, and improved agricultural technology came into use. Historians differ as to which preceded the other, but whatever the case, the result was surplus wealth.

Something revolutionary happened next: the development of large-scale commerce. The surplus led markets, fairs, and towns to flourish; local and long-distance trade enjoyed a renaissance. Credit and banking made their appearance, while clearinghouses facilitated commercial operations.

European economic activity, as with the rest of the world, was fostered within various trade complexes focused on key towns. In and around the Low Countries, these tended to be newly emerging cities: Antwerp and Brussels, Bruges and Ghent, and a handful of others. Together with the merchant associations and ports of the Baltic, these industrial centers on or near the North Sea formed an economic constellation parallel to that of Italy and the Mediterranean south. The two clusters met at the trade fairs in Champagne, in the textile-rich port of Bruges, and, most important of all, in Venice.

From this commercial revolution, which took hold over the course of many centuries, emerged the economic order, variously defined, of capitalism. Centered in Venice (from about 1380), then in Antwerp, then in Genoa, it went hand in hand with the other changes sweeping through Europe.

In the emerging Europe, commerce occupied a central role. Italians, with their close ties with the Muslim world, were the first to master its tools. Merchants from the German port towns traveled to Italy, or sent their children there to be instructed.

"Credit," a "net price," a "discount": these were among the words in the new vocabulary that the Italians had learned and now taught. Realizing the importance of mathematics for doing business, the Italians learned from Arab masters and, grasping the advantages of using the Arabic numeral system, adopted it.

Double-entry bookkeeping was widely employed in Italy from the 1300s on. The first printed European arithmetic book appeared in Treviso in 1478, and in 1494 a more comprehensive work was published in Venice, dealing not only with arithmetic but also with the double-entry system, which was termed "in the written manner of Venice."

A Portuguese work published in 1519 states its practical purpose in the author's dedication: "I am printing this arithmetic because it is a thing so necessary in Portugal for transactions with the merchants of India, Persia, Arabia, Ethiopia, and other places discovered by us."

In the five or six centuries after 1000 the introduction of gunpowder gradually brought about alterations in military technology that rendered feudalism obsolete. Indeed, changes in technology triggered changes in almost all aspects of life.

Ways of living were transformed, and along with them ways of thought. Classical learning became the ideal; and while Aristotle and the other Greek and Latin classics never had been completely forgotten in western Europe, when brought back to the West's attention by scholars of the Greek and Muslim East, the ancients, pagan though they were, were recognized as intellectual masters.

With classical learning came secularism: the restriction of religion and the supernatural to their own sphere. Niccolò Machiavelli, a sometime official of the republican city-state of Florence, in his writings described politics with unblinking realism. Thomas Hobbes, translator of Thucydides into English, later followed in Machiavelli's footsteps; but both the sixteenth-century Florentine diplomat and the seventeenth-century Englishman were walking in the footsteps of the ancients.

Though only recently reintroduced to the classics, and despite consciously following in their footsteps, Europeans still rebelled against them at times. Challenging Aristotle, Galileo Galilei dropped objects from the leaning tower of Pisa to determine the speed of their fall, thereby introducing the experimental method into science. No longer was theoretical proof sufficient. People began asking questions such as "What evidence is there to prove it?" and "Does it work?" Trial and error replaced abstract reasoning as the proper mode of conducting scientific inquiry.

The Englishman Francis Bacon is associated with the practice of arriving at conclusions on the basis of induction, the accumulation of evidence. The Frenchman René Descartes looked to the mathematics in everything.

Descartes's intellectual path was indicative of the direction in which a certain distinctive kind of European thought was moving; he was the proponent of radical doubt and the systemizer of skepticism. Michel de Montaigne was another. Seeing the dangers and errors which passionate beliefs can lead to, he became the philosophical exponent of moderation.

An enlightened self-interest, a practical turn of mind, a disposition to base judgments only on facts and hard evidence, skepticism in thought and moderation in action—here is the synthesis towards which Europe was reaching as it emerged from the long sleep of feudalism.

Throughout the Middle Ages, Europe took its time from the tolling of church bells. But then mechanical timepieces were invented. By the 1600s the clock industry was booming. Europeans no longer were oriented by their churches; they had learned to tell time for themselves.

Gibbon adduced at least two dozen explanations for the collapse of Rome. But the one he most wished to be associated with surely was that embodied in his most famous image.

A literary artist, the historian tinkered with his account of how he came to be inspired to tell the story of Rome's decline and fall. In his final version (which probably was as fictitious as the others), he claimed that the vision appeared as he was contemplating the ruins of the Capitol in Rome one autumn evening. He saw barefoot friars singing Vespers in what had been a pagan temple, and there it was: the clerics without shoes, therefore uncivilized; the Capitol, civilization incarnate, but in ruins.

To Gibbon, the early Christians had been the barbarians within the gate who had helped pull Rome down. In his view, much of religion was superstition. The triumph of his own world—the second and best great era of civilization as he saw it, the third European civilization as others see it—was due to its rejection of superstition.

What we might well find suggestive is the notion, implicit in Gibbon's outlook, that one of the most important things that happen in history over long periods of time is a change in worldview. In looking at the story of the modern world, one might well say: in the beginning was the mindset. It was rationalism that brought us from 1000 A.D. to 2000.

The skepticism and moderation of Europe's thinkers in the age of Gibbon were reflected in the relatively effective balance of power which brought to that world a certain amount of stability. How did Europe achieve this? Why did only Europe, then America, become progressive in both thought and deed?

In the beginning of our century, the sociologist Max Weber set out (in the words of our contemporary Daniel Bell) "to explain the historical puzzle of the past 500 years, the question why a total revolution in the organization of society—law, administration, the economy, the arts and religion, and the development of science—occurred only in the West, not in other sections of the world."

Today we would ask other questions. Among them: how and why did the modernism that began in the West spread to countries all around the world?

Many Europeans five hundred or a thousand years ago believed that greatness lay only in the past. Not so; in fact, one of the most glorious of historic adventures lay ahead, and it was their achievement of a rationalist outlook that was to make it possible.

Their adventure story begins.

6: UNITING THE PLANET

It was a great adventure but, as so often is the case in history, its consequences were not foreseen: Europe's takeover of the rest of the globe was neither deliberate nor intended. Only afterwards could it be seen that Europe had conquered the world; and even now we might disagree as to why it happened.

In what has been called the age of reconnaissance, Europeans not only encountered lands and peoples of whom they had been unaware, but became conscious that there were still others that remained hidden from them. Previously they had believed that the part of the world they were aware of was all that there was; now they knew better. Taking as his analogy a burial urn that lies hidden in the earth beneath our feet, the English doctor and man of letters Sir Thomas Browne wrote in 1658: "That great Antiquity *America* lay buried for thousands of years; and a large part of the earth is still in the Urne unto us."

It was not, as we might suppose, because Europeans had invented new technologies that they first set out to roam so far; for such advances by and large were made by them in the doing. Europeans were not always the pioneers in technology: the compass, for example, may have been invented first by Chinese, then by Arabs, and only later by Europeans. Nor was it, in the first instance, Europe as a whole that embarked on the reconnaissance, but only a couple of its poorest countries, animated by a crusading zeal and a desire for wealth and resources.

The move into a new age was started by restless adventurers on the edges of civilization. For Christendom, as it entered what, according to its calendar, was the second millennium, the disputed frontier ran through the Iberian peninsula. It was there that Roland, El Cid, and other warriors for the faith made themselves into figures of romance and legend. The Arab conquest of Spain and Portugal, which had begun in 711 A.D., was, from about 1000 A.D. on, in the process of being undone, stronghold by stronghold. Muslim Iberia, a temptingly wealthy land, was giving way to the assaults of Christian adventurers from the borderlands: crusaders, but also herders hungry for more grazing pastures, and classless men in search of fortune and fame.

It was a drama that bore some resemblance to the crushing of the Latin empire by German tribes of the frontier, but with the roles reversed; Catholics this time were playing the part of the rude outsiders smashing a delicate high culture. Once victorious in Iberia, the Christian warrior bands were to replay the drama overseas.

The Christian reconquest of Spain and Portugal, though mostly accomplished previously, was not completed until the eventful year 1492. It was the year in which two monarchs of Catholic Spain, Ferdinand of Aragon and Isabella of Castille, were united in marriage; and in which they expelled Jews from their kingdoms. In 1492, too, competing against Portugal, Ferdinand and Isabella financed a seaman adventurer named Christopher Columbus. Born in Genoa to a weaver of obscure ancestry, Columbus was a tall man of ruddy complexion, brave and bold, talkative, opinionated, egotistical, and possessed by fantastic visions. He was stubborn and every bit as contrary as folklore believed redheads to be. The two monarchs supplied him with the wherewithal to search for an ocean route to India. The Portuguese sea captains were sailing east; Columbus proposed to go west.

It was Portugal, the smaller and poorer of the two countries, that started the race to the Orient, though it was not what the Portuguese originally had set out to do. At first they were continuing their crusade against the Muslims, whom they pursued across the water from Europe to North Africa. Portugal successfully attacked Ceuta, in Morocco, in 1415, and unsuccessfully attacked Tangier in 1437.

Prince Henry of Portugal (1394–1460), who participated in both attacks, sponsored a systematic program of voyages of exploration down the west coast of Africa, setting geographic goals for his captains to reach or surpass. They went further and further, encouraged by Henry and later helped by developments that he sponsored in navigational instruments, map-making, and shipbuilding. At the outset, the prince's goal was to explore the possibility of outflanking the Muslim world; but then he also was moved to locate the source of the gold that camel caravans, seemingly out of nowhere, carried up through the African desert to Morocco.

In many respects Henry, a crusader and a medieval soul, was steeped in conservatism, but the enterprise he initiated provided an early example of the new spirit that was in the air. His revolutionary project has been called "planned discovery." A historian of Renaissance exploration has written that Henry was "the first rational organizer of exploration as an expanding reconnaissance based on co-operation between pilots at sea and experts at headquarters." The key word is "rational": Henry displayed the style of thought that eventually made the world modern.

In 1441, a Portuguese vessel at last brought back gold dust and slaves from the West African coast, the first solid evidence that there were fortunes to be made. Portugal was coming in contact with sub-Saharan Africa, with kingdoms and empires and cultures that had been developing since about 900 A.D., of which it knew nothing, and of which even today we do not know a great deal. Perhaps because of a lack of natural harbors in sub-Saharan Africa, these societies tended to be centered in the interior rather than on the coast. Nonetheless, on the west coast there flourished, at one time or another, powers such as the empires of Ghana, Mali, Songhai, and the kingdom of Benin. There were more; and indeed at times they overflowed with gold. Tantalizing rumors reached Iberians of a powerful Christian prince somewhere in the interior, named Prester John, who could give them the help they needed to achieve their diverse goals; but search though they did, the land of Prester John proved as elusive as a rainbow.

Starting in the 1470s, Portugal's Prince John (later King John II), a successor to Prince Henry and his enthusiasms, issued stone pillars to his sea captains to plant at the farthest point of land they reached, to stake out the claims of the Crown. The pillars provided subsequent Portuguese voyagers with a tangible goal to exceed.

At some point Portuguese seamen and their rulers became convinced that there was a reasonable possibility, and even a probability, that they could sail around southern Africa and reach India by sea. At the time, India was the great trade center of southeast Asia and the Pacific. Spices, from the Moluccas in the East Indies, as well as other highly prized commodities, were purchased in India by Arabs and other Muslim merchants, who controlled the carrying trade and brought their goods across the Middle East to the Mediterranean, where they sold them to the trading houses of Venice and Genoa. Collectively, the middlemen—Hindus, Muslims, and Venetian and Genoese Christians and their Muslim partners in Egypt—enjoyed a monopoly on essential commodities such as pepper. Europe either bought from the monopolists, or else had to do without.

But shipping by water remained vastly more efficient and inexpensive than transport across the Middle East by land; so that if the Portuguese could pioneer a trade route to and from India by sea, they could purchase an abundance of spices and herbs at affordable prices. As the low-cost purveyors, they then could put Venice, Genoa, and the Arabs out of business.

To the motives for pursuing voyages of exploration—the crusading impulse, the search for Prester John, and the lust for African slaves and gold—Portugal added the quest for spices and a desire to take over from Italy control of Europe's trade with the Orient.

One of Portugal's—and Europe's—outstanding seamen was Bartolomeu Dias. We know little of his antecedents and early life; we know what he did, but little about who he was. It was to him that King John entrusted the task of finding the southern tip of Africa. Leading an expedition of two caravels (small sailing vessels with little storage space) and prudently taking along a supply ship, as well as a complement of able pilots, he succeeded just after New Year's in early 1488. He discovered that, not the Cape of Good Hope, but Agulhas, to its east, is the southernmost cape of Africa. The sea route to the Orient lay open to Portugal. Dias had pointed the way to the other side of the Muslim world, from which it could be enveloped. The great coup in global geopolitics and geoeconomics of which Prince Henry had dreamed now was at hand.

But the Portuguese crown took nearly a decade to follow through on Dias's success. In the meantime Lisbon probably received valuable news about the way eastward from Pedro de Covilhon, a Portuguese agent sent overland to India via Africa. On his way back, Covilhon stopped in Cairo, and from there, disguised as a Muslim pilgrim, journeyed to forbidden Mecca. He went on to Ethiopia, where he remained. Perhaps he sent back word of what he had found out, even though he himself was never to return.

In Portugal, meanwhile, in 1493, the caravel *Niña*, one of Columbus's two remaining ships, unexpectedly emerged from an Atlantic storm in which she nearly went down, and dropped anchor off Lisbon.

Even though Columbus was in the service of Spain, a rival, he was received with highest honors by Portugal's king, to whom he reported that he was returning from Japan, which (he explained) was a chain of islands off the coast of Asia that could serve as stepping stones to China. Of course the islands from which the *Niña* was returning really lay off the coast of the Americas, but Columbus did not know that. The Portuguese crown, skeptical of Columbus's account of his voyage, was uncertain what to make either of it or of Spain's intentions.

Rodrigo Borgia, the Spaniard who became Pope Alexander VI in 1492, negotiated a treaty in 1493 between Spain and Portugal, by the terms of which the two countries divided between them the mysterious new lands they were discovering.

· · ·

At the Portuguese court, counsel was divided and intertwined with factional rivalries and clashing interests, but in the end, the rulers persisted in exploring the sea road around the southern tip of Africa. It may be that, following Dias's return, other Portuguese voyages took place between 1493 and 1497 of which we know nothing. For when at last they did set out to outfit an expedition to India, the Portuguese displayed a thorough knowledge of the winds they would encounter, and a mastery of what such a voyage would require. They did not follow Dias's route, but chose a more practical course; in a number of ways they seemed to know what they were doing.

Portugal, by the Tagus, July 8, 1497: Early in the morning, the handpicked ships' crews streamed out of the chapel where they had spent the night praying. Following their priests in procession, surrounded by chanting crowds, they descended to the docks. Ferried to the ships, which rode at anchor farther out in an estuary of the Tagus River, the sailors threw themselves into preparations for departure—the unfurling of sails, the lifting of anchors—as trumpets sounded, chains rattled, and pennants flapped in the breeze. The fleet sailed under the sign of the cross, emblazoned in red on each sail, and under the ensign of Portugal's monarch, John II's successor, Manoel the Fortunate.

The expedition had been outfitted by Dias, who may have accompanied it in his caravel part of the way, but it was under the command of Vasco da Gama, a hitherto obscure figure of the minor nobility. Why he was chosen remains a mystery. Da Gama was not a navigator; his appointment to command may have shown that Portugal no longer was merely reconnoitering. In addition to a 50-ton caravel and a 200-ton supply ship, his fleet included two 120-ton *nãos:* three-masted, square-rigged sailing vessels mounting 20 guns between them. The expedition of between 148 and 170, many of them soldiers, was an armed embassy intended to open up trade and relations.

Departing from the mouth of the Tagus, and with what may have been Dias's caravel alongside for a time, the four-vessel task force sailed to the Canaries, and then ran before the northeast trade winds to the Cape Verde Islands. Working its way through the tropical calms towards favorable winds, heading southeast, then south, then southwest, with the crew marveling at such oceanic sights as whales and porpoises, it circled around so that it had the Brazil-to-Africa westerlies at its back, sweeping it the rest of the way across the South Atlantic to its landfall. It arrived only about a hundred miles away from the Cape.

Pausing for a week to rest, scrape off barnacles, take on supplies, mend, and repair, the expedition then resumed its voyage. Sailing from Africa's southern tip to Asia, da Gama entered a political and cultural world entirely new to the Portuguese, with port-states, religions, and trade alliances of which he knew nothing. His relations with the mostly Muslim merchants of the ports at which he put in were troubled. But in what now is Kenya, he managed to pick up a much-needed pilot. Until now it was believed that the pilot was Ahmed ibn Majid, an author and an authority on seamanship, who has been described as "the most celebrated Asian navigator of his day." It made a romantic story, but documents uncovered in the 1980s confirmed suspicions that it was not true.

After a long run across the Indian Ocean, the flotilla made its way safely through the coral reefs and scattered islands of the Laccadive chain in the Arabian Sea. Finally reaching southwestern India, it anchored off Calicut,[1] a town on the Malabar Coast.

As always, da Gama took precautions. Instead of going ashore himself, he sent ahead an envoy who was expendable, a convict brought along from Portugal for just such purposes. The local inhabitants took the envoy to a place where there were two Muslims from Tunis, Moors who spoke both Italian and Spanish. The often-quoted conversation they held, supposedly with da Gama himself, in fact was with the convict-envoy.

Muslims: "The Devil take you! What brought you here?"

Envoy: "We came to seek Christians and spices."

The Portuguese stayed in Calicut for about three months. There was something almost dreamlike about their experience, if one can judge by a surviving contemporary account and other fragments of evidence. They were looking for Christian kingdoms in Asia with

---

1. Not to be confused with Calcutta. Calicut, a cotton-weaving center, gave its name to the woven fabric known as calico.

which to enter into an alliance. They assumed that anybody not Muslim was Christian, but that Christians in Asia might practice rites rather different from their own. Misled by the two assumptions, they believed that many of the inhabitants of Calicut with whom they had dealings during their sojourn were Christians.

Escorted by locals to what must have been a Hindu temple, the Portuguese thought they were being taken to a church, were being shown a small image of Our Lady, were being sprinkled with holy water, and were participating in a Catholic ceremony. What their babblings about Christianity were understood to mean by the locals remains unclear and unrecorded.

The tiny Portuguese expedition led by da Gama was the first European force to reach India since that of Alexander the Great. In the intervening 1,800 years, India, like Europe, had experienced the rise and fall of great empires—among others, that of the Mauryas, just after Alexander, and that of the Guptas, which flourished as Latin Rome crumbled. Also like Europe, India often had to defend its civilization against nomad hordes, mostly from the north: White Huns, Mongols, Arabs, Turks, Tatars, and the like. Like Europe, too, India had witnessed religious conflicts and changes. Buddhism, though moving north and east to win converts throughout Asia, for reasons imperfectly understood had declined and disappeared in India, the land of its birth. The Muslim faith, brought by invaders and travelers from the Middle East and Central Asia, won over much of the country, while Jainism persisted, and Hinduism flourished as the creed of the majority.

In another major respect, however, India's experience had been different from Europe's for most of the time since their earlier encounter: starkly put, Europe had been poor, while India had been rich. This was a fact of life of which Vasco da Gama was made aware in unmistakable terms by representatives of the Samuri,[2] the ruler of Calicut.

2. A variant of Samudri Raja, literally "King of the Sea," which the Portuguese pronounced *Samorim*.

The merchants who represented the Samuri took a look at the gifts da Gama proposed to tender him—and burst into laughter. A dozen swatches of cloth, some clothes, a few strings of coral, a half-dozen washbasins, a bale of sugar, two barrels of butter—which must have gone rancid—and two barrels of honey: a meager offering, poor stuff, of inferior quality. Was the King of Portugal insulting the Samuri?

Da Gama smoothly explained it away: the gifts were from himself, a poor man, not from his great monarch. But the next day, when he appeared before the ruler, da Gama had no plausible response to the Samuri's question as to why he had brought no gifts from his king.

Portugal's goods could not successfully compete in the Indian market. The Muslim traders offered merchandise of superior quality and of a far wider range, including horses and copper from the Middle East, in exchange for the spices and jewels India could supply. This was not a problem on which Prince Henry and his successors had focused. For them, the hurdle to overcome had been to find out how to sail to the Orient. In the long years during which the Portuguese had been seeking a sea road to India, it seems never to have occurred to them that getting there was only the first of the challenges they would meet. Even with the aid of the Samuri, it was only with the greatest difficulty that da Gama and his crew conducted their trading activities.

In the years to come, the Portuguese discoverers would essay the sailing of the Pacific Ocean, and much else, but the age of reconnaissance was approaching its end. Driven by circumstances, Portugal once again was about to pioneer entry into a new era: an age of trade wars.

Seeing no way to compete against the Arab merchants, Portugal set out to destroy their trade by force of arms. Da Gama himself, Alfonso d'Albuquerque (1453–1515), and other Portuguese commanders led war fleets against their merchant rivals. Europe was in the midst of the gunpowder revolution, which gave the Iberians an edge; the cannons of Portugal's ships swept the Arabs from the seas.

Pursuant to a strategic plan of which d'Albuquerque was the author, Portugal established a chain of fortresses and commercial and naval bases on foreign soil that stretched all the way from the Middle East to the west coast of India, Ceylon, the Malacca Strait, and China. The trade monopoly with the Orient, won in victories at sea, was administered by a Portuguese fleet based in the East. As the leading recent historian of these matters has written, "only those ships carrying certificates from the captain of a Portuguese port were free from molestation" as they attempted to sail to or from Asia.

The first two phases of the adventure, first reconnaissance and then seizing control of the vital trade routes, had been pioneered by Portugal; but it was Spain that led the way into the third territorial—or colonial—phase. Where Portugal had established an empire merely of bases and outstations, Spain created an empire of conquest and occupation.

The islands that Columbus, and those who came after him, had found were off the coast of the Americas; these served as a jumping-off point. The Spaniards took control of Cuba as a principal base for expeditions to the mainland. Young adventurers made their way there, inspired by a mix of idealistic, crusading zeal and greed for fame and fortune. They had heard stories of men like themselves who had come out to these Indies with nothing and soon afterwards had returned to Spain rich on the profits of gold mines worked by Indians. One of the young soldiers of fortune, Bernal Díaz del Castillo, when asked why he had come out to the New World, replied in a similar vein to da Gama's envoy in Calicut: "We came here to serve God and the king, and also to get rich."

Díaz del Castillo, remembering in later years his first arrival in Cuba, where a kinsman of his served as governor, wrote that "On landing we went at once to pay our respects to the Governor, who was pleased at our coming, and promised to give us Indians as soon as there were any to spare. I was then twenty-four years old." Like the other young Spaniards who made their way to the Caribbean— impoverished gentlemen and younger sons—he was there to wager his life against a fortune.

Díaz del Castillo entered the service of Hernán Cortés, who

carried the European enterprise overseas to its next stage, from establishing bases to winning empires. At the age of thirty-three, Cortés set out in February 1519 from Cuba to the Mexican coast, authorized by Cuba's Spanish governor to establish colonies there. But after arriving two months later, Cortés threw off superior authority and took full command. He had brought his expeditionary force to a land held by a people who called themselves the Mexica. They ruled all the other "Aztecs": the tribes that spoke their Nahuatl language.

The empire of the Mexica was vast; it may have comprised up to thirty million people, though our best current estimate is between eight and ten million. Cortés led a band that was tiny: only a bit more than five hundred soldiers, a hundred sailors, and sixteen horses. Yet in less than three years, Cortés completely conquered the Mexica. Historians continue to wonder how he did it.

Leadership, or a lack of it, is part of the answer: Montezuma, the all-powerful Mexican emperor, was weak, indecisive, and vacillating. He allowed the Spaniards, unmolested, to cross his country, enter his capital city, and take him captive. Cortés, on the other hand, was bold, decisive, and a master of generalship.

Military technology was also a factor. The Spaniards had horses, which the Mexica never had seen before. The sight of the strange animals was terrifying, as was the sound of explosives. The Spaniards had gunpowder, metal armor, and weapons of iron and steel. They had weaponry that was lethal: cannon, handguns, and swords that could sever a head at a stroke; while the wooden weapons of the Mexica could injure but not kill. Still, the band of Spaniards was so small that sheer numbers should have been able to overwhelm it. However, chance played a role. Smallpox arrived with the Spaniards, who had developed immunity to it. An epidemic in 1521 killed more Indians than the Spaniards did.

Above all, there was the Spanish alliance with the other Aztec tribes. These evidently had been ruled with great cruelty by the Mexica. Seizing the opportunity offered by Cortés, the tribes changed sides; two hundred thousand Indians served alongside the Spaniards, which evened the odds. The European invaders were by no means so outnumbered as, until recently, historians have led us to believe.

Finally, there was the personality of Cortés himself. From his youth he was, in the language of his secretary and biographer, "a source of trouble to his parents" because he was "much given to women." He was unable at first to sail to the Indies because of an injury suffered in escaping the house of a married woman. Once in the Indies, he had to drop out of an expedition to the mainland because he had come down with syphilis. He brought endless troubles on his head by seducing a girl whose sister the governor of Cuba was courting. Imprisonment, chains, and escapes followed his breach of promise, until eventually he surrendered by marrying her.

In Mexico he obtained possession of a captured Nahuatl-speaking princess, who became his mistress. It was his greatest stroke of luck. She provided him with some of the keys to his success; she spoke for him, influenced Montezuma in his favor, and negotiated for him with the Indians. She was able to explain to him the political crisis within the Mexica empire, and guide him through the complex of relationships and resentments that he and she were to exploit by securing an alliance with anti-Mexica Aztecs: an alliance that was, in the end, to overthrow the empire.

The wealth of the Mexica empire was the stuff of fables; for centuries European adventurers had been setting off into the great unknown in hopes of finding a fortune. Now Cortés had done it. He had won for himself not just a gold mine or two, but mountains of precious things. He had shown that the dream could be a reality by locating and looting the wealth of a major civilization. Others were fired with an ambition to follow where he had led.

In 1528, bringing with him a treasure, Cortés returned to Spain to defend himself against various accusations, and to be received by his monarch, the emperor Charles V. Lifting the conquistador into the ranks of the nobility, Charles created a title for him—Marqués del Valle—and Cortés remarried into the family of a duke.

A distant relative of Cortés's, Francisco Pizarro, the illegitimate son of an army captain and a socially inferior woman, happened to be at the Spanish court at the same time. He too was there to see Charles V; his plea to his monarch was to be given a chance to become the next Cortés. Pizarro already had discovered Peru, and had heard rumors that in its mountains another golden and glorious Indian empire was to be found. He asked, and received, authority to take this empire for the crown.

Charles V gave Pizarro full backing and sent him out to South America as a viceroy. In January 1531, Pizarro set off from Panama to Peru with a force even smaller than Cortés's had been.

The golden kingdom that Pizarro encountered, at that time the only great American empire other than that of the Mexica, stretched through the Andes mountains and along the Pacific coast from what now is Ecuador all the way to what is now Chile. Its center was the valley of Cuzco, in what now is Peru. Members of its royal family were known as Incas. The rulers of the empire called themselves the Children of the Sun, the deity they worshipped. The inferior peoples over whom they reigned were called by them "the four quarters of the world," for the Incas seemed to believe that they had extended their frontiers to the ends of the earth—or at least all of it that interested them. Their outstanding leader (in the words of a nineteenth-century American historian) "carried the banner of the rainbow, the armorial design of his house, far over the borders, amongst the remotest tribes of the plateau."

Pizarro's conquest of Peru in many ways was a replay of Cortés's triumph over Mexico. Again, it was astonishing that a small band of Spaniards took control of a formidable empire against what looked like overwhelming odds. Once more European weaponry, gunpowder, horses, and the like played a major role—in this case against bows and arrows. Pizarro's bold and brilliant leadership, like Cortés's, made it possible, as did adroit exploitation of political differences—a succession crisis—within the Inca camp, and of resentments of the peoples of the four quarters against their masters. The emperor of the Children of the Sun was captured and allowed himself to be used by the Spaniards, as had the emperor of the Mexica. In Peru, the Indians also allowed Pizarro to nominate a new Inca emperor after the Spaniards strangled the old one.

So amazing were the Spanish conquests of Mexico and Peru that they impressed themselves on the world's imagination. It was easy to generalize, to conclude that such would be the result wherever

Europe, with its advanced weapons technology, encountered the rest of the world at that time. In fact, the experiences of Cortés and Pizarro were two of a kind: there would be no others like them for some time to come. They were freak episodes, made possible by special circumstances—among them, the still imperfectly understood thinking of the Mexica and Inca leaders. In the event, it was not until centuries later that modern weaponry would, by itself, allow modest groups of Europeans to routinely defeat large numbers of technologically backward people.

The flow of treasure from the New World to Spain sustained Charles V, and then his son and successor, Philip II, in their struggle for mastery in Europe. Spain was taking the gold and silver away from the Americas, and it was only a matter of time before other Europeans would move to take it away from Spain. English privateers in the late 1500s, among them Sir Francis Drake, made their names and fortunes raiding the treasure fleets that brought the output of American mines across the Atlantic to Spain.

Drake also circumnavigated the world in 1577–1580, duplicating the feat of a Spanish expedition sent out under the command of the Portuguese Ferdinand Magellan. All the European powers now knew essentially what the globe looked like, and realized that they could reach anywhere by going either east or west. Control of the trade routes became a chief prize in the worldwide rivalry of the maritime nations.

The story that began with Europe's discoveries continued with the establishment of overseas bases to control trade routes to Asia. It had gone on to a third phase: the conquest and settlement of the Americas. Now it entered a fourth phase that was to last for centuries, an era in which Europeans turned from fighting Asians and Americans to fighting one another overseas. It was to be the first era of world wars.

In the 1500s and 1600s Holland and England began to prey on Spanish and Portuguese overseas trade, sometimes acting together, sometimes alone. At times, they also fought against each other. Eventually France, too, entered the fray. Europeans always had struggled against one another in Europe; now they confronted one another all around the world. The entire globe became their theater of operations and their battlefield. In the 1770s, decisive encounters between the two greatest European adversaries at that time, Britain and France, were fought on distant continents, in India and Canada.

Until 1648, the commercial wars waged by the Europeans overseas also had the aspect of religious wars, as the Spanish-led Catholics of the south crossed swords with a coalition of Protestant states in northern Europe that tended to include England, Holland, and Sweden. After 1648 the causes of conflict were dynastic rivalries, threats to the European balance of power, and competition for the spoils of empire.

Portugal was the first to fade in the course of the worldwide wars, followed by Spain and Holland. By the late 1700s, Britain and France were the last remaining great European powers with global interests and rivalries. From the age of Louis XIV, beginning in the 1600s, France repeatedly bid for, and often won, something close to complete hegemony on the continent of Europe, while Britain, fearing a continent united against her, summoned up coalitions of European land powers to block French designs and maintain a balance of power.

The Treaty of Utrecht (1713), which brought the wars of Louis XIV to an end, aimed at establishing a balance of power not only in Europe but throughout the world. The underlying imperial principle was recognition of, and respect for, existing European positions and trade monopolies. In practice, this proved difficult, not only because of widespread cheating (for example by English and Dutch smugglers in the Spanish Caribbean), but also because instead of staying in place, the European powers continued to expand their empires overseas and clashed with one another in doing so.

By the 1800s, however, and especially in the late 1800s, the powers developed a greater ability to reach agreement on how to share newly acquired lands, an ability which they demonstrated in colonizing Africa.

. . .

Extraordinary leaps in technology brought Europeans into the fifth phase of their history as world-conquerors. New and ever more mobile and destructive weaponry made it feasible to attempt the capture of whatever overseas lands still remained unsubdued. The same advances in arms would make a war between Europeans on the continent itself so costly as to be unthinkable. To Europeans of the governing classes, expansion of empire seemed to be necessary, for a combination of economic and strategic reasons, as well as concerns of power and prestige, but not at the risk of plunging the rival powers into wars against one another for the spoils of empire.

The logic of the situation dictated a negotiated and agreed-upon partition of the lands that remained to be acquired; and that is what was eventually done.

The interior of Africa had not previously been open to conquest from abroad. Three developments by the end of the 1800s rendered it feasible. The steam-powered gunboat made it possible for Europeans to penetrate into the interior to exercise and retain power, while still maintaining their lifelines of communication and transportation to the coast. The rapid-fire guns mounted on the boats enabled them to massacre native warriors equipped only with arrows and spears. Not least in importance, the use of quinine and other drugs enabled the Europeans to survive in the African interior. Previously, disease—chiefly malaria, but also yellow fever, dysentery, and typhoid, among others—had been the curse that killed foreign treasure-seekers in the African jungle.

Able at last to annex Africa, the Europeans did so, but in concert with one another. The "scramble for Africa" initiated by King Leopold II of the Belgians, for reasons well described as "piratical," took place largely in the 1880s; and though there were threats, crises, and alarms, the Europeans carried through their division of the continent without going to war against one another.

China was next. European encroachments had begun long before: in the sixteenth century, with the Portuguese of d'Albuquerque, and had continued, fitfully, through the centuries. In the nineteenth century, with the country wracked by civil war, and rendered helpless by the Opium Wars (1839–42 and 1856–60), special concessions and monopoly privileges were wrested from the Chinese by European nations within the respective spheres that they carved out for themselves. A de facto partition of China was in process by the 1890s.

At the end of the decade, there erupted an anti-foreign movement, misnamed "the Boxer Rebellion." The Legation Quarter in Peking, in which foreign embassies were situated, was attacked by so-called Boxers in 1900. Withstanding a siege of the Quarter, the foreigners were rescued in the summer of 1901 by an international expeditionary force sent by the United States, Japan, and six European powers: Britain, France, Russia, Germany, Italy, and Austria-Hungary. The Chinese were forced to cede permanent control of the Legation Quarter to a foreign consortium.

The episode provided a vivid picture of the unity of the industrial countries and of the success of the imperial venture by which the European powers and their associates had taken control of the earth. Europeans at one time or another had ruled or settled (Antarctica aside) all the other continents. Even China managed to retain only the shadow of independence.

King George V of England ruled not only a quarter of the world's population, but a quarter of the earth; the Czar of Russia, a sixth. A historian of imperialism recently has calculated that "by 1914 over eighty-four percent of the world's land area was European-dominated." All that remained outside Europe's grasp—never settled or dominated by Europeans in the years since Columbus—was the Middle East, which was governed by the Muslim Ottoman Empire; and this was captured and occupied by Great Britain four years later. The world was won; the world was one.

By 1914, all the world belonged to the same political system, which was a new state of affairs. Alongside of it developed a world financial system, centered in the city of London, which was new as well.

The Europe of 1914 had united the world. The subject peoples around the globe no longer were any match for the industrial powers with their modern weaponry. So long as the European nations could maintain their concert, no rebellion against their authority seemed likely to succeed, as far ahead as anyone could project.

How had it happened? With a perspective that comes only from surveying events over a long period of time, it can be seen that a number of streams flowed into one another to form the great river that was to bear all of the human race on to its destination.

The first stream was an intellectual one: rationality, a way of thinking that was most effective in inquiry, observation, interpretation, integration, and organization.

Another stream was the conquest or settlement of the planet that the Portuguese initiated and other Europeans carried out, impelled by hunger, greed, ambition, and crusading zeal.

Another was the invention and use by Europeans of new technologies of seafaring and warfare, among them gunpowder and the steam-powered gunboat: tools that helped establish and expand the European empire, but do not account for the initial victories.

Another was the agricultural revival going back to the tenth century, followed by entirely new developments: the commercial revolution, and the birth of world capitalism.

Finally, there was the center stream into which all others flowed: the scientific-technological-industrial revolution. It was a movement in which Great Britain took the lead: the most consequential initiative by humans since the peoples of the Fertile Crescent invented agriculture and Sumer invented civilization.

7: RELEASING NATURE'S ENERGIES

The industrial, scientific, and technological revolution of our millennium—the modernizing revolution—transformed human life and prospects more profoundly than had any achievement since apes engendered humans, and humans invented agriculture and civilization.

The shift made by the more advanced countries in the late twentieth century away from the industrial toward the scientific and the technological, has made it evident that the ongoing revolution through which the modern world has been living began earlier, runs deeper, and may go on longer than was supposed earlier in the century. We have experienced more than the industrial revolution, which conventionally is dated from the eighteenth century. The larger revolution began with rationalist and scientific thinking, and the development of the experimental method. It began with science—nearly a thousand years ago. It continues today.

In the United States in our time, computers have become ubiquitous. They are in homes, offices, factories, libraries, shops, and, in imbedded form, in machinery of all sorts. To their users, they, and the communications networks which are their offshoots, make it possible to enter into a conversation with other users everywhere in the world. They offer access to almost unlimited information.

The industrial revolution that began with the steam engine had to do with power in a muscular sense: the power to fuel machinery to do lifting and carrying and moving. But the technological revolution, which made access to useful information instantaneous, and conversation and collaboration with others possible at great distances, has to do with the even greater power of mind and culture; it enables humanity to realize its intellectual potential.

A universe of energy in the service of human genius: it conjures up images of Faust, and appropriately it began with magic and its quests for the supernatural.

European science emerged from a murky background. In part it was nourished by the learning of medieval Islam, and of classical Greece and Rome, which the Arabs reintroduced to Europe during the extended contacts between Christians and Muslims brought about by the Crusades. Byzantium, too, particularly in the last century of its existence, tutored Latin Europe in classical culture. And, in part, science tapped the underground springs of pagan superstition and witchcraft that had survived the Christianization of Europe. Thus the Englishman Roger Bacon (1220–1292), who presciently gave instructions for making gunpowder, and outlined designs for eyeglasses, motor vehicles, and flying machines, nonetheless believed in astrology and alchemy. Indeed, gunpowder was discovered in the course of experiments in alchemy. And, in a sense, gunpowder did work magic. Used for destructive purposes by the Europeans—rather than for firecrackers, as it was by the Chinese—it put a definitive end to the nomad invasions; it helped bring down the feudal order in Europe; and it assisted western Europe in conquering the world.

Gifted students of the esoteric ended by illuminating the stellar universe for medieval Europe. The Polish scientist Nicholas Copernicus theorized that the earth circles the sun rather than vice versa. His views were championed by an Italian Renaissance man, Giordano Bruno, who believed that there are many solar systems other than ours, and that matter has an atomic basis. Bruno advocated freedom of inquiry, essential to science but a heresy in his world. Threatened with excommunication by Catholics, driven from Geneva and Paris by Calvinists and Aristotelians, respectively, excommunicated by Lutherans, he was, in the end, denounced by the Inquisition and burned at the stake by authority of Pope Clement VIII. Yet for all his advanced views, Bruno was deeply immersed in magic, kabbalah, and the so-called Hermetic tradition: occult teachings that supposedly derived from the wisdom of the ancient Egyptians as expounded by one of their high priests, a certain Hermes Trismegistus. Mystic numerology, astrology, and universal harmonies were blended in Bruno's thought with views we regard as rationalist and with presentiments of the discoveries of modern physics.

Was it a paradox that Bruno's outlook, part science, also was part superstition? Some believe so. A scholar of the Renaissance, Frances Yates, argued otherwise; she believed that the magic was inseparable from the rest. A date of basic importance was 1614, when "Hermes Trismegistus" was unmasked as a fraud. As a result of the exposure, the German scientist Johannes Kepler was able to break with mysticism and move on to mathematics as a quantitative measurement.

Galileo Galilei, pioneer of the experimental method in science, an Italian who escaped Bruno's fate by recanting; the Englishman Francis Bacon, proponent of the inductive method; the French geometrician René Descartes, who conceived of the universe as capable of being expressed mathematically; and, above all, the Englishman Isaac Newton, who supplied the mathematical formulation describing the paths and movements of heavenly bodies, were among others who led science out of magic and into rationality. It was just at the point in European history when science-based technology was about to lead to industry, when capitalism had emerged to exploit it, and when the uniting of the planet by imperialism had opened up overseas markets that would provide tempting profits to those who would create industry. Like tributaries flowing into a river, they came together.

. . .

The industrial revolution[1] started in Great Britain, and in about the middle of the 1700s. Scholars disagree as to why it began, why there, and why then.

Maybe it was the Protestant work ethic. Maybe it was the abundance of English coal, or England's network of inland waterways, or her easy access to the sea, or her long run of bounteous harvests, or her moist climate. Or maybe, as E. J. Hobsbawm has argued, it was due to none of the above.

It seems to have been based upon energy, for it started with the steam engine. Here was the first new source of energy to be discovered by humans since ancient man mastered waves and winds and harnessed other animals to do his work. French writers dubbed the development revolutionary. Friedrich Engels, the intellectual partner of Karl Marx, wrote that it was "well known" that the textile inventions together with the steam engine had given rise to "an industrial revolution."

In the nature of the case, it was more practical to bring workers to a steam engine that powered textile machines, than to bring the engines to each worker. The hand tool gave way to the power tool, cottage and small workshop gave way to factory, and artisanal small-scale production gave way, eventually, to mechanical mass production.

It was convenient for the pool of labor and the factories to be near one another, so both established themselves in cities, which expanded. The lure of jobs caused a mass migration to metropolitan centers. Farmers became factory hands. For those who formerly had lived in the countryside, the switch to urban existence brought about a profound change in the ways of work and life. Among other things, ties to the land, to family, and to the local community were broken as rural workers moved into impersonal cities, and lost touch with their roots, their past, and their identity. The social order tended toward disintegration: a theme of many a nineteenth-century novel.

1. There were more than one. I refer to the one that occurred in Great Britain between 1750 and 1850.

But wealth, population, production, demand for goods and services, productivity, and trade all grew explosively. Textiles, and manufactured food and drink, such as beer and flour, followed later by the metallurgical industries, iron and steel, led the way, driven by new technologies and improved engineering. By and large, the new devices, such as spinning machines and looms, were inexpensive.[2] It took relatively little capital to start a business. Entrepreneurship flourished.

The globalization of activity brought about over the centuries by European imperial expansion opened up a world of opportunity to the first industrial manufacturers. In Britain, government policy played a role. The building of the greatest of navies brought with it the greatest of shipbuilding industries, and stimulated the development of new technologies. Even more to the point, as Hobsbawm has pointed out, was the use to which the navy was put: the British government pursued commercial goals as an integral part of its global strategic and naval policy. The result was that in most decades of the eighteenth century, growth of export industries exceeded growth of home industries in Great Britain by a ratio of better than ten to one. Everything expanded: trade, capital, population, organization, commercial and financial structures, production, and innovation.

Improvement, efficiency, initiative, and invention were well rewarded; rationality in organization and administration was the order of the day.

The engine, powering ocean liners and railroads, introduced a new sensation: speed. It also shrank distances, uniting the planet in its way even more than European imperialism had done. Communication advanced as transportation did—in the nineteenth century the telegraph, and then the wireless, were followed by the telephone—so that now, a century later, anyone can hold a conversation with anyone else anywhere in the world. This too has had the effect of turning the planet into a neighborhood.

·   ·   ·

2. Fixed assets and overhead were low. Only variable costs—raw materials, inventory, and the like—were significant; and these could be covered by short-term bank loans. By and large, short credit was all that was available, but it also was all that was needed.

Some new developments enabled others to be made; for example, the invention of the elevator made it feasible to build skyscrapers. Even more striking were those that changed the nature of society. Isaac Merrit Singer, the nineteenth-century American inventor who developed a sewing machine, offered to sell his company's products to the public on the installment plan. His installment plan was more far-reaching than his mechanical creation. For the first time ordinary people could buy expensive goods, as new ones were invented and marketed: the refrigerator, the dishwasher, the automobile. What Singer had fabricated was the consumer society, and what he had sparked off was a credit revolution.

Releasing new energies remained central to the process of increasing human powers. In eighteenth-century England, wood, which was running short, was replaced by coal. In the early twentieth century, Winston Churchill, as First Lord of the Admiralty, ordered the ships of the Royal Navy to switch from coal to oil. Improvements in transport beginning in the 1940s made the use of natural gas in homes a feasible alternative to petroleum.

Learning how to generate electricity, a process initiated early in the nineteenth century by the Englishman Michael Faraday, resulted in lighting up the world, a process initiated by the American Thomas Alva Edison.

Keen observers at the turn of the century saw that the world had entered the age of electricity. Henry Adams, the historian who served as America's link with her past, marveled at the dynamos he inspected at the Chicago and Paris world fairs, and ventured the opinion that they might render all of human experience until his time obsolete. From the beginnings of civilization until the eighteenth century in Europe, the only power the world had had available for use was that of humans and other animals, and environmental resources such as wind and water. People now had at their disposal so much more power that it could not really even be quantified. Adams recognized that his world stood on the threshold of what might be a revolutionary transformation in the prospects and possibilities open to the human race.

Today, having learned to release nuclear energy, we are almost there. We are told that nuclear fusion, if the process can be mastered commercially—producing more than it consumes, and at a competitive price—could supply for all practical purposes an infinity of clean, safe, and renewable energy. There would be no real limit to the amount of power available to humanity. Prometheus would have brought down fire from the sun.

Like Singer, Edison created something else besides his inventions: he created inventing as a career. R&D—research and development—was born. No longer was the typical invention an accident; it was the intended result of a systematic, organized, and often lavishly funded program of discovery. As such, it was the parallel to what Prince Henry the Navigator had done in initiating the age of reconnaissance. Like the program instituted by the ex-crusader, it exemplified the rationalist frame of mind that took Europe out of medieval religion and into modern times.

It also illustrated the progressive nature of the system that Europe had pioneered in emerging from the Middle Ages and industrializing. Self-perpetuating economic growth was a characteristic of a free-enterprise system in the industrial age. So (as shown by Edison) was planning for change. It was a system in which people always were purposefully moving on and moving ahead. It was not until our own lifetime that it was seriously recognized that there might be limits to growth, or that there might be costs associated with growth that we cannot afford to pay.

Edison, the father of systematic technological advancement, born in Ohio and raised in Michigan, was a self-made man. From childhood he was partly deaf. He had only three months of formal schooling before being expelled as mentally retarded. He was taught at home by his mother, a former schoolteacher. His father found him difficult and often beat him. He started to work at the age of twelve, trained himself in telegraphy, and roamed the country taking odd jobs as a telegraph operator and repairman. At twenty-one, he read the journals of Michael Faraday, which exerted a profound influence on him. Edison was fascinated by Faraday's experiments with electricity, which he duplicated.

Edison was twenty-two, sleeping in a basement in downtown New York, when he made his fortune by inventing a reliable stock ticker for the Western Union Telegraph Company to sell to Wall Street and other brokerage houses. Seven years later he moved to Menlo Park, New Jersey, to build laboratories in which he could work full-time at inventing. He invested an immense sum of money in it and hired a team of experts to work for him. It was the first industrial research laboratory, and soon it was applying for hundreds of patents every year. In addition to the electric lightbulb, Edison invented the phonograph, improved the telephone, and fathered hundreds of other products. He also took the first step on the road to the electron tube and the electronics industry.

Edison was nearly forty when his wife died. He then remarried. It may be, as his biographer Matthew Josephson wrote, that his second wife, "a woman half his age, but of genteel background and firm character . . . took the heretofore incorrigible, tobacco-chewing eccentric in hand and made him presentable in polite society," but he remained a diamond in the rough, and apparently could be a terror to his employees when he was not inspiring them.

The Michigan-born machinist Henry Ford (1863–1947), who left school at fifteen, became in his twenties chief engineer of one of the many companies spawned by Edison—the Edison Illuminating Company of Detroit. Like Edison, Ford was an eccentric and self-made. His innovations, too, changed the way people lived and worked.

When, having left Edison, he founded the Ford Motor Company in 1903, the automobile was a custom-made, high-priced product for a small upper-class market. Ford changed that. He automated and standardized; he developed the assembly line and made use of interchangeable parts. He pioneered mass production, which lowered costs so that he could distribute to a mass market. In 1913 he sold Model T cars for $500; by 1927 he had sold 15 million automobiles.

Assembly-line production changed the way that people work, and the way they feel about their work, with implications that sociologists continue to discuss. The automobile also changed the way that people lived and behaved: because of it, Americans were able to move outside of cities and live in newly created suburbs; they enjoyed mobility, and learned to travel far and wide; and because it brought privacy, it enabled couples parked in dark lanes, far from parents and other supervisors, to make their own decisions about sexual behavior. As did so many of the new technologies, mass production and mass marketing of automobiles therefore brought about social revolutions.

Great Britain started and led the industrial revolution, and diffused it to western Europe,[3] where Germany, after its creation in 1870, became an industrial power that looked likely to overtake the British. But a century or so ago the United States took over the lead.

In the beginning, manufacturers in the American states had a problem with transport; distances were long, and to ship goods by land was expensive. Roads and canals were proposed. Britain had the advantage of its small size, its crisscrossing internal waterways, and the curious geography that placed everywhere in England close to the ocean.

The invention of railroads transformed the situation in the United States and was basic to its industrialization. 1848 was the first year that more than a thousand miles of track were built. The pace increased, especially after the Civil War. The first transcontinental railroad was completed, and service on it began in 1869. By 1893, according to the Baedeker guidebook to the United States, the U.S. had about 170,000 miles of track, or almost more than all the rest of the world put together.

Great fortunes were being made by the tycoons who owned the railroads. The train network bound the country together, opened up the west for mass settlement, and created a continentwide market that enabled fortunes to be made in other industries as well. Because the transport problem was solved, the country's enormous size

---

3. Though the pattern of the industrial revolution in the countries of continental Europe did not always replicate that of Britain.

became an asset rather than a liability, and its richness and variety could be exploited.

America's mineral wealth was enormous; it had an overwhelming abundance of coal, iron, and everything else needed for industry. Oil produced fortunes that dwarfed even those of the railroad men; by 1913 the country was producing more than 35 million long tons of petroleum, while the rest of the world combined was producing less than 20 million.

A growing population fueled the work force and the consumer market. Millions of immigrants, by their very willingness to cross the ocean and take their chances in a new world, showed initiative, adventurousness, and a strong motivation to succeed. So America attracted the quality as well as the quantity of new citizens that were needed.

Americans and their elected representatives often espoused and adopted protectionist measures. Whether or not such policies were wise at the time may not have mattered a great deal. The United States had no internal trade barriers, none among the internal states or territories, and so, regardless of foreign trade, it had a sufficiently large internal free-trade zone to give its industry and agriculture a market large enough in which to flourish.

Like any new enterprise, industrial America needed risk capital to start things off. Americans in the nineteenth century could supply some of it themselves, but for the rest they looked to Britain and the European countries. It was an advantage that the United States was relatively stable; the political risk for foreign investors was not high. On the other hand, American swindlers were notorious, and political corruption was rife; judges and legislators were bought and sold all the time. If foreign investors nonetheless subscribed to new American securities issues, it was due, of course, to the lure of high returns, but also in no small measure to the example of the New York banker J. P. Morgan, who took responsibility for watching over the honesty of the American companies for whom his firm raised funds in the London market.

Morgan was the banker who, by creating the U.S. Steel Corporation, made the industrialist Andrew Carnegie (1835–1919) one of the wealthiest people in the world. Carnegie had a sense that the industrial revolution had transformed the world in such a way as to call for a new kind of international politics. He was driven by that ancient dream: permanent peace.

The United States was the right country in which to pursue such millennial goals. By tradition, the country was opposed to militarism and to standing armies and tended to regard economic activity as virtuous and political striving as unvirtuous.

The idealistic rhetoric in which American statesmen were accustomed to indulge when lecturing the rest of the world gave rise sometimes to weariness, sometimes to derision, in the chancelleries of Europe. But as the twentieth century dawned, the vision of a peaceful world in which Americans professed to believe took on relevance.

An international system in which warfare is endemic is viable only if, as in Edward Gibbon's world, conflicts are limited, indecisive, nondestructive, and fought in compliance with agreed rules. But in 1914, a war broke out in Europe that, with intermissions, was to go on for the rest of the century; and it was not to be fought in Gibbon's way at all. All the weapons of mass destruction with which the scientific, technological, and industrial revolution had armed the human race were to be employed in the service of total war among entire populations. In the bloodbath of the twentieth century, Europe was to ruin itself—and to be obliged, in the end, to follow the United States into at least professing to believe in a new kind of politics.

8: RULING OURSELVES

After entering the First World War in 1917 under the leadership of President Woodrow Wilson, the United States became the first major power in the modern world to adopt the abolition of warfare as an immediate political goal. Wilson drew inspiration from the antiwar left-wing opposition in Great Britain, and also from his own opponents in the United States: former president William Howard Taft, defeated for reelection by Wilson in 1912, had accepted the leadership of a bipartisan movement in support of an international league to enforce peace. Wilson, an eloquent speaker but not an original thinker, was able to express the views and ideas of others more powerfully and memorably than they could themselves.

Wilson was a cold, austere man of fine features and ascetic temperament. The son and grandson of Presbyterian clergymen, he was a preacher by disposition. His religious convictions ran deep, and he was imbued with a sense that in his worldly activities he was carrying out a divine mission. A novice whose entire career in politics consisted of two years as governor of New Jersey, he won election to the presidency as a Democrat by a fluke: the Republican majority allowed itself to be split almost evenly in two, torn by the rival candidacies of President Taft on the regular ticket and former president Theodore Roosevelt heading the insurgent Progressive party. The minority candidate therefore slipped by to win with a mere plurality of the popular vote.

Wilson took office pledged to domestic reform. He had no intention of focusing on foreign policy, and proved maladroit at it when obliged, almost immediately, to deal with a tangled situation in Mexico.

The outbreak of what was to become the First World War in Europe in the summer of 1914 confronted him with a series of challenges that would have tried even a past master of international relations. There was no doubt that American traditions dictated noninvolvement in the wars that European nations waged against one another on the other side of the Atlantic. But supplying the Allies became so lucrative a trade that the United States was unwilling to sacrifice it in order to avoid being attacked at sea by the Germans. However, it was also unwilling to allow its merchant vessels to be sunk, and after a number of such sinkings by German submarines early in 1917, Wilson, albeit with misgivings, asked the Congress to declare war on Germany.

As was his habit, Wilson elevated America's quarrel with the Kaiser's government to a much higher level than that of the events themselves. He propounded the theory that the international behavior of states is an expression of their domestic political system. The United States, not wanting to be involved in the war, nonetheless was being dragged into it by Germany's attacks on American shipping, attacks that were the result of Germany's militarist political culture. It therefore was not enough for the United States to win the war; at some later point, Germany—or some other country— might attack again, bringing about another war. To make the world safe for democratic countries, the political systems of other nations would have be restructured to America's specifications.

In the past, the United States had adopted an "American system" in foreign policy: that is, it played an active role in the politics of the Western Hemisphere but rarely in the rest of the world. For many reasons, that hemispheric division no longer was workable. Advances in military technology now rendered the Americas vulnerable to attack from Europe. Britain's diminishing ability to shield the United States against such attack—a consequence of a shift in the balance of power—had the same effect.

From the outset, the United States had disapproved of the political systems of other countries. But the founding fathers had not ventured to change them; they wished merely to provide an alternative. Wilson proposed to part company with the founding fathers on this, his justification being that his was the way to permanent peace. Many disagreed. Indeed, Wilson never showed persuasively either that America could change the world, or even that if America did so, war could be abolished. By the end of the twentieth century, the political systems of other countries had changed, becoming closer to the ideal advocated by the United States; but it is by no means clear either that the United States had brought about the changes, or that they will produce the hoped-for results.

With what purpose did the founders of the United States break with the politics of their world? At first—in the middle of the eighteenth century—they objected to certain measures adopted by the government of England. Then they objected to that particular government itself, not just to some of its policies. Finally, they objected to being ruled by any kind of British government at all. The founders were able to see the implications for other peoples of what Americans were doing for themselves.

The new era in human affairs began in 1776 when the united thirteen colonies of English North America declared their independence from Great Britain. Yet the Americans of that time were of diverse views, and those who had arrived at the conclusion that they ought to rule themselves had done so only gradually, over the course of years, and for different reasons. Their quarrel with the mother country had to do with, among other things, power, taxes, and ideology. Historians disagree as to which played the greatest part in triggering the conflict.

The colonists' vision of their revolution's place in human history could be, and often was, misunderstood. Once they had taken up arms, they made great claims for what they were doing. They believed themselves (or at least so their most eloquent propagandists said) to be rejecting practically the entire political past, and making a fresh start for the human race. From the outset, three fundamental principles had characterized the organization of society: humanity had been governed almost always by kings or priests; political position in civilized society had been acquired by inheritance; and individuals had existed for the benefit of the community or the state or the ruler. The Americans, in throwing off the ties that bound them to King George III and Great Britain, were not only defying an oppressive monarchy; they were contesting politics as a whole, as it had existed from Creation to their own time. Of course they borrowed from the few republics known to history and known to them, but their system differed in being based on a belief in the natural rights of the *individual,* and in that sense it was unique.

While their doctrine claimed universal rights for the individual— all humans everywhere, it asserted, are endowed with these inalienable natural rights—the colonists took up arms to win those rights only for themselves. This seems contradictory, yet Americans considered setting an example as their only role in improving the world. They were not to fight for the rights of others; every nation would have to liberate itself.

It was in designing their own political system that the Americans brought into existence something that they, with good reason, believed to be new and exceptional in human affairs. But in their rebellion against Britain, and in the defense of their interests against the powers and politics of Europe, they played much the same game that the other countries did. They won independence by playing off France against Britain, later playing off Britain against France. The American leaders were practical men of the world—their foreign policy was not, and was not intended to be, exceptional. Though idealists at home, they were realists abroad.

At least some of them knew that a country's domestic system does not necessarily shape its foreign policy. In Number 6 of the *Federalist* papers, Alexander Hamilton reminded his readers that democracies, too, wage wars. "Sparta, Athens and Carthage were all republics; two of them, Athens and Carthage, of the commercial kind," he wrote. But they were "as often engaged in wars, offensive and defensive, as the neighboring monarchies of the same times."

True, the founding fathers were influenced by such teachings as those of Immanuel Kant and Jean-Jacques Rousseau, according to which wars were fought in the private interests of kings: interests not shared by their peoples. The dynastic wars current in the Europe of that time lent credibility to this view. The European powers also maintained standing armies, a practice that Americans found wasteful. Even though the United States itself fought wars often enough, Americans believed that their country was essentially peaceful, and usually advanced its interests through commerce; whereas the monarchies of Europe pursued the bad old politics in which warfare not only played a central role, but was endemic, normal, and usual, an essential part of the system.

The United States, then, was intended by its founders to be exemplary. Because America's freedom of opportunity was so attractive, many of the most ambitious people elsewhere in the world would flock to its shores, as did others of talent fleeing persecution. Eventually other countries might well essay to copy the American political system, but encouraging them to do so was never among the country's pre-Wilson foreign policy goals.

Much later, when other countries did in fact consider emulating the American example, it was not so much because of the system's virtues, considerable though they were, as because of the prosperity brought by the modernizing revolution to which American-style politics proved particularly conducive.

The United States became the preeminent modern society—the first twentieth-century country, so to speak—in part by becoming the leader of the industrial revolution that began in England, and in part by becoming the leader of the political revolution that also began in Britain. One of the hallmarks of America is that it took its ideas, as it took its population, from the rest of the world, but most of all from the mother country against which it had rebelled. Some of the most distinctive characteristics of the United States were copied from Great Britain, even though, like children who cannot or will not see the extent to which they resemble their parents, Americans did not and do not always acknowledge it.

It should be pointed out that the Britain that gave birth to America was not the Britain of the common majority. Many of those who sailed away to settle in the New World were dissenters and Dissenters, nonconformists and Nonconformists.[1] There were seekers of religious liberty: the Puritans of Massachusetts, the Quakers of Pennsylvania, the Catholics of Maryland. There were adventure-seekers and fortune-seekers. There also were society's outcasts, including the convicts who settled Georgia. There were those who rejected Britain, and also those whom Britain had rejected.

The settlement of North America by Great Britain was an immigration, but it also was an emigration. It was a going away *from* more than a going *to;* for many of those who embarked from England's ports, what mattered most was what they were putting behind them. The voyage to the far side of the Atlantic was an intentional break with whoever or whatever prevailed at home. In that sense, the passage to America was a rebellion that foreshadowed the revolution to come in 1776. It also set a pattern in which the United States again and again took people, ideas, attitudes, and much else from those in Britain who opposed the established order. After it became independent, the U.S. also took people and ideas in large numbers from continental Europe and elsewhere—many of them, too, fleeing whatever they left behind.

Paradoxically, it is America's historical syncretism that has made it unique. How the United States is exceptional, and to what extent, are questions endlessly debated; but in some respects, the answers should not be in doubt. The country is peopled by the descendants of immigrants from all over the world. Traditionally the goal of the immigrants was to assimilate into what was pictured as the Anglo-Saxon American archetype. American society facilitated such assimilation; it welcomed the drive for conformity. But it also recognized the right to be different: the United States has accepted, albeit at times with misgivings, immigrants unwilling to assimilate—so long as they too subscribed to the American political faith.

For the United States is more an idea than a nation, which is something new in history. To be an American is to subscribe to a set

---

1. British Christians who were not members of the Church of England.

of beliefs grounded in the Constitution, a political gospel that defines not only the society but also individual Americans.

From the beginning, the founders of the American republic inspired the belief that they were bringing forth something new under the sun. Against the background of a continent that they saw as virgin and unspoiled, settlers had come to make a fresh start, to be given a second chance in life. From there it was a simple jump of the imagination to the conclusion that Europe and mankind itself were being given a second chance in the New World. America was offering the world a new kind of politics, and new answers to the questions of who should rule and how.

On April 30, 1789, George Washington was inaugurated as the first president of the United States. That was the outcome and ending of the American Revolution. That same year, the French Revolution began. At the time, it was not unreasonable to suppose that the second rebellion against monarchy had caught fire from the first.

Gradually, however, it transpired that the two revolts were quite different in spirit, representing alternative approaches to politics. The American Revolution of 1776, like the English Revolution of 1688, was informed by moderation and characterized by continuity of laws and institutions. In both cases, an existing society that was used to playing a significant role in its own government took up arms to change its rulers. The French went further; they tried to change not only rulers, but also the society as a whole, a feudal order centered around inherited privileges and an aristocracy that had become parasitic. The French Revolution became a byword for extremism characterized by the attempt to start mankind all over again at Year One.

Revolution was a new thing in Europe. It caught the imagination, especially of the young. Its banners and anthems stirred pulses. It brought back millennial, messianic hopes that had faded with religious faith. It was a new avenue that had opened up in politics, and from 1789 on, always had to be counted among the possibilities.

The French Revolution, because of its radicalism, became the prototype of what the young and the ardent expected a revolution to be. It exemplified the real thing—undiluted, uncompromising, and uncompromised. It fed the dreams of the idealistic, the romantic, and the ambitious, and was reenacted at one time or another on the barricades of many a European capital city.

The revolutions of modern Europe, for all the differences among them, bore a family resemblance to one another; all were manifestations of a modern world trying to come into its own. They were explosions triggered when social and economic pressures, having built to an intolerable level, blew the lid off moribund regimes that had been unyielding, or that yielded too little or too late. Instead of building on whatever existed, the revolutionaries tried to demolish it and rebuild from the ground up.

But for some reason, or perhaps for more reasons than one, even though Europe's *anciens régimes* deserved to be overthrown, they were replaced, time and again, by something similar or worse. Generation after generation of young idealists have believed in the promises and then had their hopes shattered.

In our own time, the ideology of revolution has been discredited. We have been witnesses to the revelation of where the Bolshevik coup d'état of 1917 led: dictatorship, police state, corruption. At the same time, the contrast has become all the more glaring between the failure of the politics of extremism and the success of the principles of moderation and modernization.

What were the new American political principles, and what was it in them that worked? In other words, why did they prove to be so especially congenial to the modernizing revolution?

Of course, opinions continue to differ. A partial answer was provided in 1941 by the Librarian of Congress, Archibald MacLeish, when, following the Japanese attack on Pearl Harbor, he sent to the invulnerable vaults of Fort Knox, Kentucky, for safekeeping, some of the icons of the country's democracy. There was one of the four existing copies of Magna Carta, held by the United States on loan from Britain. There was a Gutenberg Bible. And there were the Declaration of Independence, the Constitution, and the Bill of Rights. These treasures, in their way, begin to define the articles of belief of the traditional American political faith.

Magna Carta, the "Great Charter," issued and reissued between

1215 and 1225 by England's rulers, is a list of rights and duties, mostly between the English king and the British aristocracy, purporting to restate the ancient law of the land. It initially was forced upon the monarch by rebellious barons in a meadow called Runnymede by the side of the River Thames, some twenty miles outside London.

To contemporaries, Magna Carta did not have enormous significance. Similar charters had been granted to the nobility in the past by monarchs, both in England and on the continent of Europe, with no great lasting effect. In the months that followed the signing of Magna Carta, it appeared to be even more ephemeral than the others, as King John, who had issued it, repudiated it, and hostilities ensued.

"In 1215 Magna Carta was a failure," writes a leading modern scholar. "It was intended as a peace and it provoked war. It pretended to state customary law and it promoted disagreement and contention. It was legally valid for no more than three months, and even within that period its terms were never properly executed."

The document itself was a muddle. A scholar of these matters writes that "Sometimes Magna Carta stated law. Sometimes it stated what its supporters hoped would become law. Sometimes it stated what they pretended was law."

From today's perspective, the document treats of a number of issues of little lasting importance. It defined the rights of only a small percentage of the population, and the questions of feudal law that it regulates are of no contemporary relevance. Why, then, is Magna Carta of such importance? In part because it seemed to justify rebellion, even against a king, if he transgressed the law. In part, too, because it later was misconstrued by John Locke and other natural-law philosophers as restating, not merely the rights of Britons, but the inalienable rights of all human beings.

It was a strength of Magna Carta that it had the capacity to grow. In what is described as its thirty-ninth chapter, it famously provides that "No freeman shall be arrested, or detained in prison, or deprived of his freehold, or outlawed, or banished, or in any way molested; and we will not set forth against him, nor send against him, unless by the lawful judgment of his peers and by the law of the land." Although it did not mean it at the time, over the course of centuries this came to apply to all persons, and to guarantee them trial by jury.

Chapter 39 also came to be a guarantee of "due process of the law," a phrase that resonates throughout Anglo-American legal history.

Due *process:* it became an article of faith with Americans that fairness of the process—which is something within our control—is more important even than the justice of the outcome, which is something not always within our control. It is analogous to our belief that the end never justifies the means—in part, because we know and can determine the choice of means, but never can know in advance what ends will be achieved.

What Magna Carta stands for above all is the rule of law. In addition to all the other merits and benefits of such a system, it transpired later that law would provide the stability that allows a modern industrial society to flourish.

The Gutenberg Bible. The communications revolution of the modern world began with the creation, in Europe, of printing with moveable type. Whether or not he invented it, such a printing press was used by Johann Gutenberg (circa 1398–1468), a German goldsmith of whom we know little. What we do know is that he lived a troubled life of debts, litigation, and failed partnerships. A creditor, having won a lawsuit, ruined him financially and took control of the type for Gutenberg's two masterpieces, a Bible and a Psalter.

The spoken word carried no further than the distance a person could shout; but the printed word could travel to the ends of the earth. It could reach everyone. By the year 1500, there were twenty million copies of books in print.

Easy access to books made it possible for people to educate themselves. It exposed them to new ideas and controversies, and encouraged people to think for themselves.

This became immediately apparent in matters of religion. Even before history began, people seem to have received the words and commands of the gods only through the intermediation of their priests. Now, Bible in hand, they could read for themselves the word of God—and interpret it for themselves, too.

A path led directly from the printing press to the Reformation; in 1517, Martin Luther nailed his Ninety-five Theses onto a church door in the German town of Wittenberg. At once it was reprinted and distributed widely in and outside of Germany.

As the Bible was translated into European languages in large printings, it had the effect of undermining the authority of the Church—or at any rate Church authorities believed that it had such an effect. William Tyndale translated much of the Hebrew Bible and the New Testament into English; for doing so he was hunted down by the clerical establishment of his day and burned at the stake.

The printing press, used at first to circulate the Bible, was later employed to acquaint the European world with works of a skeptical bent by authors ranging from Erasmus to Voltaire, David Hume, and Edward Gibbon. It also made possible the ambitious project of Denis Diderot to encompass all knowledge—and make it available to everyone—in an encyclopedia.

"Twice in this millennium, Europe was hit by a good, big idea: first the Reformation; second the Enlightenment. Both left legacies of independence of mind, a sense of individual rights before the law and other virtues," according to the *Economist*. The Reformation—broadly speaking, the reform movements within Christendom that were started in the 1500s by Luther and others—and the Enlightenment, the variously defined and unsystematic body of thought that led from the humanism of Erasmus in the 1500s to the skepticism and the questioning of authority by Voltaire and Hume in the 1700s, flowed into the making of the American mind. Benjamin Franklin and Thomas Paine, leading Enlightenment figures, both played a major role in the American Revolution.

It has been said that the American culture that emerged in the 1800s was shaped by the clashes and reconciliations of the Enlightenment with the Reformation. One thing that both movements had in common—and that is basic to the ideology of the United States—is that both, rejecting authority, emphasized the freedom of the individual—freedom of conscience, freedom to shape one's own faith, freedom of thought and inquiry.

Another thing that the movements had in common was that both, in large part, were facilitated by the printing press. And it was mass education and mass literacy that made possible the success America achieved.

The Declaration of Independence, the Constitution and *the Bill of Rights* were the basic documents uniting thirteen of the English colonies in North America into a single independent federal republic that was designed to respect the rights of its citizens. Its affairs were to be administered by a divided government of limited powers. All, even the government, were made subject to the rule of law. These founding documents expressed a philosophy shaped by English law, European thought, and American experience.

The uniting of the colonies under the Constitution created a single market without internal trade barriers, facilitating the dynamic expansion, later, of a modern economy. The focus on satisfying the individual, on the right to pursue happiness, paved the way for a consumer society.

From these icons of the United States emerged the republic. It was in large part an agrarian society with a small and homogeneous population. There were those, among them Thomas Jefferson, who believed that small polities were best for the human spirit. Smaller communities seemed to provide the environment in which the individual was most free—the purpose of politics, in the American view.

But the industrial revolution changed the character of the country. After the railroads, the oil, the steel, the full industrialization, and the mass immigration from all over the world, the United States no longer was a rural republic of small towns; it was a mass, urban democracy.

It was the changed and changing United States that, under the leadership of Woodrow Wilson, fatefully encountered twentieth-century Europe under the circumstances described at the beginning of the chapter. For decades, before the shots fired at Sarajevo that ignited the conflict of 1914, people on both sides of the Atlantic, even such practical men as the steel magnate Andrew Carnegie, believed that the modernizing revolution had made warfare between industrial powers suicidal.

Industrial civilization was capable of producing weapons so destructive that if both sides possessed them, a war between them could very well destroy both. A widespread belief during the last half of the nineteenth century was that the leaders of the industrial countries recognized this truth and had drawn the appropriate conclusions from it. Confirmation of the belief was provided by the Concert of Europe: by the harmony with which the great powers of Europe worked together to defuse international crises. It seemed to show that the advanced countries shared an interest in preserving peace.

Around the turn of the century, an abundance of treaties were negotiated providing for the arbitration of differences between countries. Carnegie poured millions of dollars into a campaign to encourage the peaceful settlement of international disputes, and created institutions to promote and facilitate such accords. An English publicist named Norman Angell wrote a book in 1910 called *The Great Illusion*, famously arguing that war does not pay anymore. Many of his readers concluded that in a modern industrial society, war could not occur.

At the turn of the century, as Carnegie and others campaigned for peace, Great Britain presided over a world balance of power. Britain was the sole supernation, exercising total command of the world's oceans, and therefore was able to exert power on the coast of any continent. London was the center of world finance. It was not a world order of which an American could approve, for Americans— ignoring the existence of their own imperial sphere in Central America, the Caribbean, and the Pacific—believed that people should rule themselves: should not be ruled, in other words, either by kings at home or by imperial mother countries from abroad. But the system functioned.

Afterwards, the British felt nostalgia for the freedom of that pre-war world. The historian A. J. P. Taylor wrote that "until August 1914 a sensible, law-abiding Englishman could pass through life and hardly notice the existence of the state, beyond the post office and the policeman. He could live where he liked and as he liked. He had no official number or identity card. He could travel abroad or leave his country for ever without a passport or any sort of official permission. He could exchange his money for any other currency without restriction or limit. He could buy goods from any country in the world on the same terms as he bought goods at home. For that matter, a foreigner could spend his life in this country without permit."

The French academic André Siegfried, it was reported, recalled that before the war, "he had once gone around the world with only one piece of identification: his calling card!" The economist John Maynard Keynes remembered how easy it had been, on an impulse, to send a servant to the bank for gold, and then go "abroad to foreign quarters, without knowledge of their religion, language, or customs," and how the ordinary Englishman "would consider himself greatly aggrieved and much surprised at the least interference. But, most of all, he regarded this state of affairs as normal, certain, and permanent. . . . The projects and politics of militarism and imperialism, of racial and cultural rivalries . . . were little more than the amusements of his daily newspaper, and appeared to exercise almost no influence at all on the ordinary course of social and economic life, the internationalization of which was nearly complete in practice."

The outbreak of war came as a surprise. As late as July 1914, it remained unthinkable. Yet that August, seemingly out of nowhere, it exploded into being, like some universe of its own. Life changed forever. The nineteenth century, born politically in the French Revolution of 1789, came to an end in the First World War of 1914–1918. The world at war stopped being Romantic or Victorian or Edwardian and began to be modern. Governments took command of national economies. Labor was regimented. Social barriers collapsed. Obscure people did well out of the war; were courted, and went everywhere. Authors no longer affected a high style, but adopted the language of the street or even of the gutter. In such countries as Britain and the United States, women threw off inhibitions imposed by dress and society; changed into something comfortable; smoked, drank, or swore; took jobs; and eventually got the vote.

After the ceasefire of 1918 there was an uneasy intermission in the fighting. Following a brief, delirious spree—the 1920s—the world underwent an economic and financial collapse that many blamed on the war. Plagued by mass unemployment and widespread despair, Europe in particular entered into an age of dictators; the Soviet Union, Germany, Portugal, Spain, Italy, Yugoslavia, Greece, Hungary, Romania, and Poland were among the countries that were subjected to authoritarian or totalitarian rule.

The war resumed in 1939–1945 and Germany lost again. But on the morrow of victory, the winners found that they were unable to agree on peace terms in Europe. The Soviet Union insisted on retaining control of the European territories and countries it had overrun in winning the war. The United States demanded that the Soviets relinquish their domination of those lands. No compromise proved to be available. The quarrel assumed global dimensions, and from the outset was associated with ideological ones. Each side stood its ground, confronting one another in a Cold War until the Soviet Union backed down in 1989, and then withdrew its last troops from Germany on August 31, 1994. The great worldwide war that had begun in 1914 finally was over; a settlement had been reached at long last. The war, and such real or apparent consequences as the Depression, the release of colonies in Asia and Africa from European empires, the achievement of a global economy, the transfer of the center of finance from London to New York, and an enormous acceleration in the growth of science and new technologies, were, in essence, what happened in the twentieth century. War defined the century's dates: from August 1914 to August 1994. It was a short century, lasting only eighty years; but it was the bloodiest in history.

All of the great powers—the United States, Russia, Britain, France, Italy, Germany, Japan, and China—were belligerents in the great war that raged throughout the twentieth century and defined it; and all but America were ruined by it. The United States won every conflict, and alone came out of it unscathed.[3]

3. Great Britain, too, triumphed in all phases, but its victory was pyrrhic, costing it its empire and its worldwide naval and economic supremacy. Germany lost in 1918 and 1945; Japan lost in 1945; France, bled white in 1914–1918, lost in 1940; China lost in 1931 and, though continuing to resist, was losing in 1937–1945; Russia lost in 1918, and in effect surrendered again by dissolving the Soviet Union and its empire in 1989–1994.

When the war began, America was a debtor country with a small navy and practically no army. When the war ended, the United States was not only the world's wealthiest nation, the center of the global economy and of global finance, but also the only remaining superpower, able militarily to dominate the planet. America was the one and only winner.

It was not what Americans had intended; they had not wanted to be involved. In both 1914 and 1939, they planned to remain neutral. In both 1919 and 1945, they demobilized and disarmed. It was only in 1949, when the United States received its third summons to defend western Europe, that Americans sent armed forces overseas to stay.

Once drawn into overseas conflict, Americans had not believed that they were reaching for world mastery, even though that in fact was what they were doing and, in the end, achieving. In their ideology, politics was supposed to seek to realize ideals. Americans liked to believe that their quarrel with other great nations was one of principle. Certainly the rival political revolutions of the modern world expressed very different philosophies, and that of the United States stood in stark contrast to the others.

The American Revolution stood for the primacy of the individual; the French, of the nation broadly conceived; the Bolshevik Russian, of the industrial working class; the Italian fascist, of the state; the Nazi German, of the master race and its one leader. On the plane of ideas, the United States deserved to win, and did so: in particular, it was in large part a loss of faith by the Soviet Union that led it to concede victory. Raymond Aron, a great French thinker, addressed a London meeting of the Institute for Strategic Studies in the 1980s, and posed a question about political belief. Reminding the conference of what Machiavelli had said about armed prophets being much more likely to succeed in this world than unarmed prophets, he asked, as regards the Soviets, what would happen if the armed prophet, once in power, kept his arms but lost faith in his religious message.

Within years, we had the answer. It was one of the most astonishing events ever. The most formidable, armed-to-the-teeth, totalitarian empire the world had ever known dissolved itself of its own volition because nobody, not even its rulers, believed in it anymore.

However, it was the prudent deployment of American power around the world for decades that kept the Soviet Union at bay until its collapse took place. And with such aggressors as Nazi Germany and fascist Italy, it was power—and not merely the contrast of America's bright vision with the darkness of that of its adversaries— that brought victory to the Allied cause. But above all it was geography and the American economy—shielded by an ocean on either side, and therefore given time to mobilize—that proved to be invincible. The Soviet Union collapsed in an effort to keep up with the American economy: it was the other major reason for the self-destruction of the USSR.

Like a series of killer earthquakes, the various phases of the twentieth-century war brought down and leveled the political structure of the world outside the western hemisphere. The features of global politics to which the United States always had objected were among those that collapsed in the fighting. It will be remembered that, at the outset of the century and of the war, Woodrow Wilson had argued that the world had to be remade to America's political specifications in order to achieve peace. In the course of the century, the world was remade in an American fashion. The old order that Europe had imposed upon itself and the world went up in flames. The hereditary principle of rule was discarded. Kings were overthrown; those few who retained thrones mostly did so as mere figureheads. Aristocracies followed their sovereigns into the dustbin of history. Empires were dissolved; colonies obtained their independence. Constitutions were adopted. Parliaments were installed. Markets were opened. Elections were held. By the end of the twentieth century, except for China, all of the great powers were parliamentary democracies. By and large, people, at last, now rule themselves.

Today's world is the world that America wanted, but it is not a world that America made. The United States did not overthrow the kings or free the colonies. Things happened to fall out the way Wilson and his countrymen desired. It may have been luck. In part it may also have been that the country is so allied with modernization that where the modernizing revolution takes the world is where the United States wants the world to go.

A major test still lies ahead. The United States is, in international affairs,[4] a satisfied country that desires permanent peace. The modernizing revolution—or, at least, so many people believe—compels peace between the industrial powers: biological, chemical, and nuclear weapons, if used in anger, could bring life on earth to an end.

As has often been the case, America wants what the scientific-industrial-technological revolution needs. But can it be done? Can a world of states that are independent live together in peace? What of the innate disposition of groups to hate and try to destroy one another?

In the middle of the millennium now coming to an end, Europe began to conquer or colonize the rest of the world. It is one of the main stories in the tale of humanity's politics. The program took five centuries to accomplish; by the first quarter of the twentieth century it was completed, by the last quarter it had been undone.

Thrilled by the disintegration of the Soviet empire, Americans did not always keep in view the achievement of their more long-term goal: the bringing to an end of all European empires. Yet it was on this astonishing note of triumph that our century and our millennium draw to their close. It is well worth summarizing the extent to which our hopes have been realized.

Ever since 1776, the United States has wanted to see Europe's conquest of the planet undone, and ever since 1945, it wanted the Soviet Union and its bloc to unravel; and both events came to pass in the twentieth century. The greatest mass liberation in history took place in our time. China with its 1.2 billion people;[5] the three states that were once British India, with their 1.2 billion; the countries of Africa with 732 million; Indonesia with 206 million; all of these and many more achieved full independence.

4. In domestic affairs, there are major challenges that—it should not even need saying—the country as yet has failed to meet.

5. In theory China always retained its sovereignty, but a century ago the country was to a considerable extent dominated by foreign powers.

Of the European powers, Britain alone, in the first few decades after 1945, surrendered 5.2 million square miles of colonial territory with almost a billion inhabitants. The United States itself granted independence to the Philippines, and released Germany and Japan from occupation and tutelage.

The world was free. But it was a far different world from the one Europe had found and taken in hand centuries before.

Looking back, what happened in modern history was that a millennium ago, Europe began to develop a distinctive mentality. That mentality, rationalism, enabled Europeans to triumph in two enterprises.

The first enterprise, after their survey of the rest of the world, was the one just summarized: their settlement or conquest of the globe. Their armies and navies brought the whole world for a time into a single political system; and their bankers and investors fashioned a single financial system.

Their second enterprise was the modernizing revolution that began with science and went on to industry and technology. Modernization was born in Europe, of rationalism and science. In many respects "Europeanization," "westernization," "Americanization," and "modernization" all mean the same thing.

But it was the United States that developed a special vocation for modernization. Traditional American politics and values seemed best suited to the task: the focus on universal education and mass literacy; meritocracy; freedom of inquiry, thought, and expression; and other aspects of an open society.

In ancient history, there had been a variety of civilizations. Such pluralism had been healthy for the human race, providing viable alternatives to those who ran up against dead ends. Modern history has witnessed a narrowing of the options, to the point that civilization now runs in a single channel. Sumerians and Egyptians and others invented civilization independently and for themselves; but there is only one scientific-industrial-technological revolution. As Ernest Gellner used to point out, it has its imitators, but there is no other original.

Today the alternatives are gone: that, perhaps, more than anything else, is what has happened in the last five hundred to a thousand years. Now we're all in the same boat. It may be a seaworthy boat; but it would be less worrisome if there were more than one.

Visitors from the ancient world might notice a few big changes other than the girdling of the globe by one civilization.

They would observe the enormous power that humanity now exercises over its natural environment.

In the Northern Hemisphere, they probably would marvel at the unprecedented wealth of the average person. They would be struck by the strides made towards the equality of women. They might find it remarkable that so much of the population is middle-aged or older.

If they were people who took the long view, they might remember that conscience, asserting itself in religion and philosophy, had been the great ethical development of the world of antiquity. They might recognize its parallel in the present day. They might see that freedom, asserted in politics and by the force of arms, has been the theme of the modern world, that the philosophy of its leading country is based on the rights of the individual; and that its dominant powers at the end of the twentieth century profess to believe that the state exists to serve the individual rather than, as in a Greek city-state or a Persian empire, the individual to serve the state.

Would they recognize that all of these marvelous achievements are closely associated with the modernizing revolution that still continues on its headlong course? And would they sense that winning such prizes as freedom, wealth, and power might prove dangerous? They might well; for it was the ancients, the Greeks of antiquity, who taught us to fear the goddess they called Nemesis: a daughter of Night who envies good fortune and exacts retribution for it.

PART THREE: FUTURE

9: ANTICIPATING WHAT COMES NEXT

Madame Sosostris, famous clairvoyante, . . .
Is known to be the wisest woman in Europe,
With a wicked pack of cards. Here, said she,
Is your card. . . .
. . . Fear death by water.

—T. S. ELIOT, *The Waste Land*

What's going to happen next?

Mankind always has been fascinated by the possibility that this question can be answered. There have been fortune-tellers throughout history; always and everywhere there has been a demand for their services.

In the past, people who gazed into crystal balls hoped to foresee the future without much hope of changing it. They believed there were precautions that might usefully be taken, but that, in the end, there was no way to avoid meeting one's fate.

Scientific man is different, recognizing that, over time, everything changes. Wise men in other civilizations perceived this truth as well, but unlike them, we welcome change, believing it to be a good thing; we initiate it and lay plans both to anticipate it and to bring it about. In order to plan for the future, we make forecasts. In business and government, we continuously look ahead, project demographic and other trends, and emerge with detailed short-run predictions. We take action and initiate policies on the basis of such predictions. Betting on the accuracy of futurology—that sector of it that is based on current trends—is one of the characteristics of rational modernism. We do it routinely and successfully, especially over time spans that are short.

Can it be accomplished in politics as well? Can the political future be foretold? When it comes to specific events, the record has not been very good. Many if not most of the major happenings of the twentieth century took the world by surprise. When the First World War broke out in 1914, cabinet ministers and general staffs expected it to be over in weeks. Instead it lasted for four terrible, seemingly endless years. The Bolshevik seizure of power in 1917, from which so much followed in our century, was an unforeseen and unforeseeable event. Insiders in German politics in the early 1930s thought the Nazi movement was not to be taken seriously; Hitler was a buffoon who would allow himself to be used for a time by serious politicians, then be cast aside and forgotten. In the 1930s the French army was rated the strongest in Europe, but in 1940 it disintegrated in a few weeks as France was ripped apart by the Nazi blitzkrieg. When Germany invaded the Soviet Union in 1941, the best military minds in America advised President Roosevelt that the Red Army could hold out for no more than a few weeks; instead, after waging nearly four years of combat, it proved to be the most powerful army of all. Starting in 1989, the collapse of the Soviet Union and the Soviet bloc, as it happened, and when it happened, was completely unexpected.

Yet some of the main lines of the twentieth century were sketched out accurately, albeit in broad strokes, long in advance. In 1835, young Alexis de Tocqueville, traveler in the New World, foresaw that by the next century Russia and America would emerge as the world's two great powers; that each of them would "sway the destinies of half the globe"; and that their contrasting qualities—America's freedom and Russia's authoritarianism—would become one of the principal themes of international politics. It was a fair picture of the age that ended when the Berlin Wall came down. The Frenchman's inspired forecasts were far from wild speculation; again and again, they were borne out by history.

Tocqueville was in his middle twenties when he and a companion voyaged (1831–1832) to the United States to study the new country. Of an old Norman family that was elevated to the peerage in 1827 by the reactionary Bourbon monarch Charles X, Tocqueville nonetheless was an understanding, if not always sympathetic, observer of the democratic and egalitarian trends he witnessed. His seeming clairvoyance came from working out the logical consequences of the main features and trends he observed in social and political life. What appeared to be a vision of the future was largely a clear-eyed analysis of the present and of where the course of events would lead if continued. That is what business and government forecasters do today within their own spheres, except that they then go on to take action on their predictions. And that is what we must do in politics too: not merely expect future events, but anticipate them.

In the Western world before, during, and after the turn of the present century, science, with its universe of possibilities and dangers, suddenly caught the public imagination. At that time, in looking ahead, people tended to dwell on the wonders of the technology that tomorrow would bring. Hence Jules Verne, and hence H. G. Wells.

Wells (1866–1946) scored his first success as the author of what have been called "scientific thrillers." His luck was that his tales appeared just as the public developed a hunger for scientific fantasy and speculation. Self-made, born into a family of servants and small shopkeepers, poorly schooled, Wells managed to convey his own sense of excitement and discovery as he himself encountered and acquired knowledge.

Though he made his success as a journalist and novelist, he was driven to be a pedagogue, a social critic, and a prophet; and he combined all three in his futurology.

In the immediate aftermath of the First World War, Wells plunged into an outline of the world's history and future. He wrote it in a million words in a great burst of energy in 1920. *The Outline of History* has retained its fame throughout the century. As history, it does not stand up under the scrutiny of modern scholarship; but as conceptualization, it still deserves respect and admiration.

It pictures history as a story of progress. This is not a popular view today among academics. Yet it should be undeniable—if you are prepared to grant that an increase in human power over nature is a good thing. Wells portrays the great enlightening forces in history as religion and education. These are broad generalizations that can be disputed, but not disproven. My own equally broad generalization is that the development of conscience was a theme of ancient times, and the pursuit of freedom, a theme of modern times. Put either way, ancient times were the age of faith and its enemies, and modern times, the age of reason and its enemies.

Wells was a rationalist and an optimist. His *Outline* sprang from a belief that science would be all-important in the modern age, and that understanding the directions in which science would develop presented the key to seeing where the human race would go.

The long-term trend, as he saw it, was towards enlargement of political units. It had been brought about by transportation and communications bringing people together. Now science had given the human race weapons of mass destruction. As a result it was of vital importance to prevent nations from taking up arms against one another ever again. In the wake of the First World War, it was clear that soon science would need the establishment of a world community, and of a world state that would bring the rule of law to the whole planet, in order to do away with suicidal warfare.

Broadly speaking, he may not have been far wrong. But today we would want to amend and add to his vision. We have become aware that achieving a global government, a global state, and a global community in order to accommodate the requirements of a global civilization puts all eggs in one basket—with obvious consequences if we drop the basket. We also would point out that there are social trends at work in the direction of breaking up political units,[1] rendering them smaller—not, as Wells deemed necessary, larger. We also would want to explore the extent to which human power over nature creates new responsibilities that the human race may not yet be capable of assuming. We would want to caution that we cannot take progress for granted, our accomplishments are too recent, civilization remains fragile, and human beings and their societies, as

---

1. So much so, that today there are many more independent countries than there were when the Wells book appeared. At its zenith in the 1920s, the League of Nations had 54 members. The United Nations in 1997 had 185.

we have seen in the past, are as capable of regression as they are of progression.

The force of rationalist logic, in looking ahead to the needs of the future, cannot be denied. But the claims of the mind and of Edwardian optimism having been recognized, we have become aware that we also must take account of human nature—of animal nature—in politics.

Beginning in the last half of the nineteenth century, a literature that includes the works of Nietzsche, Freud, and Kafka focused on the power of the irrational and the persistence of the absurd. The monstrousness of the massacres, the mass hysterias, the wars, and some of the politics of the twentieth century have validated at least some of the insights of that school of thought. The dark side of human nature, we now know, persists.

Then, too, we have discovered that there is much to be learned about our drives, instincts, and behavior from other species, especially those closely related to us.

Two things that we know are seemingly contradictory, but both are true: humans are very much like the other primates, and humans are very much unlike them.

Scientific evidence, especially that gathered in the last part of this century, shows us to be so close to other animals in genetic structure as to indicate that there are only a small number of innate differences. In a DNA analysis, chimpanzees, our closest living relatives, differ from us genetically by a mere 1.5 to 2 percent. Of course in a crucial way this ratio misleads—that 2 percent may contain everything that matters. Nonetheless the genetic similarities provided good reason for Jane Goodall and other pioneer field workers to draw on the behavior of chimpanzees in reaching conclusions of relevance to ourselves—even of political relevance. For while we have little in common with the germ that was our ancestor, and neither do apes, today's humans have a great deal in common with today's chimpanzees.

One of the similarities is an intense interest in ourselves. Chimpanzees being raised for research purposes as wards of the United States government are supplied with television sets to amuse them;

and it tells us something about them (and about ourselves) that their favorite programs are those, such as *National Geographic* specials, that are about chimpanzees.

Jane Goodall, born in London in the early 1930s, was schooled in Bournemouth. Instead of going on to college, she worked as a secretary to earn enough money to send herself to Africa. Once there, in 1957, at the age of twenty-three, she met and went to work for the great prehistorian Dr. Louis Leakey, at first in the Natural History Museum in Nairobi, and later in the field. Her passionate sympathy for animals impressed him; and he arranged for her to be sent to study groups of chimpanzees that lived on the shores of Lake Tanganyika. "Louis told me," Goodall later wrote, that "the remains of prehistoric man were often found on a lake shore and it was possible that an understanding of chimpanzee behavior today might shed light on the behavior of our stone-age ancestors."

Venturing alone into the forest, Goodall aroused first the fear and then the hostility of the chimpanzees. But after more than a half year, they accepted her, and allowed her to befriend them with gifts of bananas. Her book *In the Shadow of Man*, describing the first decade of her life in the forest with the chimpanzees, was a pioneering work. Soon other researchers followed her lead, undertaking similar studies of other groups of primates in their natural environments.

Contrary to what then was thought and taught, Goodall discovered that chimpanzees eat meat and make tools: forms of behavior still believed at that time to be distinctive of man. In a surprising number of ways, she found that, in body language and behavior, the animals with whom she lived were "human."

Living together is difficult unless there is agreement on who makes the rules. Goodall observed that her chimpanzee society had its elaborate social hierarchy—each male had his rank and knew his place. When she first made contact with the animals, she called the chief male Goliath. She observed that if Goliath and another ape both started towards a banana, it was the other who gave way and let Goliath take it. And, "If Goliath met another adult male along a narrow forest track, he continued—the other stepped aside."

At the other extreme was Mike, a male adult at almost the bottom of the hierarchy, who was threatened and attacked by practically every member of the band. But Mike eventually thought of a novel tactic for turning the tables.

Within their group, chimpanzees who fight tend to win by scaring, rather than actually hurting, their opponents. Dragging a branch along the ground is their normal method of producing a frightening sound to unnerve the adversary. Mike discovered that metal kerosene cans he came upon in Jane Goodall's camp, if banged together, make a much more terrifying sound. Apparently counting on that, he challenged the leadership of his tribe, charging his superiors while clanging his cans, causing terror and bringing about surrender.

Goodall's account of the final half-hour showdown between Mike and Goliath has something of the drama of a duel at high noon on the main street of a frontier cowtown. In its own terms, it was a sort of western—except in its outcome. For in the end, Goliath lost his nerve, and offered submission to Mike.

Not only did Mike become the new leader, but, as a consequence, a chimp who had been his friend in the old days rose in the hierarchy with him. Such is politics, a subject famously described by a Yale sociologist a generation ago as "Who Gets What, When, How."

At the heart of politics is the tension between the two aspects of leadership. On the one hand, leadership unites individuals, making it possible for all primates to live in groups and for humans to function as groups. On the other hand the question of who shall be the leader divides the group: rivals, each with supporters, fight it out.

What Jane Goodall witnessed in the forests of East Africa, as Goliath beat his tree branch and Mike clanged his cans, was rudimentary politics: behavior going back tens of millions of years to the first primates, and focused then as now on the dual and conflicting aspects of the question of leadership, which both unites and divides.

Within groups of early human hunter-gatherers, presumably one would have found the social cohesion, the cooperation, the food-sharing that also was so attractive in the chimpanzee society that Jane

Goodall studied. The eighteenth-century followers of Rousseau, the back-to-nature Romantics of the nineteenth century, and the flower children of the 1960s might have found their ideal in Goodall's chimps. Indeed, when *In the Shadow of Man* first appeared, it inevitably raised the question of whether we have lost touch with our roots, of whether we might not be well advised to recover some of our lost humanity by imitating, in some respects, our animal cousins.

It transpired that the first picture taken by Goodall had been shot in too soft a focus. Further observations led to a modification of her initial conclusions. "Had my colleagues and I stopped after ten years," she remarked recently, "we would have been left with the impression that chimpanzees are far more peaceable than humans." It turned out that, like ourselves, the other members of the ape family have a dark side to their nature.

Chimpanzees, in particular, though helpful, generous, and even loving with members of their own group, behave murderously towards members of other groups. In 1970 Goodall witnessed a killing, as chimps of one band skirmished with those of an adjacent territory. She observed raids in which the invaders sought to destroy, or at least permanently incapacitate, their enemies. This was in striking contrast to leadership combats within a group, in which losers are not injured seriously, or not injured at all. Goodall remarked that chimpanzees share with humans "an unusually hostile and violently aggressive attitude toward non-group individuals."

Like ourselves, then, chimpanzees have not one kind of politics, but two: the politics of comradeship within groups, and the politics of hostility between groups. Some students of animal behavior explain it on the basis of genetics: each group protects the purity of its genetic inheritance by a hatred of other groups so intense as to preclude intercourse among them. If so, the chimpanzee wars that Goodall witnessed were literally blood feuds. Their purpose might have been to preserve the variety upon which evolution through natural selection is said by Darwinians to depend.

By a curious coincidence, as members of Goodall's team were making and pondering these observations in their encampment far from civilization and its conflicts, they were attacked by fellow humans. In a midnight raid in May 1975, about forty Marxist guerrillas of a group based in Zaire, and calling themselves the Popular

Revolutionary Party, crossed Lake Tanganyika and kidnapped three students and a staff member to attract attention to their obscure cause.[2]

The raid was a striking reminder that there is no place on earth, not even in the forests and among the animals, that is beyond the reach of warfare and the brutal side of politics. Yet the illusion persists: a glass that refuses to be shattered, even when thrown against the hard brick wall of reality.

Robert Louis Stevenson, adventurer, escapist, romantic, wanderer, author of *Treasure Island*, and incorrigible optimist about what might be found over the horizon, spent his last years in the Samoa Islands of the South Seas, where he died in 1894 at the age of forty-four. Although in general for Stevenson, "happiness was elsewhere," Samoa, after he settled there, seemed as close to a paradise as the world had to offer. Yet even in Samoa, surrounded by an ocean called pacific, he could not escape the world's deadly political quarrels. Germany, Great Britain, and the United States all sought control of the Samoa Islands at the time, and each backed its own local chief.

War among the chiefs erupted in 1888 and again in 1892; and Stevenson wrote to his friend Mark Twain, "I wish you could see my 'simple and sunny heaven' now . . . with severed heads and men dying in hospital." To Henry James, another friend, he explained that "You don't know what news is, nor what politics, nor what the life of man till you see it on so small a scale."

It was fitting that the two morally opposite faces of man in society—characteristically helpful and friendly to those in our own group, but hostile, sometimes murderously so, to those in all others—should have been remarked upon by the author of *The Strange Case of Dr. Jekyll and Mr. Hyde*.

It is tempting to believe that we are back where H. G. Wells and his rationalist colleagues started, before and immediately after the First World War. The twentieth century, 1914–1994, was a sort of war

---

2. The hostages later were released.

between those who desired progress and freedom and those who did not, in which the former won. It can be regarded as a long and terrible detour. Can we now get back to the main highway of political life? Can we go back to being Edwardian or early 1920s optimists? Should we convince ourselves that the problems are within reach of being solved?

It was by no means surprising that in the aftermath of the western victory in the Cold War, Francis Fukayama should conclude that history has come to an end; or that Samuel Huntington should argue that world politics of the type we have known until now—conflicts among countries—has come to an end. It was surprising only that the expression of such views was unexpected.

If we are to use the past and the present as our basis for guessing what lies ahead, then we have to say that in the next century and perhaps even the next millennium, people will continue to live with conflicts and contradictions, and are unlikely to resolve them all. Human history has been so brief—only six thousand years, in a universe billions of years old—that there hasn't been enough time to arrive at definitive decisions about many of the big issues. A look back at the eight turning points discussed in this book so far will confirm that: none of them constitutes an irrevocable move or a final stopping point: mankind has climbed eight rungs but still could fall back off the ladder.

Becoming human is a process that may be continuing. Or it may be coming undone: humanity may be on the road to becoming something else—and not necessarily something of which we would approve.

To some extent we may have slowed evolution by employing medical technologies that allow those who otherwise would have fallen by the way to survive and perpetuate their genetic traits. But there is no reason to believe that evolution has come to a complete stop. Moreover we may soon be able to speed it up ourselves. Biologists are learning enough to tamper with the evolutionary process in humans for our own purposes—with all the ethical and other questions that may raise.

Change, for better or for worse, may well come about from an altered environment. The living surface of the earth, moving, rising, falling, imposing new strains and exposing old faults, may transform the world around us. So may the atmosphere. As an example: *The New York Times* reported on June 29, 1996, "A University of Chicago astrophysicist says the solar system . . . having spent a few million years passing through calm and relatively empty space . . . is headed, in about 50,000 years, for what may be trouble—a cloud of interstellar dust and gas a million times denser than the space it occupies now." The turbulence may be severe. Cosmic-ray bombardment may increase. Some new form of life, immune to such disturbances, might replace us.

In a more cheerful vein, it has been suggested that the increased integration of individuals with miniaturized mobile machines offering continuing communication with others worldwide, and also access to data banks, will make humans something of a new and higher species.

Inventing civilization was an enormous human advance that long was contested on the battlefield by nomad horsemen out of the wastelands of northern Eurasia. Now the barbarians dwell inside the walls: the urban areas of the world still fight for sheer survival, but wage their battles against challenges from within. Cities have become the arena in which all society's needs, wants, and ills are addressed. That is because, increasingly, the cities are where the masses of humanity live.

Reports from a United Nations conference on cities, attended by delegates from 171 countries, that ended the last week of spring in 1996, suggested the topicality and even urgency of the urban crisis—which is more a crisis of society than of the metropolises that society inhabits. According to one dispatch, "While close to half the world's population already lives in urban slums, people of the developing world still pour into the cities" at such a rate that by 2015, the ten largest cities on earth, with the exception of Tokyo, will be located in the (curiously misnamed) developing world.

According to another reporter, "The United Nations estimates that two-thirds of the earth's population will be living in cities by 2025, straining the ability of urban society to provide shelter and sanitation."

But the point made by one civic leader is that such challenges are more effectively met in an urban than a rural setting. "From electricity to water to sewer to heating to garbage collection . . . costs are much lower per person in cities than in rural areas." Moreover, cities, with their economies of scale, are more effective producers of the new wealth needed to deal with these problems than are rural areas.

Developing a conscience has run up against limits. In certain areas the human race has been notably unable to overcome the basic instinct in men and monkeys that makes people so hostile to members of alien groups that they believe it right to kill them. The clearest example is international politics. Though examples may be made of a few highly visible individuals, for the most part hideous atrocities essentially go unpunished. In part, this may be due to the pervasiveness of the problem: there are so many perpetrators that it would be impractical to go after them all. But mostly it is because we tend not to condemn what is done in the course of public conflicts. "That's war," we say, sadly perhaps but acceptingly. A civilian who kills is a murderer; but a person in uniform who kills is a soldier.

It could be that, like the Greeks described by Thucydides, we have been brutalized by our wars and are becoming less good rather than more good.

We go on *seeking a lasting peace*, but find ourselves no closer to reaching that elusive goal than we were before—and possibly even further away. Limited-scale wars break out all the time, less civilized and more bloody than the eighteenth-century wars of which Edward Gibbon wrote. It is true that in the 1990s the eruption of a conflict between the major powers seems to be out of the question; but in the 1890s it seemed so too, and yet, not long afterwards, the world war began.

Looking back, *The Economist* on August 3, 1996, observed, "The 20th century was the century that should have known better, did know better"—but did it anyway. It essentially was one long war, punctuated by mass murders, and darkened by the fascist, Nazi, and communist regimes in which criminals were the police. On the occasion of the approaching turn of the century, and of the many hopes and wishes of which it will be the occasion, *The Economist* beguiled itself and its readers with the suggestion that we program our super-powerful computers to "make it 1900 again, but use the wisdom that has been so bitterly acquired to get the 20th century right this time around."

In point of fact it was the twentieth century that for the first time adopted as an immediate goal of great-power politics the bringing of international warfare to an end—forever. It was a program promoted after both world wars by the leaders of victorious countries: The United States, the world's strongest and wealthiest state, and Great Britain, its most extensive empire. It inspired the creation of the League of Nations and the United Nations.

That these efforts, even though supported at times by great powers, failed to stamp out warfare, suggests the elusiveness, and perhaps even the practical impossibility of achieving, the objective that they sought.

Achieving rationality is another goal in which we were set back often in this century. Moreover, we seem to have learned that we are far less advanced along the road than previous generations believed.

After Christianity in the Dark and Middle Ages apparently spread to encompass all of Europe, it was discovered that it had spread too thin: that despite its formal and official acceptance, beneath it persisted a substratum of paganism and superstition. So it is with modern science. Science is said to be the faith of the modern world, it is the basis of our hopes for the future; yet many of us—probably most of us—either do not understand it, or do not accept as true that which it tells us.

Almost a third of elected school-board members in the United States are inclined to take Genesis literally, rejecting the evidence not only of biology, but of archaeology and anthropology. Disregarded is the testimony of fossils, bones, unearthed human remains, buried tools, and DNA.

This is one aspect of being blinded, rather than enlightened, by faith. There are others. More than three centuries after wars of religion supposedly came to an end at Westphalia in 1648, and two centuries after religion was taken out of politics in the American Constitution in 1789, religion again has broken out of what the rational modern mind had regarded as its proper sphere—the conscience of the individual—and is back in politics, in wars, and at the barricades.

Across Muslim Eurasia and the Pacific, from Algeria to Indonesia; in Hindu India; and, indeed, all around the world, hundreds of millions of people now challenge science, secular government, and modern civilization—the only civilization we still have—in the name of an outdated fundamentalism that has no relevance to the way we live now.

Education may provide the answer. Yet it is arguable—or at any rate, it often is convincingly argued—that education in the United States and other advanced countries is declining rather than improving.

Uniting the planet is something that the modernizing revolution did in the economic and transportation-communication areas, and that the entertainment, consumer-goods, and tourist industries accomplished in the social sphere, but that—despite widespread predictions that it would happen—did not happen in the political sphere during the twentieth century. Quite the reverse occurred.

The disintegration of Europe's overseas empire, however welcome to all who believe in liberty, undid much of the work of unification accomplished long before. Instead of the world today consisting of fewer and larger countries, as one would have expected in the early part of the century, countries are becoming smaller and more numerous.

· · ·

The extent to which we can go on *releasing nature's energies* remains an open question. Nonrenewable fossil fuels still are available in abundance; there is time to continue the search for an alternative, which we assume one day will be affordable nuclear fusion. It goes without saying that if no such alternative ever is found, the human race at last will have lost the wager it placed on civilization, and its way of life.

Ruling ourselves is something that the United States espoused as a global principle, and that was accomplished, in America's eyes, for most of the world during or after the great war of the twentieth century. The United States advocated independence, but only for countries that had been ruled by other countries: self-rule, but not self-determination.

So for the United States, the goal was reached. Others, however, believed in independence, not for countries, but for nations. These advocates of modern nationalisms demanded the right to secede from their respective countries to form independent states of their own; and the right to expel from their own state all groups other than themselves. Each people would rule itself within its own territory; and each would be ethnically pure. The clash between these two conceptions looks as if it will be carried from the twentieth century into the twenty-first. On the one hand is America, champion of the existing political structure of the world, on the other there are forces of disintegration and of terror: nationalism, separatism, ethnic cleansing, secession, and religious and ideological factionalism.

When H. G. Wells looked at history, he saw progress. The regressions into barbarism that have been so conspicuous a feature of the twentieth century suggest that instead he should have seen—and we should see—fluctuations. There are tensions rather than resolutions, continuities rather than conclusions, retreats as well as advances. The United States prefers not to look back at all. "Democracy," wrote Tocqueville, "gives men a sort of instinctive distaste for what is ancient." We tend to believe that the past can be disregarded. "It's history," Americans say dismissively, meaning that the matter is closed and need concern us no longer.

This is an error on our part. Many supposedly lost causes, though buried, are not dead; they may have to be confronted once more, or even many times more. The price of enjoying the fruits of past victories is our readiness to fight the battles again if necessary.

With our weakness comes a strength. "Democratic nations care but little for what has been," de Tocqueville continues, "but they are haunted by visions of what will be." Instead of "haunted," should we not say "inspired"? For being forward-looking may well be our best quality.

Death by water, death on land, death from the sky; in our time, the wise have outlined an amazing variety of imaginative new scenarios for the imminent destruction of the human race. Some are plausible, some farfetched. A few will be looked at in the chapters to come.

What will the future bring? Looking ahead in the way that de Tocqueville did, we can see that what is happening now—indeed what has been happening throughout modern history—is the revolution that began when science separated itself from magic a thousand years ago. Like a stream fed by tributaries that grows into a great river, the modernizing revolution has come to dominate the lives of those who live on its banks. As the Nile proved central to the history of Egypt, so science, industry, and technology were to the making of the modern world—and they go on making the world of the future.

The modernizing revolution widens, deepens, and accelerates all the time. Looking at the course of its flow provides a reasonable basis for prediction in the de Tocqueville style: farsighted analysis instead of tea leaves or crystal balls. The consequences of science are among the things that we face in our future, for good or ill. Other things will happen that we cannot predict. What we *can* foresee is that the continuing flow of science, and our reactions to it, will shape the centuries to come.

Our reactions—and our anticipations. For as rationalists we believe in looking ahead as best we can, not merely to satisfy curiosity or to delight in the prospect of the new conveniences that science may make available to us, but to begin thinking now about how we will deal with those consequences of the continuing modernizing revolution that can be expected to pose dangers for us, some of them quite terrible. At the same time we should be cheered by the knowledge that science is likely to provide us with powers that, if wisely used, can enable us to go from triumph to triumph.

Ancient history is the story of how the human race experimented, invented civilizations, and then created more and more of them. Modern history is a tale of elimination rounds, with the number of civilizations contracting until only one remained. Of course there may be someplace in the world, like Europe in the Dark Ages, where the seeds are being planted of what someday will be a successor civilization, but if so, it is not visible today.

Can mankind adapt to the requirements, and cope with the consequences of the functioning of the sole currently surviving civilization? The foreseeable future will be concerned with the directions in which science is taking society: some of them risky, described in chapters 10 and 11, and some hopeful, outlined in chapter 12. That is as much of the future as we can reasonably hope to foresee.

What does it hold in store for us?

10: HOLDING PEOPLE TOGETHER

Ever since the industrial revolution began, people everywhere have noticed—could hardly have failed to notice—that it, and the scientific and technological revolution of which it was a phase, were transforming life, work, beliefs and behavior. Tocqueville's contemporary Auguste Comte was one of the seminal thinkers who believed he could read the riddle of where these engines of change were taking humanity.

There was no question in Comte's mind; he was sure that the future could be foretold. He wrote that "no enlightened person today could doubt that . . . human intelligence has always followed a clearly determined course . . . which would . . . have enabled a sufficiently informed intelligence to predict . . . the basic advances reserved for each age."

Comte was the child of deeply religious, royalist parents. He broke with their beliefs, projecting his own story onto the events of the world. He believed mankind to be on the threshold between the waning medieval world of kings and priests and the scientific era that was dawning.

Though he had left the religious convictions of his parents behind, Comte brought away from them a belief that history follows a design: a more or less inevitable evolution. To this he added the modern notion that the design is one of progress. He believed that the entire world was destined to become an industrial society, a prediction hard to argue with now.

We know that nature's tendency is to diversify. However, in Comte's vision, humanity's tendency is to unify. The design of history, as he envisioned it, is for the human race to become united as a single people.

The long-term trend, as H. G. Wells also was to argue, has been for political units to grow larger and larger. In the beginning there were city-states. Then there were empires ruling many city-states. The empires grew larger and larger: Assyria's was the greatest the world had ever known to its time, Persia's, even bigger, was overthrown by Alexander of Macedon, whose empire was greater still. So it went until, by the early 1900s, Britain's was the largest yet.

As de Tocqueville explained, "If none but small nations existed, I do not doubt that mankind would be more happy and more free; but the existence of great nations is unavoidable. . . . Small nations are often miserable, not because they are small but because they are weak. . . . Physical strength is . . . one of the first conditions of the happiness and even of the existence of nations. Hence . . . small nations are always united to large empires in the end, either by force or by their own consent."

The emergence of global infrastructure and, in our own time, of a global economy, provides compelling new reasons for the creation of international authorities. Communications, transportation, and other systems now operating on a worldwide basis require regulation, or at least some sort of coordination.

Air-traffic controllers and aircraft pilots have to adopt the same procedures and, to some extent, the same language all around the world. Rules have been adopted to govern mining the bed of the oceans, and now have to be drafted for mining the moon. Our politics need to be enlarged to match the size of our technology and our economics. Otherwise, if decisions cannot be reached by cooperation, and if the issues are important enough, countries will go to war over them.

For the twentieth century, which was co-extensive with the greatest war in history, the principal question in international relations has been how to put an end to war before (as we often have been warned) war puts an end to us. Idealists, originally taking their lead from such diverse personalities as Andrew Carnegie, William Howard Taft, and Woodrow Wilson in the United States, and Lord Robert Cecil and Gilbert Murray in Great Britain, proposed to achieve perpetual peace by the creation of international organizations, chiefly the League of Nations and, later, the United Nations.

In the past, warfare has been stamped out only within countries, and even there not completely, for civil wars do occur; so if the past is to be our guide, only the creation of a world state might bring permanent peace. Such a state might arise through peaceful and voluntary federation, as did the United States, or through conquest, perhaps after a ruinous future war. One way or another, if the shape of history turns out to be what Comte, H. G. Wells, and others imagined it to be, a world state is in the cards for us—eventually.

In Comte's view, the industrial revolution shaped life everywhere in the same way, causing cultures to converge. This is a widely shared belief today. Not only industrialization, but the post-industrial processes currently at work in the service-industry era, the computer epoch, and the information age tend towards global homogeneity.

In superficial ways, people everywhere are already becoming one. As remarked elsewhere, with modernization comes common tastes: blue jeans, sneakers, T-shirts, soft drinks, hamburgers, rock music, Hollywood films. Does the sharing run deeper? In Iran, Malaysia, Singapore, Japan, and elsewhere, there are those who argue that they can undergo the scientific-technological-industrial revolution, as did the western world, without, on the other hand, being shaped by it, as was the west.

Samuel P. Huntington of Harvard claims that "the image of an emerging . . . universally Western world" is "misguided, arrogant, false, and dangerous." Regarding the increasing standardization of what people eat and wear and what entertains them as trivial, he argues that at the level of values, the differences remain. They certainly seem to, but values change—and can be changed. Accepting what the western world offers does shape both ways of life and values. Thus the paid annual vacation, an innovation of the French Popular Front regime led by Léon Blum in the summer of 1936, far from remaining confined to France or even to Europe, spread everywhere, and eventually gave rise to the world's largest industry, tourism. Taking time off from work each year in order to travel or to spend time with family or friends is now an essential part of existence.

Dishwashers, washing machines, dryers, frozen meals, and the like—not to speak of restaurants, a product of the French Revolution—are more than a bunch of inventions: taken together, they go a long way towards doing away with housework. They have broken the restrictions that kept women at home; and a world in which women as well as men leave the house and work at the same jobs is a profoundly different world. The point is not just that people everywhere are experiencing change, but that in experiencing the same changes they are becoming more and more alike.

The automobile changed the way people live, work, travel, and have fun. The computer is driving us at high speed to a destination which, although unknown, we all will share.

The universal availability of credit, from installment plans to credit cards, taken together with television and household and office appliances of everyday life, have shaped a consumer society that creates its own special values. They are materialist values, and they are attractively propagated by film, video, the Internet, popular songs, and all the other media of mass communication; and they have come to be shared all around the world.

These come into conflict with the values and codes of conduct of traditional cultures and religious societies, but, over time, the powerful appeal of the consumer society may well overcome all obstacles.

Yet from the beginning of the industrial revolution it has been clear that the way we live now has a central flaw: the cohesion of our society has been eroding, even though it is only through working together as a community that we can sustain culture.

The home, the family, the village where everyone knows everyone else, the rooted traditions and shared values and beliefs; all of these, as we often have been told, were left behind when mankind moved, first to the anonymous big city where the jobs were to be found, and later to the suburbs.

Work on the assembly lines of the industrial age is repetitive, hence unsatisfying, and produces the alienation of which Karl Marx famously wrote. According to Tocqueville, democracy breeds "individualism," a word that he used to mean a selfish and exclusive withdrawal into personal concerns and a lack of care for the interests of others or for the community as a whole. The attraction of fascism, communism, and nationalism in the modern world has been their ability to provide a purpose in group solidarity for lives lacking an individual sense of meaning. In this respect pluralist democracy, for all its other virtues, falls behind the competition. It is not an easy thing that it calls upon its citizens to do. Americans must indeed develop their own faith individually, define their own purposes individually, find for themselves the meaning of existence individually.

It has become commonplace to observe that the urban industrial democracy into which the United States has been leading the rest of the world—the single global society that Comte foresaw—generates self-destructive tendencies. In one way it brings people together, but in another way it pulls them apart, driving them away in search of the certainties or absolutes that an open society cannot provide.

So that while the modernizing revolution leads humanity on to ever greater unity, it also leads in the opposite direction by destroying social cohesion and stability. Paradoxically, two of the major trends in the modern world are the objective need for concentration of power to deal with the global economy and the global environment, and the diffusion of power that results when the glue holding societies together grows too thin. The clash of these two principles seems likely to be a theme of the next century, and perhaps of the next millennium.

Comte predicted human unity. Wells, as noted, foresaw fewer and larger political units, and argued persuasively that mankind both needs, and eventually will have, a world state. Oddly, events have been moving in the opposite direction. A century ago there were only a few dozen countries. Now there are close to two hundred. The franchise in international affairs has been extended to every continent. At the same time that the division of the planet into separate states has come to be looked upon as anachronistic, further divisions have been taking place: independence has been granted to one group after another. This is the century that has seen the rebirth of the city-state, Singapore and Kuwait, to cite two examples, as well as such island states as those of the Pacific—Nauru, the Marshall Islands, and Palau among others—and of the Caribbean.

In large part, this is due to the fulfillment of America's political program. A handful of empires were dissolved into a large number of independent political communities. The 185 countries of the United Nations exist as separate entities in a world political structure that the United States willed into being.

But having arrived at this state of affairs, America upholds the existing structure, while there are forces set loose in the world by the modernizing revolution that may subvert it.

One of the most striking and alarming tendencies in world politics as we head into the next century is an aspect of the trend toward the diffusion of power. It is the widespread process of political fission, in which a country splits into two or more hostile groups who refuse to go on living together. At first we called this a revival of nationalism—until it was remembered that in times past, nationalism often pulled peoples together, rather than tearing them apart. The creation of Czechoslovakia and Yugoslavia after the First World War was a product of the old nationalism; their dissolution after the Cold War was a product of the new. "Ethnic" became the word for the special kind of nationalism that caused the fissiparism of the post-Soviet world, and yet in its most notorious recent episode—the "ethnic cleansing" of Bosnian Muslims by Bosnian Serbs—religion was the dividing line. Muslims and Serbs are both ethnic Slavs. The Muslims are descendants of those in the local population who converted to Islam during the centuries of Ottoman rule, while the Serbs, also Slavs, are descended from those who did not change their faith.

In Algeria, in Egypt, and all across the Muslim world it is most conspicuously religion, rather than ethnicity, that sparks violence within the country. Meanwhile, in states as diverse as Belgium, Canada, and India, language differences bring threats of secession.

These reversions to the bloody clannishness of early times represent, whatever their sociological or psychological wellsprings, a revolt against the modern world. For what the world economy and the world environment now require are wider rather than narrower units[1]: regional and global regulatory bodies corresponding to the worldwide activities of business and utilities.

This type of nationalism demands the creation of countries that would be too small to be viable. Even existing countries are in important respects too small. That is why the United States all along has encouraged the creation of a single Europe, not only to resolve the dangerous problem of Germany's relations with its neighbors, but also to create a viable economy for America's European partners. In the American view, only a continent-wide market can enable Europe to trade with Japan and the United States on an equal footing. But it looks as though the road to European political unity will be a long and difficult one at best. As the opening battle of the twenty-first century, the conflict between Europe and its nationalisms should provide both a preview and a paradigm of the dramas that will be played out in the new century.

Federal governments may well win their struggle to survive; but the important point is not that they may win, but that their survival will be at stake. For a central question in the politics of the twenty-first century throughout the world will be the tension between holding together and pulling apart: between the centripetal pull of a modern global economy that requires regional and planetary organization, and the centrifugal push of atavistic tribalisms. It is a conflict that pits rational interests against irrational emotions. Whatever the outcome, what seems likely to distinguish the twenty-first century from its immediate predecessors and to give it its special character, is that this internal struggle, rather than a conflict between great powers, seems likely to be the overriding issue.

. . .

1. I continue to believe in the argument I advanced in my first book, *The Question of Government* (1975)—that at the same time, government is too big in many areas, and that devolution of powers to local authorities should take place wherever possible to give people more control over their own lives.

One of the obvious long-term trends in technology has been the increasingly destructive power of weaponry. For decades mankind has been haunted by the threat of a war between rival world coalitions in which nuclear, biological, or chemical weapons are used. It might still happen; but now a new, parallel danger also threatens our stability.

The related long-term trend in technology has been an increase in the amount of damage that one person, or a small number of people, can inflict on others. Weapons have become more powerful: a lone machine-gunner can mow down waves of attackers, a handful of men in an airplane can drop a bomb that will destroy a city.

Earlier in the twentieth century we saw this lead to a focusing of power in dictatorial hands. Coercion of the masses through state terrorism; employment of a political police force to sustain an oppressive regime; the use of modern technology to enable a relatively small but organized elite to establish totalitarian control over whole countries—these were features of, for example, the pre-1990s Soviet regimes. They demonstrated how the growing power of weapons could lead to a concentration of power in the hands of a small elite. But paradoxically, the technology also enables the opposite result. The dramatic image with which the politics of the twentieth century drew to a close was that of the Afghan guerrilla armed[2] with ground-to-air missiles shooting down troop-carrying Soviet helicopters. It opened up a new era in which small bands of militants with lethal weapons inflict enough damage so that large occupying armies are forced to withdraw. The twenty-first century could well be the golden age of secession.

Developments in weaponry also make it possible for the coming century to be the age of the terrorist—of the individual with the mini–nuclear bomb who can destroy New York or Mexico City or Tokyo. Technology has simultaneously empowered us and made us more vulnerable. Parallel to the tension between the drive toward unity and the pull of secession, there will be a tension between

---

2. Armed, it should perhaps be mentioned, on a clandestine basis by the United States and several other countries associated with it in this endeavor.

technology used to control and technology used to disrupt, while a fellowship is likely to develop between diverse governments faced with common enemies within.

An unanticipated result of the end of the Cold War is that, peace among the great powers having made it unnecessary to maintain vast inventories of weaponry, the industrial powers are deluging the globe with lethal weapons. They are arming every rebel and every cause that can pay cash or can obtain credit.

In the twenty-first century it may seem that there has arisen an enormous proliferation of new social, economic, and political causes: a sort of ideological fission to parallel the political fission bringing about the breakdown of nations. But it really will be a proliferation of new powers, not of new issues—of explosives detonated in the name of obscure heresies and long-ago-discredited causes, forcing the world to pay attention to views that had been—rightly—forgotten.

In time the disorder introduced by the multiplication of causes should bring about a reaction, a desire for a return to stability. The overarching issue, as the twenty-first century may come to see it, will not be one cause as against another, or one power against another, but order versus anarchy, government versus lawlessness. The world may welcome tyrants as saviors.

Terrorism has haunted the last half of the twentieth century, and seems likely to continue, bedeviling us in the years to come, flourishing if it continues to be sponsored by states. A parallel but different danger stalks civilization as our world moves into the twenty-first century: the specter of organized crime in command of governments. In part it is a consequence of the sheer volume of cash generated by the trade in illegal narcotics. Nobody has ever seen such sums before. The closest parallel is with Prohibition in the United States in the 1920s; on the almost limitless profits from selling bootleg alcohol, the mobster Al Capone was able to purchase control of the city of Chicago. Today, drug racketeers routinely buy police forces, armies, prosecutors' offices, and elected officials with the oceans of money available to them.

Then, too, the collapse of authority in parts of the former Soviet bloc and elsewhere has left a vacuum that is being filled by brute forces of gangs of thugs and their bosses. The rise of these gangster duchies and kingdoms is one of the least expected manifestations of a world slipping out of control.

From the outset the United States has been identified with the cause of the larger polity. The original thirteen colonies saw that, as independent sovereignties, they would become the playthings of the European powers unless they merged into one powerful entity. Abraham Lincoln held the Union together for the same reason.

When threats to the countries of the world emerged in the twentieth century, American statesmen took the lead in advocating the creation of an international organization: a global authority to deal with global issues. Holding up America as a model in this respect as in so many others, writers in the idealist tradition argued that we should set out on the road to a United States of the World.

However, there was a kind of large-scale entity that the United States always had opposed: the European overseas colonial empire. America was born of a revolt against it, and what emerged from the successful revolt was a stable state. The thirteen colonies retained their frontiers and identities even when merging, but that was because the colonists had the good fortune to have shaped their colonies themselves. That was not the case elsewhere.

In Latin America, for example, administrative borders and other frontiers were drawn by Spain and Portugal to suit their own desires, needs, and convenience. These units of government did not necessarily correspond to social realities. When, however, Iberian America liberated itself from the mother countries, it became clear that, inappropriate though the borders were, to attempt a redrawing of frontiers would be to embark on an endless bloodbath.

Latin America adopted a policy grounded in Roman law. Known, for short, by the words *uti possidetis*, taken from a Latin phrase, it denotes a recognition that a statute of limitations has run out. Its injunction is that, whatever the frontiers were, that is what they must remain; they can no longer be questioned. The former administrative borders of South America became international borders. Anything that had borders around it became a country. All persons who lived in the country were obliged to try to become one people.

Africa, faced with a similar problem, has adopted the same solution. Africa is tribal, but the units into which Europe divided it were not. When the continent won freedom in the last half of the twentieth century, its newly liberated countries adopted *uti possidetis* as their policy too. The strain that this imposes on politics within the artificial states is enormous. Already there are signs that frontiers may be crumbling as tribes massacre each other. It is by no means certain that in Africa the rule of *uti possidetis* will continue to hold. Yet failing to adhere to it could usher in an age of more and more mass murders.

The latest whiff of danger in the air arises from a tendency in Eurasia not to follow Africa's example in accepting *uti possidetis*. Most Middle East governments, for example, never really accepted the legitimacy of the states and the boundaries established in the region by the European powers in the early 1920s—and the Middle East has been in turmoil ever since. Now, in Eastern Europe, the tragic ethnic feuds that followed the collapse of the Soviet Union and the Soviet bloc in 1989, and of Yugoslavia, illustrate the Middle Eastern sort of dangers from which Africa and Latin America have escaped, at least until now, by adhering to Roman law.

What if the unraveling of the Caucasus and the Balkans portends a growing belief elsewhere in the doctrine, rightly or wrongly associated with the name Woodrow Wilson, of national self-determination? In this view, each nation is entitled to be an independent country if it so wishes. But who is to decide which groups are nations? In recent years we have seen Bosnia secede from Yugoslavia, and then itself disintegrate; and Slovakia secede from what had been Czechoslovakia; while Afghanistan, which dissolved some time ago into Pathans, Tajiks, Uzbeks, Hazaras, Baluchis, and Turkomans, all apparently at odds with one another, is being offered a chance to restore its unity—but only on the basis of fundamentalist religion, not of nationality. Self-determination, we see, can become a sorcerer's apprentice.

The foreign-affairs advisor to the president of Kazakhstan, one of the formerly Soviet states of Central Asia, warned not long ago that his country, which contains a hundred nationalities, could burst apart into "1,000 Yugoslavias." Nigeria consists of 250 ethnic or linguistic groups. With Belgium strained to breaking point by the tension between merely two language groups, what will happen to the Sudan, in which 1,008 languages and dialects are spoken? Or to the world as a whole, with its 8,000 languages?

At least 3,500—more likely 5,000—groups now call themselves nations; and more seem to spring up all the time. If all of their claims were to be accommodated, the world would have to be split into about twenty or thirty times more countries than exist today. As their claims conflict, the world would dissolve into hopeless blood feuds.

And all this for something that at best is elusive and at worst illusory. "Nationality," as the *Encyclopaedia Britannica* (11th ed.) tells us, is "a somewhat vague term" that "represents a common feeling and an organized claim rather than distinct attributes which can be comprised in a strict definition."

It often is said that the modernizing revolution has rendered the nation-state obsolete. In these pages we have been discussing the tug between the functional need for it to be larger—to expand into regional federations or a world state—and the human need to regroup into smaller and more meaningful units. In an ideal world, we could do both: an enormous variety of nationalities, enjoying some amount of autonomy, and international status as distinct formal entities, could function constitutionally within a global federation.

Looking at that possibility suggests what is wrong about saying that the nation-states of today's world are obsolete. By and large the nation-state—if by that we mean a state that contains just one nation—is not so much obsolete as nonexistent. Great Britain is not just the English; it is the Scots, the Welsh, and the Ulster Irish. China has the Tibetans, and the Muslims of Turkestan. India is a patchwork of nationalities, religions, and language groups. Few countries are without significant ethnic or racial minorities. Hence the disintegrative tendencies of the modern world, the drift to ethnicity, the wars of secession.

It is not entirely improbable that ahead lies a nightmare of nationalist, religious, and language-group wars, leading only after a thousand years of almost unimaginable suffering to a regrouping of humanity along true clan, tribe, and ethnic lines. Then, finally, mankind might start along the road to an eventual world federation: the direction, according to H. G. Wells, in which the human race must eventually go, no matter what horrors it has experienced in the interim, what valleys of death it may have traversed, or what wrong turnings it may have taken.

But surely there is an easier and better way to get there. Isn't the American program—transcending national and religious differences to achieve unity—far more attractive?

11: TAKING NATURE'S PLACE

The story of mankind, we learned as children, was the tale of humans conquering Nature over the course of history. Winds, waves, and animals now worked for us. Instead of waiting in the hope that good things would come our way, we had taken steps to make sure that they did. No longer taking a chance on finding grains, vegetables, fruits, or nuts in the wild, we grew our own crops, ensuring a supply of what we wanted to eat when we wanted it. Rather than search for hospitable caves, we created our own housing to shelter us from the elements. We developed weapons against what otherwise might have killed us: arms against animals, medicines against microbes. As a result, our population grew.

We were told that it was an error to believe that the effect of all this was to upset the balance of nature, giving rise to new dangers. We were also taught that the nature of the error was illustrated by the case of Thomas Robert Malthus (1766–1834), an English curate and economist, who warned that population was increasing more rapidly than food supply, so that one day there would not be enough to go around. He was wrong; technology, by increasing agricultural production, solved the problem. Time and again, Malthusians have been discredited. Until now, civilization has continued to wager its future on the proposition that technology always will solve the problem, whatever the problem might be.

In the preceding chapter, reference was made to thinkers who, as early as the 1800s, saw that the modernizing revolution, though it brought progress and prosperity, did so at the cost of society's growing inability to hold people together and to give meaning to work and to lives. Societies found it more and more difficult to remain communities. Only in our half of our century has it become generally acknowledged that there are other costs as well. The technology of everyday life often damages and sometimes destroys not only our relationships but also our environment.

Not long ago natural processes still flushed out industrial pollution. People didn't have to think about the problem since nature took care of it. At some stage in the industrial revolution, however, that stopped being true. The scale of human activity grew too large; it had an impact that the environment could no longer absorb.

It is surprising how long it took to recognize that impact. It began only about a century ago. In the United States, after the western frontier was officially closed (1890), a sort of Malthusian mood seems to have taken hold—a feeling that the country was running out of untouched nature, that virgin territory was a finite resource being exhausted. After the turn of the century President Theodore Roosevelt and his Secretary of the Interior, Gifford Pinchot, channeled this sentiment into the conservation movement. Its object was to preserve what was left of the wilderness, and it expressed itself in the creation of national parks.

The next stage—much later—was the publication, first in *The New Yorker* magazine, and then as a book, of Rachel Carson's *Silent Spring* (1962). It brought to public attention concerns that had been confined to specialists. It also marked an ideological transformation; what had been the conservation movement now was inspired with something broader than a simple desire to keep the wilderness wild. It went on to embrace the cause of the global environment.

Rachel Carson, scientist and author, became fascinated by the outdoors as a child. Born and raised in Pennsylvania, she grew up to be a marine biologist. Her professional career was in the U.S. Bureau of Fisheries, later the U.S. Fish and Wildlife Service, of which she became the Chief. She pursued a successful literary career at the same time; her *The Sea Around Us* (1951) won her a wide public.

Silent Spring, which appeared when Carson was in her middle fifties, focused attention on pollution, and specifically on the harm caused to plants and animals, and thus eventually to humans, by the use of such pesticides as DDT. It was lent poignancy by the author's death from breast cancer a couple of years after its publication.

Others emerged to build on Carson's accomplishment. By the 1970s the environmental movement, going beyond pesticides, had identified and denounced a broad range of contaminations. It also had expanded its agenda. Returning to the issue with which conservationists had begun—the depleting of finite resources—ecologists such as Barry Commoner in his *The Closing Circle* (1971) argued the need in general for recycling rather than exploiting and discarding. In that way, he wrote, industrial civilization could bring human activity back into harmony with nature.

But the movement that Carson had started went in other directions as well. For some, *Silent Spring* was a primer in an ecology that led to regulation and legislation. For others, it was an attack on technology itself—a call to return to an earlier and simpler world.

In the early 1970s a group of concerned private individuals calling itself the Club of Rome commissioned a computerized study of how much longer economic growth could continue in a world of finite resources. The initial report, submitted to the Club under the title *The Limits to Growth*, seemed to show that those limits were close at hand; that if economic growth keeps on, the natural resources upon which industry depends soon will be exhausted, bringing about collapse.

It was a doomsday scenario, not only closing the door to the Third World—for which economic growth is the only possible strategy to rise out of poverty and despair—but warning the industrial countries that their success was coming to an end. The policy which the report advocated called for the slowing of the world economy, and for everyone to live on short rations until synthetics could be developed to substitute for the range of natural resources that are about to be used up. Alternatively, one could conclude that the entire scientific, industrial, and technological revolution has been shown to be, not the road to the future, but a dead end.

But when the report was made public, its assumptions and methodologies came under withering fire. Its conclusions did not hold up. The tide of opinion seemed to turn; it was persuasively argued, among other things, that technological innovation could solve the problems singled out in the report. The error of Malthusianism apparently had been exposed again.

Now largely forgotten, *The Limits to Growth* deserves credit despite its faults for its leap of imagination in attempting to picture the human enterprise as a whole. It was a stepping-stone on the road from conservation to ecology.

Environmentalism, as distinct from conservation, won public attention in the 1970s with the popular dissemination of doomsday scenarios. Thus it was claimed that, given the current state of exhaust systems, if everybody in China turned the keys in an automobile's ignition, the entire human race would choke to death. This was followed by speculation as to other lurid possibilities.

Death from the sky. The process of depleting the ozone layer, ultraviolet radiation destroying life on Earth ... Sometime or another, an asteroid from outer space smashing into the Earth and destroying it ... Loss of the Earth's oxygen supply ... Smothering to death from smog ... Nuclear missiles, fired in anger or by accident ... Global warming, melting the polar ices and flooding the planet ...

Death on land. Nuclear radiation and fallout. ... Overpopulation ... Mass starvation ... Disease ... Tens of millions from the slums of the Third World fleeing in human waves to the industrial north ... Death of the rain-forests ... The end of species diversity ...

Death by sea. Poisoning of the world's oceans ... Pollution of the drinking supply ... Contamination of all seafood ... Lack of clean water ... Lack of water ...

There are more, and most of them must be taken seriously. A

couple of hundred years ago, these, with few exceptions, were not issues at all, let alone issues that figured in politics. That they do so now is a measure of the speed with which the modernizing revolution flows on.

The revolution continues to rush forward. Like some great river, it brings blessings. But one must beware its perils. Today we fear that the quickening waters that sweep humanity on to its future may be rapids; and that the roar from around the bend may be the thunder of falls.

The effects of modern technology are not merely global but international: they create friction between countries. Acid rain and overfishing, two otherwise unrelated issues, are among those that have moved the question of regulating potentially harmful activities from the national plane to the level of international relations.

It is a fundamental rule of public international law that a country must not allow its territory to be used as a base from which activities take place that harm the territory and inhabitants of another country. If Mexico were to permit terrorist groups to set up staging areas on its side of the Rio Grande from which they fired nuclear missiles into Texas, and if Mexico refused American demands to put a stop to it, the United States would be entitled to declare war, and to send its armed forces south to deal with the situation. If the United States were to permit its factories to emit poisons that the wind carries over the border into Mexico, and if the American authorities were to refuse Mexican demands to put a stop to it, the principle would be the same.

Now consider a more difficult case. Country A, which is desperately short of both jobs and housing, experiences a population explosion that its government does nothing to curb or reverse. In the millions, its young people, looking for work, flood across the border of neighboring country B, threatening to bring down the social order in B. If A persists in taking no appropriate action to reverse its population growth, despite repeated demands, is B justified in declaring war? But isn't A's population-control program entirely A's own business?

Another case: Two major world powers go to war. It is a fight to the death, and neither side will consider agreeing to mediation or to a compromise peace. They employ tactical—i.e., low-level—nuclear weapons against one another, and the danger exists that they may use strategic ones as well: the doomsday weapons. What can or should, neutral countries do to save the lives of their own inhabitants? Should they go to war against one or both of the belligerents?

Until recently, environmental issues arose one at a time. There was the shrinking of the wilderness, and then pollution. There were the many dangers posed by nuclear and biological warfare. There was the exhaustion of nonrenewable resources, and the threatened extinction of species and variety. There was global warming and ozone depletion. And always there was the problem of population explosion on an already crowded planet.

Now perspectives seem to be widening. The stage appears to be set for a transformation in outlook similar to that which took place in economics in the 1930s. Until then, theory had postulated that in a completely free economy full employment would come about automatically; society and government did not have to make any effort themselves to achieve it. With millions out of work in the Great Depression, and social and political order in danger, the world lost patience with the explanations, however valid in theory, of why this did not work out in practice. In time, governments took up full employment as a goal that should be achieved by policies consciously adopted in order to get there.

Similarly, a healthy overall global environment may have to be a consciously set goal requiring, at a point in the future, some kind of overall governing body. The state of the earth's environment may have to be continuously monitored, regularly assessed, and per-haps even managed on a full-time basis. In this context, what mechanisms are employed—free market, or regulation by govern-ment—becomes less important than the assumption by society of responsibility for the planet in its entirety. Having destroyed nature's balance, we may have to create our own. In that sense, humans will have to play God.

. . .

When the Iron Curtain was lifted in the 1990s, environmental horrors were revealed. A closed society that felt no responsibility for the health of its population or the cleanliness of its soil, air, or water had managed to keep the rest of the world from realizing the extent to which it was destroying the large portion of the earth and of the earth's population that it governed. This pointed to the conclusion that mankind's future in successfully dealing with ecological issues is tied to the fate of open societies.

Once again, the road to follow seems to be that pioneered by the United States and its allies. For all its faults, the American way may prove to be the only viable one to deal with the consequences of the modernizing revolution. If so, the world is in luck, for continuing American leadership, like it or not, seems to be what the world has got.

12: ENTERING YET ANOTHER
AMERICAN CENTURY

Two of the major events of the twentieth century were the growth of American power and the spread of American ideas. These are the reasons that the publisher Henry R. Luce may have been right in claiming in a 1941 edition of *Life* magazine that he was living in "the American century." If he was right—if indeed the twentieth was the American century—what will the twenty-first be? Until recently it was commonly predicted that it would be the Japanese century. Then we heard that it was to be the Chinese century. Now there are some who claim that it will be Europe's century.

Of course, entering a new century, or even a new millennium, does not of itself entail making a break with the past. The arrival of the year 2001 is unlikely to signal a change. It will not even mark a milestone. It isn't an anniversary. It is not as though mankind or history or civilization began exactly two millennia before the Times Square crowds could be expected to burst into cheers. It is not as though Christ were born two thousand years before that midnight; Denis the Little,[1] the churchman who in 525 A.D. invented the Christian calendar, got the date of Jesus' birth wrong.

---

1. Known also as Dionysius Exiguus.

American power continues to grow. American ideas continue to spread. Major reversals in direction tend to take time; so neither movement seems likely to come to a stop at midnight on December 31, 2000. For the first part of the century at least, and perhaps for all of it, it is a reasonably safe bet that we will have more of the same, that the twenty-first will be, not Japanese or Chinese or European, but another American century.

For the moment—the continuing historical moment—the power of the United States and of the political, legal, and economic ideas it espouses are interrelated. But this need not continue to be the case in the future.

Most of these ideas, including due process of law, free-market economics, the abolition of slavery, and the establishment of a league of nations, originated in Great Britain; they are part of the shared heritage of the English-speaking world. Others derive from continental Europe or the classical Mediterranean—and the Middle East, from which we take letters and numbers, literature, religion, and civilization.

This tradition, known as western although it draws upon the east as well, underlies the modernism that is called Americanism because the United States is its most formidable champion in the contemporary world. Should the New World fall below the level of its ideology, another power may pick up the fallen banner and become the new America of the future. A suggestion of the sort of failing that might bring about that scenario: Arthur Schlesinger tells us that "in 1900 the United States was the most literate nation in the world; today, according to the United Nations, it is the 45th." A failing of another sort is illustrated by the sorry record of U.S. involvement in Central America and the Caribbean for most of the past hundred years, in support of dictatorship, corruption, and much else that runs counter to the principles we normally regard as American. The United States neither deserves to lead, nor is likely to lead, in the twenty-first century if it pursues such policies again.

For countries, as for people, becoming too wealthy or too powerful tends to be dangerous. One can forget what one stands for. With the knowledge that at times the United States has done that in the past, we have to allow for the possibility that it will do so again—and may lose its primacy in the world as a result.

The political ideals and constitutional ideas that America appropriated from Britain, and that others are appropriating from the United States, are spreading to the rest of the world because of their intrinsic attractiveness. They constitute an ideology that—to the extent that the country has been true to it—has strengthened America and can strengthen others. The rest of the world will continue turning (if indeed it does so) to the credo of the modernizing revolution—the rule of law, representative government, government by consent, countries ruling themselves—on its own merits, and because it works in today's world, rather than because it was and is espoused by the United States. It is not so much because the United States is powerful that its beliefs flourish; in large part it is because of the power of its beliefs that the United States succeeds in a world to which its views are singularly well adapted.

In economic and social matters the United States has become the model; its market economy and its consumer society are emulated and copied around the world. America found the common denominator: its food, clothes, best-sellers, and entertainments have achieved global status. As observed earlier, everybody wears blue jeans, sips diet soda, and gyrates to the same sounds. America's sloppy casualness has been adopted by a formerly buttoned-up Old World in manner as well as dress; European, Asian, and African public figures, instead of appearing serious of visage, unsmiling, high-minded, and dignified, now, American style, grin into the camera and wave to the crowd.

Of course all is not well with life in the United States today. The witches' brew that blends racism, poverty, joblessness, drug addiction, and crime continues to poison part of the society, and to haunt the rest. So far, American approaches to these problems have not worked, yet nobody has shown convincingly that turning away from the country's constitutional arrangements and political system would enable it to deal with such matters more effectively.

· · ·

In international politics, it was by conscious design that the New World shaped a new structure for the twentieth century. The United States, inspired by ideas borrowed from England, was an early advocate of establishing international organizations. These now circle the planet, coordinating or regulating a world infrastructure, an international financial structure, and a global economy. The creation of the United Nations was the result of an American initiative. Its General Assembly provides a forum designed to allow all the countries of the world to voice their views about world politics, while its Security Council offers an institutional process in which the great powers can achieve consensus in pursuit of a common program of action.

Today's structure of global politics as we prepare to enter the twenty-first century is an international order that now—at long last—is in line with American ideas: a world of independent countries, in which existing states rule themselves and preserve their unity, and from which the hereditary principle of government has been banished. For the most part, though with conspicuous exceptions, it is governed by secular regimes that, as in the United States, leave matters of religion to the individual conscience. Whatever they may do in practice, governments tend to claim that regional or global freedom of trade, of business, and of investment are their ultimate goals; that open markets are their ideal; that matters of common concern should be dealt with by regional or international organization and cooperation; that disarmament is to be desired; and that politics among countries should be conducted without the threat or use of force except in self-defense.

That is the political world and the political creed that the United States wanted to create in its image. It came into being only on August 31, 1994, when the last Russian troops left German soil, bringing the world war of the twentieth century—finally—to an end. Now that Americans have secured the triumph of the politics in which they believe, it will be seen whether the ideas and the principles the United States has championed will survive the strains and challenges of reality. Not only America, but Americanism presumably, will be tested in the years ahead. So will be the international system that the United States established and which it leads. Looking back a thousand years from now, our progeny may say that the twenty-first was the American century because in it, for the first time, American ideas were put into practice on a worldwide scale.

Critics of the American endeavor to achieve world governance through international cooperation rightly point out that in the end cooperation cannot be counted on to work all of the time. It breaks down when vital national interests are at stake or high passions are aroused. Like chimpanzees, human beings are disposed to hostile and often murderous behavior in dealing with members of groups other than their own. The foundering of idealistic projects in the twentieth century convincingly showed that perpetual peace, at least in our time, is a mirage. Few of us believe that a world-state—the only permanent solution to the problem of war—is within reach.

The authors of American internationalism did not set goals for themselves that were that high. Presidents Franklin Roosevelt and Harry Truman recognized that wars would break out from time to time in the future. Their objective was to keep the peace between the great powers for a long time to come, and in this they largely succeeded.

International institutions such as the International Monetary Fund and the newly created World Trade Organization may function imperfectly, as may the processes through which the leading industrial countries negotiate the coordination of financial policy; but the harmonization of economic, trade, and investment policies among sovereign states on the basis of reciprocity and cooperation, however inadequate to meet the problems of the far future, for the moment seems to be working well enough.

Anglo-American politics, as championed by the United States, therefore should continue to be prevalent throughout much of the world well into the twenty-first century and perhaps beyond. American ideas continue in the ascendant. So should American power, given a continuation of current trends.

. . .

Diffusion of force seems to be taking place practically everywhere around the world. The continuing fragmentation of central and eastern European communities shows a pattern of conflict between peoples living side by side, between majorities and minorities, between indigenous and foreign work forces, and between neighboring countries. If this process continues, it is likely to lead to alliances between local forces threatened by a common enemy: a multiplication of balances of power. They will be unstable balances because unpredictable: unpredictable, because too complex: too complex, because there will be so many players, each playing a different game.

Yet the balances of power will provide all the stability that the world of the twenty-first century is likely to be able to achieve, rent as it may be by passionate tribalism, and by such seemingly insoluble issues as that posed by mass migration from the South to the North and from the farm to the city. There may be mass population transfers, such as those between Greece and Turkey in the aftermath of the First World War: "cures" so terrible that one can forget that the disease is worse. It may well be a time of troubles, in need of a unifier to reverse the forces of history—an Alexander or a Muhammad, a world conqueror or a prophet armed.

A great change that might come about as a result of the emerging conflicts between peoples who live side by side—and which may, by their intense nature, take primacy over their other conflicts—is that political rivalry could well be mostly internal or regional. This could bring about a turning back from global politics. After decades in which the United States and the Soviet Union dueled with one another across the oceans, most great powers may have to focus on protecting themselves against forces on their own frontiers—or within them.

The new century should prove to be a testing time for the modern state system, but the test will differ from region to region. Europe's countries are pulled toward merger by a common culture, a common religion, a common economy, and a common fear of where German independence or a Russian resurgence might otherwise lead, but are pulled apart not merely by historic and authentic nationalisms, but by racism and ethnic separatism. Common wisdom has it that the choice is between a European Germany and a German Europe, a European Russia and a Russian Europe, but it may be neither. Europe may not be pulled together on any basis; the continent may come apart.

Africa, left to itself, could be torn between tribe and country; the Middle East, between state and religion. Asian politics remains centered on complex power equations: Russia, China and Japan, India and Pakistan, Korea and Vietnam, and on the relationships they will forge with one another. The multiplicity of emerging great powers should incline them to focus on tensions with one another. If the United States is wise enough to keep a low profile, the other great powers may find themselves fully occupied with local concerns, pinned down and pulled back, unable to pursue ambitions abroad.

The Western Hemisphere, isolated by its oceans, may stand apart. In the past its geography gave the United States a privileged political position within the world balance of power. The American colonists of 1776 were able to play off the powers of the European continent against Great Britain in order to gain independence; and then to play off Great Britain against the powers of the continent in the century thereafter in order to consolidate American hegemony over the western hemisphere.

The geographic position of the United States, shielded by an ocean on either side, may again allow it to stand aside from conflicts raging elsewhere. The chaotic circumstances (if that is what they turn out to be) of Eurasia and Africa could have the effect of making the United States, if it remains stable and intact, the lucky country of the twenty-first century. Freed in our time from the overseas threats posed first by Germany and then by Russia, it should be saved by the politics of fragmentation from any new threat from outside the Western Hemisphere. As it seems unlikely that any country within the hemisphere will threaten it either, America might enjoy a security comparable to that with which it was blessed in the administration of William McKinley—and seldom has known since.

Like Europe, the United States on its southern frontier will continue to be vulnerable to mass immigration of the poor from other countries. But by acting to build prosperous economies in Mexico, Central America, and the Caribbean, the country may perhaps be able to meet and overcome that challenge.

Like other countries, the United States also will continue to be threatened by ethnic and linguistic separatism. But America is more experienced than other states in assimilating immigrant masses, and has had a history—as other countries have not—of successfully dealing with these matters. It is a country built on a diversity of backgrounds, and that has learned to live with diversity. The task at hand will be primarily in education: in focusing on the common Constitutional ideals, legal heritage, and language that define the United States as a country. The American maxim should continue to be: Out of many, one.

The third principal condition of American fortune in the coming century will be the health and strength of the economy. Maintaining it should not be beyond the country's abilities; the United States has done it before. Much more difficult will be holding the nation together if other countries are coming apart, and building prosperous economies for our neighbors to the south. But if the three conditions *can* be met, then the United States should enjoy a luxury such as few nations in the history of the world ever have known: freedom to choose.

Until now the country has been forced, like it or not, to face challenges. In the twentieth century, Presidents Wilson, Roosevelt, and Truman had little choice but to pick up the standard of liberty. But America, if it meets the challenges of the new century, will enjoy the luxury of being able to choose its path in world affairs.

The country may be tempted to return to its traditional, almost exclusive concern with the Western Hemisphere from which Theodore Roosevelt tried to awaken it when he sent the fleet to Manila in 1898. The president elected in 2000 may wish to focus attention and energies on a domestic and hemispheric agenda: the building of the North American common market and the economic encouragement of America's southern neighbors.

It should be evident to foreigners that Americans find this alternative appealing, and that should allay some of the anxiety that other countries are bound to feel at the spectacle of so disproportionate an accumulation of power in the hands of one nation. So far, other countries have resisted the normal impulse to band together against the United States—at least in part because of America's isolationist sentiments. It should be reassuring that the United States tends not to want to use its power outside its hemisphere.

But a return to isolationism is not, and will not be, a realistic option. The United States is at the center of a global economy and a planetary infrastructure. It has interests everywhere, and must defend them. The internationalist world that came into being in accordance with American desires is likely to function only if the United States continues to provide it with leadership. The country's national interest, as well as its moral vision, require it to defend the world political structure that now is in place; it will have to defend regional balances of power if they are ever endangered.

The national focus on English as the common language that binds us together may suggest a more viable political avenue to future Americans: the creation of an English-speaking union of compatible countries embracing, among others, Australia, New Zealand, Canada, past and present Commonwealth members in Asia, Africa, and the Caribbean, the United States, and—especially if Europe fragments rather than unites—Great Britain. It would make good geopolitical as well as cultural sense, and would consolidate the English-speaking democracies as a leading force in the world working towards shared ideals of constitutional and open politics. If English continues to be the second language most widely spoken elsewhere in the world, it will become the lingua franca essential to an eventual global unity.

Freed from the kind of national-security concerns that arise from great-power rivalries, the United States also will be able to concentrate on the mission with which it began: the exploration of what lies below, above, and beyond. The bottoms of the oceans and the outer space above the skies hold out hopes of a future that perhaps only America will have the wealth, the technology, and the freedom from political concern to pursue. It is an endeavor for which, historically, the United States has a vocation. And it makes practical sense: satellites already are commercial ventures, and plans to mine both the seabed and the moon are in an advanced stage.

The exploration of space should be pursued as a quest for knowledge, not merely about what lies above and beyond, but about ourselves and our planet. It should better enable us to put ourselves in context. Were we to discover, for example, that there is life of some sort elsewhere, it might well revolutionize our perspective on our only-six-thousand-year-long experiment in human civilization, and even on the somewhat longer run that we have had as an apparently unique species, with our own special genius and peculiarities. We might come to see life on earth as a manifestation of something much larger in the universe.

This may sound like a fantasy. But the time may not be not far distant when it will sound plausible to propose flying into space in search of wealth, new opportunities, and even a better world. Issues and conflicts in international affairs can be left behind; many of them may disappear.

Colonies may be established on the road to the stars. It is an option that suits the country's history, nature, and driving energy. Disengaged from the internal politics of the other continents, and free to pursue a career as an oceanic and outer-space power, America—if not in the immediate future, then in the distant future—might find itself again as the country of the frontier, pioneering, settling, and moving on again.

Reconciling the country's past with its current concerns in the quest for the only kind of future in which the New World ever has believed, the United States could try to unlock the shackles of history and undo the constraints of human nature in this world's politics: something it always has wanted to accomplish.

The gift for frontier life is still to be found in America. The resourcefulness and shrewdness of the frontier persist.

Walter Fairservis[2] once described one of the frequent rides he took in the mountains of Afghanistan. It is a rugged country, inhabited by tribesmen who may be the fiercest warriors in the world. In

2. Chapter 1, page 4.

the nineteenth century they bloodied the armies of Great Britain, then at the height of its global power; and in the twentieth century they confronted and triumphed over the Soviet Red Army.

Fairservis traveled on his own, accompanied only by another American, a leathery former Marine colonel. At some point, having lost their way, the two dismounted to examine tracks on the ground. Looking up after a few moments, they saw a band of mounted tribesmen on a nearby crest. The tribesmen stood motionless, looming over them. They had appeared noiselessly, knives in belts, rifles in hand, seemingly out of nowhere. They radiated menace.

The Marine smiled. He moved slowly. He kept his hands where the tribesmen could see them. From his saddlebags, he produced a large coin, and then took down his rifle. He threw the coin high in the air. Then he swung up his rifle and fired one shot. The coin fell to the ground next to the tribesmen. One of them dismounted, inspected it, and showed it to the others. There was a bullet hole dead center through it.

The warriors turned and rode away.

Fairservis and the Marine remounted. The Marine patted his saddlebags. "You never know when they're going to come in handy," he said: "I always bring along coins with holes in them."

Resourcefulness is an aspect of the frontiersman's eye for opportunities: for trails that can be blazed where none run now. Again, the myth of the New World, and of its ever-expanding west, finds its parallel in today's rocket ships journeying to the far sides of the sky. The exploration of outer space could open up frontiers that never disappear—and that correspond in that respect to the vision of endless possibilities that always has typified the American outlook on people, politics, and future prospects.

This American optimism runs counter to, and sometimes looks foolish in the light of, the traditional wisdom of the race, according to which nothing really changes and therefore nothing improves. "The thing that has been, it is that which shall be; and that which is done is that which shall be done; and there is no new thing under the sun": so we are told by the Preacher of Ecclesiastes (1:9). It is an unjust world, but it is futile to try to correct it, for "That which is crooked cannot be made straight" (1:15). The projects of the human race are not worth pursuing: "I have seen all the works that are done under the sun; and, behold, all is vanity and a striving after wind" (1:14). Merit is not rewarded in this world, nor is wickedness punished. Power prevails, and power oppresses; such, the Preacher tells us, is the way things are.

But the Preacher's vision of existence as the same old story endlessly repeated, runs counter to what modern science shows: that everything in the universe always is changing. Of course the Preacher sought only to describe life in this world: life, in his phrase, "under the sun." He was unaware that a universe existed outside the earth, and could not have imagined that spaceships might one day soar into it, thus escaping the world under the sun.

In immediate terms, however, the message of Ecclesiastes always has had the ring of truth about it. A human lifetime is short, while changes often become visible only after a long time; so the Preacher's view corresponds to what we think we see. It is true to much of our experience, and provides a sobering corrective to American optimism. Like other illusions that we live by—that the ground we stand on is unmoving, or that the sun rises in the morning and falls at night—the view that nothing changes or can be changed in human nature or politics can be a useful proxy for the truth; the truth being that such changes do take place, but often only over a time period much longer than we have in mind.

The entire six thousand years of civilization and history are no time at all compared to the six million years it took for a two-legged chimpanzee to produce a human descendant. But when thought of in terms of a single lifetime, the six thousand years themselves seem to be forever.

Arbitrary rule, the divinity of kings, the hereditary principle: these were among the burdens of the human race for almost the whole of political history, burdens that therefore seemed to be unchangeable. It would not have been far wrong for an ancient Egyptian or Sumerian to predict that such burdens would always be with us. Not far wrong, but wrong nevertheless; in the era ushered in by the American and French revolutions of the eighteenth century, such things were brought to an end.

So there are two bodies of wisdom to bear in mind: the American, according to which everything can be changed in time; and the traditional, according to which nothing can be changed within the length of time that we can foresee. The difference between Old World pessimism and New World optimism comes down, then, to a question of time: one is truer to short-term, the other to long-term, experience. That makes all the more relevant the observation made by Henry Adams and others a century ago that the pace of history is accelerating. The generation of Americans to which he served as mentor, and the generations that followed, lived through greater changes than any preceding them. More now happens in decades than once happened in centuries or millennia.

It is, of course, science that has hurried us along. If it continues to do so, then American wisdom will prove more applicable to world realities, and traditional wisdom less so, as time goes on.

In individual cases, which wisdom to follow depends on whether the limits imposed by human nature in politics are real or merely apparent. The sound barrier could be broken, but we are told that the light barrier cannot; what elements in politics corresponds to these? Which limits are absolute, and which are challenges that can be overcome? Slavery was an institution as old as civilization, and seemed to many to have been woven into the fabric of existence, but it turned out that it was man, not nature, that created and sustained it; therefore, it was a practice that human beings could end.

When the issue of giving women the right to vote came to the forefront of politics in Britain a century ago, it was argued by Winston Churchill, then a junior army officer, that "it is contrary to natural law and the practice of civilized states." He was voicing a point of view common at the time. He added, "If you give women votes you must ultimately allow women to sit as members of Parliament."

Later, as a rising young politician, he changed his mind on the issue several times. But he returned to the familiar argument that extending the franchise to females was neither wise nor feasible because it was not natural. "At one political dinner party," wrote one biographer, "attendants rushed in to Churchill with the news that suffragettes were chaining themselves to railings in the public square and would stay there until they received the vote. Churchill answered loudly, 'A man might as well chain himself to the railings of St. Thomas Hospital and say he wouldn't move until he has had a baby.'"

In Britain and elsewhere today, women vote, while men still do not give birth. Clearly one was a practice that society could change—and without destroying itself—while the other was not.

Closely related to the women's suffrage movement, especially in Britain, was the drive to prohibit or restrict the consumption of alcoholic beverages. In the United Kingdom, temperance advocates eventually won restrictions on the hours during which such beverages could be sold in bars and restaurants. The United States notoriously went much further and in the aftermath of the First World War banned alcohol completely. The experiment proved to be a disaster. Human nature resisted it. The inability of the government to enforce the laws against alcohol brought about a general collapse of law and order in such cities as Chicago in the 1920s. In the 1930s the law and the constitutional amendment were repealed, and order was restored.

Prohibition was an extreme symptom of a general American view that anything can be changed by passing a law, a view that ignores rooted realities of human nature. It was much like the British liberal view satirized by George Bernard Shaw in *John Bull's Other Island*. The Irishman Doyle, bitterly meditating the anguish and tragedy of life, exclaims: "I wish I could find a country to live in where the facts were not brutal and the dreams not unreal." The English liberal Broadbent responds: "Don't despair, Larry, old boy: things may look black; but there will be a great change after the next election."

The same obliviousness to reality was evident in Woodrow Wilson's proposed Covenant of the League of Nations in 1919 and Secretary of State Frank Kellogg's Peace Pact of 1928–1929. Ignoring entirely the basic causes of conflict among nations, both documents assumed that warfare could be abolished simply by getting countries to sign a pledge not to use force against one another. Needless to say, the pledges did nothing to stop the wars and invasions of the 1930s.

·   ·   ·

Traditional wisdom tells us that the United States is a country, like any other; that it will occupy its place in the sun for a limited time only; and that it will decline, like England and Spain before it, or disappear, like the Roman Empire.

It is true that one of the areas in which history has brought few changes since civilization began is international politics, with its rhythms and recurrences, its rises and falls. The textbook on international relations first published by Hans Morgenthau in 1948 is as applicable to the interstate dealings of the Sumerians of 4000 B.C. as to the international politics of the twentieth century, and seems likely to be a valuable guide to the world affairs of the twenty-first as well. There is good reason for this: when states are independent of one another or of any higher authority, but interact continuously, there are only a limited number of themes and variations to be found in their mutual behavior.

The appearance and disappearance of states and civilizations is one of these themes. At the height of their glory, great powers seem to be a permanent feature of the international landscape. Yet like castles built in the sand, they are leveled without a trace by the next tide.

Will the United States, too, prove to be a transitory great power?

If we are talking about hundreds or thousands of years from now, nobody can know the answer, and indeed it may be that the human race, if it still exists, may have abandoned the state system altogether by that time, and may have adopted some other form of political organization. In the shorter run, assuming that the scientific revolution roars onward, and that the United States remains a leader in that revolution, the country should continue to play the role of a great power for a long time to come.

Even if someday the United States should fall by the wayside, there are reasons to believe that basic elements of America's politics—which, having originated in England, should be called Anglo-American politics—will endure. It would not be the first time in history that a message has survived the messenger, or a cause its champion.

The checks and balances of the country's Constitution, at the heart of its political arrangements, are based on a realistic view of human flaws and propensities to folly, and are much in line with traditional wisdom. The balance-of-power principles that it embodies have been valid throughout history; there is no reason to believe they will cease being valid for as far ahead as we can see.

The American plan of government is flexible. It is federal, not national. As a union of states, it is a model for a world that in certain vital areas needs wider government authority. Its emphasis on local government, and its goal of securing freedom of the individual, provides a model for a world that in other areas needs smaller government, less government, or no government at all.

Explicit or implicit in the American scheme are the freedoms—of thought, inquiry, and communication—that fuel what is being called the information revolution, and which seems likely to increase the powers of the human race to an extent not even imaginable today.

The ascendancy of Anglo-American politics, and perhaps even of the United States, which flies its colors, therefore may be less impermanent than has been the case with great powers and their ideologies in the past. The pattern of great-power rise and fall may be, at least for a time, suspended.

The tale, told in the time it might take a shaman around a Stone Age campfire, is over. It has consisted in singling out eight of the giant steps that have moved the human race along the course of its life thus far: those that have moved it in the direction of the scientific revolution in which we are caught up now. There has also been a look at four more steps that project what our course of action ought to be in dealing with the consequences of modernity in the next century and in centuries to come.

Irony is a major theme of history. Those who helped to move mankind along its eight giant steps were quite unaware of what they were doing. There was nothing inevitable about what happened. One of the many virtues of William H. McNeill's classic book *Plagues and People* is that it reminds us that accident (in the cases described in his work, the outbreak of diseases) often dictates the course of history.

At the turn of the last century, Americans, Englishmen, and other westerners celebrated the growing triumph of civilized values. Shortly thereafter the world plunged into barbarism such as had never been seen before. Regressions are frequent.

Did these giant steps actually move the human race in a particular direction? Was the move progressive?[3] Yes, as I define it. It should first be said that any American who reads a morning newspaper finds cause for despair every day in the reports of crime, pollution, hatred, corruption, suffering, injustice, and warfare. But over the long term—whether thought of in a historian's terms, from the birth of civilization to today, or in personal terms, over the course of a lifetime—a different and more cheering picture emerges.

In the United States, Britain, and the other industrial countries, people are healthier and wealthier than they were before. They live longer and remain youthful to a later age. More of them take part in the political process. They are more mobile, enjoy more leisure time, and possess entertainments of a sort and on a scale hitherto unknown. Sanitation is more widespread. Education is more widely available. Career opportunities have been opened. Fewer barriers exist for persons not born to privilege.

For the few at the top, life once was better, but for the many, it is otherwise. Most people are materially better off than their forebears, and more live a good life as they define it. More men and women than ever live life as they choose, rather than as government or society chooses for them. More of the world's peoples than ever before enjoy political freedom.

These are not inconsiderable achievements, and from the point of view of liberal democracy, they represent progress. The eight steps defined in this book are, in that light, steps forward and up. Moving into the new century, the world may or may not make further steps in that direction.

I have argued that all we can foresee of the future is that in large part it will be shaped by the ongoing scientific revolution, with all its perils and promises. Anglo-American politics—though, like all others, lacking a solution to the problem of international warfare—

---

3. I believe that there are areas such as art in which progress does not take place. I believe that there are other areas in which progress can, but has not, taken place. In the text I write of progress only within defined areas.

seems to me to be less ill-suited than any other to deal with the problems and opportunities afforded by the civilization of science. But even these politics may not prove effective in solving such problems as the threats to social cohesion and to the natural environment. In other words, our best efforts may not be good enough.

Yet although open societies, the rule of law, and the cooperation of independent states based on reciprocity and rational self-interest will go only so far, the point is that they go in the right direction. In Jacob's dream, the ladder reached up to heaven. The rungs of progress up which the United States might lead the world cannot reasonably be expected to reach that high; but at any rate they, too, point, as Jacob's ladder did, up to the sky.

Cheerful rationalists at the turn of the last century were wrong to view the future through rose-colored glasses, even though in the end all came out well. Along the road to the world of the 1990s, there have been times when the United States and the principles for which it stands might have been sent to the scrapheap at the bottom of the ocean, like those American merchant vessels that German U-boats torpedoed in both world wars. The spring of 1941 was such a time. The whole of Europe, save only neutral Sweden and Switzerland, was in the hands of Hitler and his allies. The coalition of Nazi Germany, the Soviet Union, imperial Japan, fascist Italy, and the other continental dictatorships, commanded armed forces that dwarfed the military resources that the two holdouts, Britain and the United States, could field. A realistic prediction at the time would have been that the coalition would complete its conquest of the world. A reasonable supposition is that only Hitler's astonishing blunder in betraying his Soviet ally kept it from happening. The worst could have occurred, and in a sense *should* have occurred, and only an accident kept it from doing so.

In the 1910s or 1920s it was wrong to be optimistic. In the 1940s it was wrong, instead, to be pessimistic. *Horizon*, the British literary periodical of the 1940s, published its last issue in December 1949/January 1950. A despairing note appeared in it, penned by its editor, Cyril Connolly, announcing that the cause of the West also was coming to an end. Man, he wrote, had lost faith in religion, but then had been betrayed by science. Everything was going to get worse, he predicted, and this, he said, was the message of the 1940s. He summed it up in a memorable and much-quoted phrase: "it is closing time in the gardens of the West."

Even at the time, it was not true. On the contrary, the middle and late 1940s were years of triumph: of victory in the Second World War, and of the heroic age of U.S. foreign policy that gave birth to the Marshall Plan and to the strategy of containment that eventually brought down the Soviet Union.

It is, if anything, less true now. Far from being cast down, the western alliance and its principles are more dominant than countries and their ideologies ever have been before. The United States enjoys a primacy in world affairs such as no nation has known in the past. The beliefs that it champions are affirmed in all parts of the globe. Most other countries now accept the American contention that an open society, the rule of law, and a market economy are the keys to success.

What is to be feared is overconfidence. We ought to remind ourselves of the serious failings of our society and of the real dangers that lie ahead.

As of now, however, Connolly has it wrong. The doors to the gardens, far from being closed, have been flung wide open, and crowds course through them. The gardens are in full bloom. People come from all over the world to admire them, but also to take away seeds, bulbs, and cuttings to transplant later in their own soil.

Where are we? The preceding pages have situated us in an American era, at some indeterminate point in a continuing scientific revolution that began about a thousand years ago. How did we get here? In my synoptic view, it was in the eight giant steps that serve as chapter headings for Parts One and Two. Where are we going? If we continue in the same direction, and are to be successful, I think it will be by taking, among others, the additional steps that serve as chapter headings in Part Three.

The world has become one now, as has civilization; therefore, so has history. No longer is it limited to tales of the tribal, the dynastic, or the national. Instead it is, at its most expansive, the story of the human race in its world.

It follows that the future too, will almost certainly be one. Whatever the future may bring, it is likely to bring it to the whole world.

This view of matters—the view outlined in this book—may have the strength, but certainly has the weaknesses, of any theory based on an interpretation of scholarship and science. It derives from evidence; and the evidence is both incomplete and changing. New data may require a shift in view. To be modern is to live with the uncertainty caused by our awareness that all of our rational convictions are provisional.

The shamans who have inspired the human race since the murkiest days of prehistory lacked our knowledge, but they could offer a faith that gripped and compelled. You could do that today only by throwing away rationalism and turning your back on the modern world. Of course, from time to time people do just that.

In certain settings, blind faith in magic and the supernatural can be contagious. A case in point: a story told some years ago by a retired British magistrate. Over drinks at a wine bar off one of the Inns of Court in London, he was recalling his youthful experiences as a colonial administrator in what now is Ghana but then was called the Gold Coast. He told about a time when he had a crew working on constructing a road. One day he went up to look at the progress being made and found the crew seated and doing nothing. A curious marker stood where they had stopped.

A witch doctor had put the marker there, he was informed. It meant that demons and curses blocked the way. The only way to deal with it, according to the crew, was to employ the services of the witch doctor to propitiate the evil spirits.

He told the men that this was a lot of nonsense, mere superstition. He pulled up the marker, cast it away, and drove the men to resume work.

The next day he came down with a fever of 103 degrees. Nothing helped. To please the natives, he offered gifts to the witch doctor and made peace with him. The fever lifted.

"From then on," the magistrate said, "whenever I saw a marker, I stopped right there, pending negotiation with the spirits. It wasn't that I believed in the mumbo-jumbo," he added, downing his drink and signaling for another, "it's just that I didn't want to come down with one of those damn fevers again."

page

CHAPTER ONE

6   **More than half the adults:** *The New York Times*, May 24, 1996.

"some 85 percent": John Noble Wilford, "Looking Back 11 Billion Light-years, a Glimpse at Galaxy Birth," *New York Times*, September 5, 1996, A18.

astronomers have peered even further: Warren E. Leary, "Light from a Tiny Galaxy Is the Most Distant Object Ever Seen from Earth," *New York Times*, March 13, 1998, A14.

7   **"crawled or slithered":** Nicholas Wade, "The Sea Yields a Clue to the Origin of Life," *New York Times*, August 23, 1996, A23.

8   **These events occasioned a proliferation:** Kathy Sawyer, "A Novel Theory of Biology's 'Big Bang,'" *International Herald Tribune*, July 26–27, 1997, 1.

"We are living . . . long after": Barrow 1994, xi.

9   **For Ovid:** *The Metamorphoses.*

the Roman novelist: Apuleius, *The Golden Ass.*

Evidence . . . from Lake Victoria: Carol Kaesuk Yoon, "Lake Victoria's Lightning-Fast Origin of Species," *New York Times*, August 27, 1996.

In the Galápagos: Ibid., Weiner 1995.

An experiment with lizards: Nicholas Wade, "Leapin' Evolution Is Found in Lizards," *New York Times*, May 1, 1997, A27.

10 **"He'll try all kinds of escape":** Homer, *The Odyssey*, transl. by Robert Fagles (New York: Viking Penguin, 1996), 137–9.

11 **weighing . . . between 90 and 110 pounds:** *New York Times*, April 18, 1997, p. A15, "Fossil Shows Apes Emerged Far Earlier."

11–12 **footprints of an anatomically modern human:** John Noble Wilford,

"Ancient Trail of Footprints in Africa," *New York Times*, August 15, 1997, 1.

13   **"What the devil determines":** Weiner 1995, 214.

      "Today, biologists call": Ibid.

14   **genetic materials . . . atmospheric forces:** Ibid., 217.

16   **controversial new evidence . . . thirty thousand years ago:** John Noble Wilford, "3 Human Species Coexisted Eons Ago, New Data Suggest," *New York Times*, December 13, 1996, 1.

      An astonishing . . . find in northwestern Australia: John Noble Wilford, "In Australia, Signs of Artists Who Predate Homo Sapiens," *New York Times*, September 21, 1996, 1.

      What may have been a flute: John Noble Wilford, "Playing of Flute May Have Graced Neanderthal Fire," *New York Times*, October 29, 1996, C1.

      Computer studies . . . a mere 2 percent: Leakey 1994, 98.

19   **the discovery in northwest Australia of tools:** *New York Times*, September 21, 1996, 1.

      aura of spiritualism: This was immediately remarked upon by Alexander Marshack in an interview.

21   **But the latest excavations:** John Noble Wilford, "Ancient Spears Tell of Mighty Hunters of Stone Age," *New York Times*, March 4, 1997, C6.

      the Nuer: Mair, Lucy. *Primitive Government*, rev. ed. (Harmondsworth, Middlesex, England: Penguin, 1970), 63.

      the Turkana: Ibid., 76.

      "Practically every behavior pattern": Topoff, Howard R. "The Social Behavior of Army Ants," *Scientific American* 227, no. 5 (November 1972), 79.

23   ***"Uilikande":*** Claude Lévi-Strauss, "The Social and Psychological Aspects of Chieftainship in a Primitive Tribe: The Nambikuara of Northwestern Mato Grosso," in Ronald Cohen and John Middleton, editors, *Comparative Political Systems: Studies in the Politics of Pre-industrial Societies* (New York: Natural History Press, 1967), 52–3.

CHAPTER TWO

27   **Dogs . . . had been domesticated:** Nicholas Wade, "Man Has Older Friend Than Thought," *New York Times*, June 13, 1997, A12.

35   **"Sadly, it also seems":** Crawford 1991, 13.

36   **"Because of . . . irrigation":** Ibid., 9.

39   **scholars now question whether predynastic:** Baines and Malek 1980, 31.

40   **"There is no evidence":** Fairservis 1992, 4.

      "In all . . . there is little to differentiate": Ibid.

      "the able Prince Cheng": Geoffrey Parker, *The Military Revolution: Military Innovation and the Rise of the West, 1500–1800*, 2nd ed. (Cambridge: Cambridge University Press, 1996), 3.

43   **Variations in economic behavior . . . examined by students of comparative civilization:** Colin Renfew, review of Bruce G. Trigger, *Early*

Civilizations: Ancient Egypt in Context (Cairo: American University in Cairo Press, 1993), in *American Journal of Archaeology*, January 1997, 164.

43 **perhaps twenty thousand years . . . before Columbus:** John Noble Wilford, "Human Presence in Americas Is Pushed Back a Millennium," *New York Times*, February 11, 1997, 1.

CHAPTER THREE

47 **A more recent theory . . . the Black Sea:** John Noble Wilford, "Geologists Link Black Sea Deluge to Farming's Rise," *New York Times*, December 17, 1996, C1.

48 **a widespread Semitic custom:** Sarah P. Morris, "The Sacrifice of Astyanax: Near Eastern Contributions to the Siege of Troy," in Jane B. Carter and Sarah P. Morris, editors, *The Ages of Homer* (Austin: University of Texas Press, 1995), 221.

50 **conceived immaculately:** Witter Bynner, *The Way of Life According to Lao Tzu* (New York: Perigee, 1944), 11.

54 **such sayings as:** Confucius 1997, 5, 16.

55 **"Everything flows and nothing abides":** "You cannot step twice": Heraclitus (Fragments 20 and 21), Philip Wheelwright, *Heraclitus* (New York: Atheneum, 1964), 29.

56 **a professor of moral philosophy:** R. M. Hare, *Plato* (Oxford and New York: Oxford University Press, 1982), v.

57 **"still hangs unmistakable":** Stark 1954, 5.
"the greatest perhaps": D. S. Carne-Ross, *Pindar* (New Haven and London: Yale University Press, 1985), 183.

58 **"Creatures of a day":** Ibid.
"Thing of a day": H. D. F. Kitto, quoted in Starr 1968, 97.

59 **Pericles . . . *Funeral Oration:*** Thucydides 1954, 115 et seq.

60 **"the catastrophe was so overwhelming":** Ibid., 126.

61 **"The strong do":** Ibid., 360.
"So far as . . . the gods": Ibid., 363.
"Allow us to be friends": Ibid., 365.

62 **"the inner side of a great conquest":** Murray 1946, 87.
"How are ye blind": Ibid., 84.
"In the same winter": Thucydides 1954, 367.

CHAPTER FOUR

66 **A boy could not eat:** Murray 1946, 111.
"able despot": Ibid.

68 **"best young Greek philosopher":** Hammond 1980, 21.
"Be wary of assumptions": O'Brien 1992, 20.
"Aristotle taught ethics": Tarn 1948, 1:2.
"a matter of faith with Aristotle": Jaeger 1962, 121.

70 **"one of the vainest men":** Renault 1975, 42.

71 **"a spear-won prize":** Hammond 1980, 61.

72 **According to . . . Tarn:** Tarn 1948, 1:117.
"It was . . . a dream": Ibid., 2:448.

74　**"The forty-three years"**: Rostovtzeff 1941, 1:23.
　　"a strong state meant": Tarn 1951, 5.
76　**"All this to carry"**: James 1884, ch. 26.
　　"An appropriate monument": Fromkin 1975, 46.
78　**"passive inertia"**: Jones 1964, 2:1061–2.
　　The army was needed . . . to occupy: Isaac 1992.
　　"Without such an army": Rostovtzeff 1957, 1:25, 40.
　　"verge of starvation": Brown 1971, 12.
79　**"more tax-collectors"**: Ibid., 25.
　　"never asked whether it was worth": Rostovtzeff 1957, 1:532.
　　"A wave of resignation . . . ": Ibid., 523.
80　**"lost all control"**: Dill 1899, reprint edition (Cleveland: Meridian, 1958), 229.
81　**"as long as there are men"**: Ammianus, quoted by Jones 1964, 2:1025.
　　"who can doubt that the end": Lactantius, quoted in Ibid.
81–2　**"the brightest light"**: Ibid.

CHAPTER FIVE

89　**"less than five feet tall"**: De Beer 1968, 34.
　　"remarkably ugly": Ibid., 114.
　　Infirmities: Ibid., Appendix A.
91　**"temperate and indecisive contests"**: Gibbon 2:441.
　　"the progress of knowledge": Ibid.
　　"in a free . . . country": Saunders 1961, 49.
　　"one great republic": Gibbon 2:439.
　　"these partial events": Ibid., 440.
92　The same result was achieved in theory: Dr. Mark Hassall of the faculty of the Institute of Archaeology of the University of London.
93　**"It cost less to bring a cargo"**: Brown 1971, 13.
　　"one of the very few great states": Ibid., 22.
　　"The savage nations": Gibbon 2, 440.
94　**"unknown dangers may *possibly* arise"**: Ibid.
99　**"monasticism became virtually extinct"**: Holmes 1988, 101.
105　**"between 700 and 1000 A.D."**: Parker 1996, 1.
　　"over two hundred kings": Holmes 1988, 82.
106　**"a sense of the extraordinary vigour"**: Ibid., x.
108　**"it was our wars of religion"**: Kamen 1984, 208.
110　**"a thing so necessary in Portugal"**: Swetz 1987, 25.
111　**mechanical timepieces:** Kamen 1984, 15.
112　**"to explain the historical puzzle"**: Daniel Bell, "The Protestant Ethic," *World Policy Journal*, vol. 13, no. 3 (Fall 1996), 35.

CHAPTER SIX

113　**the age of reconnaissance:** Parry 1964.
　　"That great Antiquity": *Hydriotaphia*, ch. 1.
115　**"planned discovery"**: Wilford 1981, 57.
　　"the first rational organizer": Ibid.

118   **Portugal . . . July 8, 1497:** The account that follows owes much to Lucas 1943 and Parry 1964.

119   **"most celebrated . . . of his day":** Parry 1964, 157.

        documents uncovered in the 1980s: Subrahmanyam, 1997, 121–8.

        in fact was with the convict-envoy: Ibid., 129.

120   **Escorted by locals . . . Hindu temple:** Ibid., 131.

        Samudri Raja: Ibid., 138.

121   **barrels of butter:** Ibid., 136.

122   **"free from molestation":** Ibid., 161.

        an empire merely of bases and outstations: See Fernandez-Armesto 1995.

        "We came here to serve God": Elliott 1964, 53.

        "promised to give us Indians": Díaz del Castillo 1956, 4.

123   **Historians continue to wonder:** See Windschuttle 1996, 41 et seq.

124   **"much given to women":** *Encyclopaedia Britannica*, 15th ed., s.v. "Cortés."

125   **"the banner of the rainbow":** Prescott n.d., 33.

128   **"piratical":** A. J. P. Taylor, *The Struggle for Mastery in Europe 1848–1914* (Oxford: Oxford University Press, 1954), 294.

129   **"over eighty-four percent":** Headrick 1981, 3.

CHAPTER SEVEN

133   **argued otherwise:** Yates 1964.

        A date of basic importance: Ibid., 398.

        Kepler: Ibid., 443.

134   **Hobsbawm has argued:** Hobsbawm 1969, 34–55.

        There were more than one: Coleman, 1992, 44.

135   **a ratio of better than ten to one:** Hobsbawm, 1969, 48.

138   **"a woman half his age":** *Encyclopaedia Britannica*, 15th ed., s.v. "Edison, Thomas Alva."

        Model T cars . . . for $500: Ibid., s.v., "Ford, Henry."

140   **more than 35 million long tons:** Marian Kent, *Oil and Empire: British Policy and Mesopotamian Oil: 1900–1920* (London and Basingstoke: Macmillan, 1976), Appendix VIII, Table 3.

CHAPTER EIGHT

150   **"In 1215 Magna Carta was a failure":** Holt 1992, 3.

        "Sometimes Magna Carta stated law": Ibid., 300.

151   **twenty million copies:** Hugh Thomas, *A History of the World* (New York: Harper & Row, 1979), 200.

152   **"Europe was hit by a good, big idea":** *The Economist*, November 16, 1996, 50.

        shaped by the clashes and reconciliations: Henry F. May, *The Enlightenment in America* (New York: Oxford University Press, 1976).

154   **"until August 1914":** A. J. P. Taylor, *English History 1914–1945* (Oxford: Oxford University Press, 1965), 1.

155   **André Siegfried:** Fernand Braudel, *Afterthoughts on Material Civilization*

and Capitalism, trans. Patricia Ranum (Baltimore: Johns Hopkins, paper-back, 1979), 104.

155 **John Maynard Keynes:** *The Economic Consequences of the Peace* (New York: Harcourt, Brace and Howe, 1920), 11–12.

CHAPTER NINE

166 **"sway the destinies of half the globe":** *Democracy in America*, vol. 1, ch. 18.

167 **"scientific thrillers":** *Encyclopaedia Britannica*, 15th ed., s.v. "Wells, H. G."

170 **their favorite programs are those:** *New York Times*, February 4, 1997, 1.
"Louis told me": Goodall 1971, 19.
"If Goliath met another": Ibid., 71.

171 **a Yale sociologist:** Harold Lasswell, *Politics: Who Gets What, When, How* (New York: McGraw-Hill, 1936).

172 **"Had my colleagues . . . ":** *National Geographic* 188, no. 6 (December 1995), 110.
"hostile and violently aggressive": Goodall 1986, p. 534.

173 **"happiness was elsewhere":** Ian Bell, *Dreams of Exile* (New York: Henry Holt, 1992), 31.
to . . . Mark Twain: Ibid., 258.
To Henry James: Ibid., 274.

175 **it has been suggested . . . mobile machines:** Prof. Ralph Buultjens, in the course of conversation with the author.
"While close to half": Neil Pearce, "A Future for the World's Cities," *International Herald Tribune*, June 17, 1996.
"The United Nations estimates": Kelly Couturier, "UN Conference Adopts Blueprint on Urban Growth," *International Herald Tribune*, June 17, 1996, 10.

176 **"from electricity to water":** Neil Pearce, "A Future for the World's Cities," *International Herald Tribune*, June 17, 1996, 8, paraphrasing Janice Perlman, founder of Megacities organization.
cities, with their economies of scale: Ibid., and "A Survey of Cities," *The Economist*, July 29, 1995.

179 **"Democracy . . . gives men":** *Democracy in America*, vol. 2, bk. 1, ch. 17.

180 **"Democratic nations care but little":** Ibid.

CHAPTER TEN

182 **"no enlightened person today":** Aron 1985, 82.

183 **"If none but small nations":** Ibid., 195.

184 **Samuel P. Huntington:** "The West: Unique, Not Universal," *Foreign Affairs* (November/December 1996), 28.

193 **"1,000 Yugoslavias":** *The Economist*, December 5, 1992, 33.

CHAPTER TWELVE

203 **"in 1900 the United States":** Arthur M. Schlesinger, Jr., "The Ultimate Approval Rating," *New York Times*, December 15, 1996, 46, 51.

214 **"contrary to natural law":** Randolph S. Churchill, *Winston S. Churchill*, Vol. 1, Companion Part 2, *1896–1900* (London: Heinemann, 1967), 765. **"At one political dinner party":** Robert Lewis Taylor, *Winston Churchill: An Informal Study of Greatness* (Garden City, N.Y.: Doubleday, 1952), 237.

215 *John Bull's Other Island:* just before the end of Act 1.

Selected Bibliography

CHAPTER ONE

Barrow, John D. 1994. *The Origin of the Universe*. New York: Basic Books.

Dawkins, Richard. 1995. *River Out of Eden: A Darwinian View of Life*. New York: Basic Books.

Dennett, Daniel C. 1995. *Darwin's Dangerous Idea: Evolution and the Meaning of Life*. New York: Simon & Schuster.

Gould, Stephen Jay. 1989. *Wonderful Life: The Burgess Shale and the Nature of History*. New York: Norton.

Johanson, Donald, and Blake Edgar. 1996. *From Lucy to Language*. New York: Simon & Schuster.

Leakey, Richard. 1994. *The Origin of Humankind*. New York: Basic Books.

Marshack, Alexander. 1972. *The Roots of Civilization: The Cognitive Beginnings of Man's First Art, Symbol and Notation*. New York: McGraw Hill.

Stove, David. 1995. *Darwinian Fairytales*. Aldershot, Hants., and Brookfield, Vermont: Avebury and Ashgate.

Weiner, Jonathan. 1995. *The Beak of the Finch: A Story of Evolution in Our Time*. New York: Vintage.

Wilford, John Noble. 1995–96. *New York Times*. Articles in the Tuesday "Science Times."

Wolpoff, Milford, and Rachel Casparin. 1997. *Race and Human Evolution*. New York: Simon & Schuster.

CHAPTER TWO

Algaze, Guillermo. 1993. *The Uruk World System: The Dynamics of Expansion of Early Mesopotamian Civilization*. Chicago and London: University of Chicago Press.

Baines, John, and Jaromir Malek. 1980. *The Atlas of Ancient Egypt.* New York: Facts on File.

Blunden, Caroline, and Mark Elvin. 1983. *Cultural Atlas of China.* New York: Facts on File.

Crawford, Harriet. 1991. *Sumer and the Sumerians.* Cambridge: Cambridge University Press.

Diringer, David. 1962. *Writing: Its Origins and Early History.* New York: Praeger.

Fagan, Brian. 1995. *Time Detectives: How Archaeologists Use Technology to Recapture the Past.* New York: Simon & Schuster.

Fairservis, Walter A. 1992. *The Harappan Civilization and Its Writing: A Model for the Decipherment of the Indus Script.* New Delhi: Oxford & IBH.

Ferry, David. 1992. *Gilgamesh: A New Rendering in English Verse.* New York: Farrar, Straus & Giroux.

Keegan, John. 1993. *A History of Warfare.* New York: Alfred A. Knopf.

Maisels, Charles Keith. 1990. *The Emergence of Civilization: From Hunting and Gathering to Agriculture, Cities and the State in the Near East.* London and New York: Routledge.

Roaf, Michael. 1990. *Cultural Atlas of Mesopotamia and the Ancient Near East.* New York: Facts on File.

Schmandt-Besserat, Denise. 1992. *Before Writing.* Vol. 1. *From Counting to Cuneiform.* Austin: University of Texas.

Starr, Chester G. 1965. *A History of the Ancient World.* New York: Oxford University Press.

CHAPTER THREE

Breasted, James Henry. 1934. *The Dawn of Conscience.* New York and London: Scribner's.

Confucius. 1997. *The Analects.* Translated by Simon Leys. New York and London: Norton.

Dundas, Paul. 1992. *The Jains.* London and New York: Routledge.

Ghirshman, R. 1954. *Iran: From the Earliest Times to the Islamic Conquest.* Harmondsworth, Middlesex: Penguin.

Herodotus. 1954. *The Histories.* Translated by Aubrey de Selincourt. Harmondsworth, Middlesex: Penguin.

Jaspers, Karl. 1962. *Socrates, Buddha, Confucius, Jesus: The Paradigmatic Individuals.* Edited by Hannah Arendt. Translated by Ralph Manheim. New York: Harcourt, Brace & World.

Lao-Tzu. 1993. *Tao Te Ching.* Translated by Stephen Adiss and Standley Lombardo. Indianapolis and Cambridge: Hackett.

Maccoby, Hyam. 1979. "The Bible," in Elie Kedourie, ed., *The Jewish World: History and Culture of the Jewish People.* New York: Abrams.

Murray, Gilbert. 1946. *Euripides and His Age.* 2nd ed. London, New York, and Toronto: Oxford University Press.

Sophocles. 1982. *The Three Theban Plays: Antigone, Oedipus the King, Oedipus at Colonus.* Translated by Robert Fagles. New York: Viking.

Stark, Freya. 1954. *Ionia: A Quest.* London: Murray.

Starr, Chester G. 1968. *The Awakening of the Greek Historical Spirit.* New York: Alfred A. Knopf.

Thucydides. 1954. *History of the Peloponnesian War.* Translated by Rex Warner. Melbourne, London, and Baltimore: Penguin.

CHAPTER FOUR

Bosworth, A. B. 1988. *Conquest and Empire: The Reign of Alexander the Great.* Cambridge: Cambridge University Press.

Brown, Peter. 1971. *The World of Late Antiquity: From Marcus Aurelius to Muhammad.* London: Thames and Hudson.

Dill, Samuel. 1899. *Roman Society in the Last Century of the Western Empire.* 2nd ed.

Fox, Robert Lane. 1974. *Alexander the Great.* New York: Dial.

Fromkin, David. 1975. *The Question of Government: An Inquiry into the Breakdown of Modern Political Systems.* New York: Scribner's.

Hammond, N. G. L. 1980. *Alexander the Great: King, Commander and Statesman.* Park Ridge, NJ: Noyes.

Haywood, Richard Mansfield. *The Myth of Rome's Fall.* 1962. New York: Apollo.

Isaac, Benjamin. 1992. *The Limits of Empire: The Roman Army in the East.* Revised edition. Oxford: Oxford University Press.

Jaeger, Werner. 1962. *Aristotle: Fundamentals of the History of His Development.* 2nd edition (paperback). Oxford: Oxford University Press.

James, Henry. 1884. *A Little Tour in France.*

Jones, A. H. M. 1964. *The Later Roman Empire, 284–602: A Social Economic and Administrative Survey.* 3 vols. and maps. Oxford: Basil Blackwell.

Mazzarino, Santo. 1966. *The End of the Ancient World.* Translated by George Holmes. New York: Knopf.

Murray, Gilbert. 1946. *Euripides and His Age.* 2nd ed. London: Oxford University Press.

O'Brien, John Maxwell. 1992. *Alexander the Great: The Invisible Enemy: A Biography.* London and New York: Routledge.

Renault, Mary. 1975. *The Nature of Alexander.* Harmondsworth, Middlesex: Penguin.

Rostovtzeff, M. 1941. *The Social and Economic History of the Hellenistic World.* 3 vols. Oxford: Oxford University Press.

———. 1957. *The Social and Economic History of the Roman Empire.* 2nd ed., 2 vols. Oxford: Oxford University Press.

Tarn, W. W. 1951. *The Greeks in Bactria and India.* 2nd ed. Cambridge: Cambridge University Press.

———. 1948. *Alexander the Great.* 2 vols. Cambridge: Cambridge University Press.

CHAPTER FIVE

Brown, Peter. 1996. *The Rise of Western Christendom: Triumph and Diversity A.D. 200–1000.* Cambridge, MA, and Oxford: Blackwell.

———. 1971. *The World of Late Antiquity: From Marcus Aurelius to Muhammad.* London: Thames and Hudson.

Cunliffe, Barry. 1979. *The Celtic World.* New York, San Francisco, and St. Louis: McGraw-Hill.

De Beer, Gavin. 1968. *Gibbon and His World.* New York: Viking.

Gibbon, Edward. *The Decline and Fall of the Roman Empire.* 3vols. New York: Modern Library.

Grousset, René. 1970. *The Empire of the Steppes: A History of Central Asia.* Tr. Naomi Walford. New Brunswick: Rutgers University Press.

Jordan, David P. 1971. *Gibbon and His Roman Empire.* Urbana, Chicago, and London: University of Illinois Press.

Kamen, Henry. 1984. *European Society: 1500–1700.* London and New York: Routledge.

Macaulay, Thomas Babington. 1907. *Critical and Historical Essays.* 2 vols. Everyman's Library ed. London: Dent, and New York: Dutton.

Mansfield, Peter. 1985. *The Arabs.* London: Penguin.

Parker, Geoffrey. 1996. *The Military Revolution: Military Innovation and the Rise of the West, 1500–1800.* 2nd ed. Cambridge: Cambridge University Press.

Saunders, Dero A. (ed.) 1961. *The Autobiography of Edward Gibbon.* New York: Meridian.

Swetz, Frank J. 1987. *Capitalism and Arithmetic: The New Math of the 15th Century.* La Salle, IL: Open Court.

CHAPTER SIX

Braudel, Fernand. 1981–84. *Civilization and Capitalism: 15th–18th Century.* 3 vols. Transl. Sian Reynolds. New York: Harper and Row.

———. 1977. *Afterthoughts on Material Civilization and Capitalism.* Baltimore: Johns Hopkins.

Díaz del Castillo, Bernal. 1956. *The Discovery and Conquest of Mexico.* Trans. A. P. Maudslay. New York: Farrar, Straus and Cudahy.

Elliot, J. H. 1964. *Imperial Spain: 1469–1716.* New York: St. Martin's Press.

Fernandez-Armesto, Felipe. 1995. *Millennium: A History of the Last Thousand Years.* New York: Scribner's.

Headrick, Daniel R. 1981. *The Tools of Empire: Technology and European Imperialism in the Nineteenth Century.* New York and Oxford: Oxford University Press.

Lopez, Robert S. 1966. *The Birth of Europe.* New York: Evans.

———. 1971. *The Commercial Revolution of the Middle Ages, 950–1350.* Englewood Cliffs, NJ: Prentice Hall.

Lucas, Mary Seymour. 1943. *Vast Horizons.* New York: Viking. (*Note:* Although written for school-age young people, this book is based on a wide reading of primary sources.)

Parker, Geoffrey. 1996. *The Military Revolution: Military Innovation and the Rise of the West: 1500–1800.* 2nd ed. Cambridge: Cambridge University Press.

Parry, J. H. 1964. *The Age of Reconnaissance.* New York: Mentor.

Prescott, William H. 1847. Reprint edition: n.d. *The Conquest of Peru.* Dolphin Books. Garden City, NY: Doubleday.

Subrahmanyam, Sanjay. 1997. *The Career and Legend of Vasco Da Gama.* Cambridge: Cambridge University Press.

Thomas, Hugh. 1993. *Conquest: Montezuma, Cortés, and the Fall of Old Mexico.* New York: Simon & Schuster.

Wilford, John Noble. 1981. *The Mapmakers.* New York: Knopf.

Windschuttle, Keith. 1996. *The Killing of History: How a Discipline Is Being Murdered by Literary Critics and Social Theorists.* Paddington, Australia: Macleay.

CHAPTER SEVEN

Coleman, D. C. 1992. *Myth, History, and the Industrial Revolution.* London: Hambledon.

Hobsbawm, E. J. 1969. *Industry and Empire: From 1750 to the Present Day.* London: Penguin.

Mathias, Peter, and John A. Davis, editors. 1990. *The First Industrial Revolutions.* Cambridge: Basil Blackwell.

Yates, Frances A. 1864. *Giordano Bruno and the Hermetic Tradition.* Chicago: University of Chicago.

CHAPTER EIGHT

Draper, Theodore. 1996. A *Struggle for Power: The American Revolution.* New York: Random House.

Fischer, David Hackett. 1989. *Albion's Seed: Four British Folkways in America.* New York and Oxford: Oxford University Press.

Holt, J. C. 1992. *Magna Carta.* 2nd ed. Cambridge: Cambridge University Press.

Malone, Dumas. 1948–81. *Jefferson and His Time.* 6 vols. Boston: Little, Brown.

May, Henry F. 1976. *The Enlightenment in America.* New York: Oxford University Press.

Wright, Esmond. 1986. *Franklin of Philadelphia.* Cambridge MA, and London: Harvard University Press.

CHAPTER NINE

Ghiglieri, Michael P. 1988. *East of the Mountains of the Moon: Chimpanzee Society in the African Rain Forest.* New York: Free Press.

Goodall, Jane van Lawick. 1986. *The Chimpanzees of Gombe: Patterns of Behavior.* Cambridge, MA: Belknap Press, Harvard University Press.

———. 1971. *In the Shadow of Man.* London: Collins.

Wells, H. G. 1921. *The Outline of History: Being a Plain History of Life and Mankind.* 3rd ed. New York: Macmillan.

CHAPTER TEN

Aron, Raymond. 1965. *Main Currents in Sociological Thought: Montesquieu, Comte, Marx, Tocqueville—The Sociologists and the Revolution of 1848.* Translated by Richard Howard and Helen Weaver. London: Weidenfeld and Nicolson.

Gellner, Ernest. 1983. *Nations and Nationalism.* Oxford: Basil Blackwell.

CHAPTER ELEVEN

Carson, Rachel. 1978. *Silent Spring.* New York: Fawcett.

Commoner, Barry. 1971. *The Closing Circle: Man, Nature and Technology.* New York: Alfred A. Knopf.

Nash, Roderick. 1990. *American Environmentalism: Readings in Conservation History.* 3rd ed. New York: McGraw Hill.

CHAPTER TWELVE

Roberts, J. M. 1976. *The Hutchinson History of the World.* London: Hutchinson.

———. 1993. *Shorter History of the World.* Oxford: Helicon.

Acknowledgments

In 1980 Leigh Bruce, who shortly before had become an assistant editor of *Foreign Policy*, asked me to write a piece for his magazine on a topic of my choice. He asked for something lively and provocative. I responded by submitting an article called "World Politics in the 21st Century"—a title rather more startling a couple of decades ago than it would be now. For whatever reasons, the magazine passed on it, and I filed it away. I remain grateful to Leigh for having inspired me to write it.

Early in 1993, James Chace took over editorship of *World Policy Journal*. James had read everything I have written, ever since we were discharged from the army an improbably long time ago: and, remembering the twenty-first-century essay, he chose it to be the lead article for the first issue he edited. As it happened, my predictions had held up reasonably well in the intervening years; so, with relatively few changes, we were able to publish it in the Spring 1993 issue. It is owing to James, therefore, that it saw the light.

Wilmer Thomas, an investment banker with a gratifying enthusiasm for history and historians, phoned to urge me to expand the piece into a book. Had it not been for his urging, I might not have entertained the notion.

I brought the idea to Suzanne Gluck, my agent at ICM, with the thought of beginning with the sort of synopsis of history that I have to do for my university students at the start of each course; and then linking that to, and ending with, the twenty-first-century section. Suzanne gave the project shape and direction, and as always took charge of all practical matters. For me as for others, she is the indispensable person.

At about the same time that we were going forward to draft a formal book proposal, but in an entirely different context, Wallace Sellers arranged a luncheon appointment for the two of us with hedge-fund manager Craig Drill; I had questions I wanted to put to him about a technology investment. Postponing that discussion until later, Craig asked about the subject of my next book, and then launched into the speech and challenge recorded at the start of the first chapter. He gave me my opening paragraph.

My thanks to Ashbel Green for being the most helpful of editors and best of friends. Jennifer Bernstein, Ash's assistant until the raw manuscript phase, and Leyla Aker, who took it from there, were founts of cheer and models of efficiency.

Francesca Marx managed to read manuscript pages anybody else would have found illegible; and typed it, draft after draft, into a word processor, often working nights and weekends when we came up against deadlines. With her perceptive stylistic, substantive, and copy-editing suggestions, she was more in the nature of a collaborator than a typist.

Nobody deserves more thanks and credit than those who endure the tedium of reading and criticizing early drafts. My profound thanks in this connection to my sister Sari Magaziner; to James Chace; to Prof. Ralph Buultjens of New York University; to retired Prof. Alain Silvera of Bryn Mawr College—all of whom read the manuscript in its entirety—and to Dr. Mark Hassall of the Institute of Archaeology, University of London (who read Part One); to Prof. Sir Hans Kornberg, Boston University (who read Chapter One); to Prof. Laura Maclatchy, Boston University (who read Chapter One); and to those who helped by making necessary introductions, notably Prof. Harry Gelber, then at Boston University; Prof. Thomas J. Barfield, Chairman of the Department of Anthropology at Boston University; and my old friends Reed and Jane Rubin.

But for whatever shortcomings the book may have, the sole responsibility is mine.

Index